MODERN HUMANITIES RESEARCH ASSOCIATION
TEXTS AND DISSERTATIONS
VOLUME 83

THE SIGNIFYING SELF:
CERVANTINE DRAMA AS COUNTER-PERSPECTIVE AESTHETIC

MODERN HUMANITIES RESEARCH ASSOCIATION
TEXTS AND DISSERTATIONS

Established in 1970, the series promotes important work by younger scholars by making the most accomplished doctoral research available to a wider readership. Titles are selected and edited by a Board of distinguished experts from across the modern Humanities.

Editorial Board

English: Professor Catherine Maxwell, Queen Mary, University of London
French: Professor William Brooks, University of Bath
Germanic: Professor Ritchie Robertson, University of Oxford
Hispanic: Professor Derek Flitter, University of Exeter
Italian: Professor Brian Richardson, University of Leeds
Latin American: Professor Catherine Davies, University of Nottingham
Portuguese: Professor Thomas Earle, University of Oxford
Slavonic: Professor David Gillespie, University of Bath

Managing Editor: Dr Graham Nelson

The Signifying Self:
Cervantine Drama as Counter-Perspective Aesthetic

by
Melanie Henry

Modern Humanities Research Association
2013

Published by

The Modern Humanities Research Association,
1 Carlton House Terrace
London SW1Y 5AF
United Kingdom

© *The Modern Humanities Research Association, 2013*

Melanie Henry has asserted her right under the Copyright, Designs and Patents Act 1988 to be identified as the author of this work. Parts of this work may be reproduced as permitted under legal provisions for fair dealing (or fair use) for the purposes of research, private study, criticism, or review, or when a relevant collective licensing agreement is in place. All other reproduction requires the written permission of the copyright holder who may be contacted at rights@mhra.org.uk.

First published 2013

ISBN 978-1-78188-002-9 (hardback)
ISBN 978-178188-003-6 (paperback)
ISSN (MHRA Texts and Dissertations) 0957-0322

www.texts.mhra.org.uk

CONTENTS

Acknowledgements vi

Introduction
Cervantes: Writing Drama on the Margins 1

Chapter One
Encuentro con Lope en el Camino: *La entretenida*, *El laberinto de amor* and *La casa de los celos y selvas de Ardenia* 15

1.1 '¿Todo aquesto es burla?': Shattering the Spectacle and Sustaining the Self in *La entretenida* 16

1.2 Expressive Selves in *El laberinto de amor* 37

1.3 Manipulative Magic in *La casa de los celos y selvas de Ardenia* 52

Chapter Two
Staging *Libertad* in Cervantes's *Comedias de Cautivos* 75

2.1 Playing the Past in *El gallardo español* 76

2.2 All that Glitters is not Gold: *La gran sultana Doña Catalina de Oviedo* Re-considered 91

2.3 Staging Spain in *Los baños de Argel* 103

Chapter Three
Shaping the Self in *El rufián dichoso* and *Pedro de Urdemalas* 128

3.1 'O sé rufián, o sé santo': Transformative Craft(iness) in *El rufián dichoso* 129

3.2 *Pedro de Urdemalas*: A Cervantine Counter-Perspective 139

Conclusion 157

Bibliography 160

ACKNOWLEDGEMENTS

I would like to acknowledge the support of the following people who made this project possible:

First, and foremost, I would like to express my gratitude to my doctoral supervisor, Professor Isabel Torres. I am hugely grateful for the invaluable guidance and support she has generously extended toward my work. My love for all things Golden-Age was ignited in Isabel's undergraduate courses and the enthusiasm and rigour with which she approaches her work is a constant inspiration. I would hope to repay the debt that I owe one day — but I am sure that could never be the case. Mil gracias, Isabel.

Special thanks are due to the staff of the Dept. of Spanish and Portuguese Studies at Queen's University Belfast. I am appreciative of the consistent support offered throughout the course of my studies and for funding towards research trips and conferences. I would also like to extend a word of thanks to Dr Jonathan Thacker, Oxford University, whose advice and interest in this project has been both helpful and valued.

These acknowledgments would not be complete without mentioning my friends at Queen's (postgrads both past and present) who kept me going and often put everything into perspective. Thank you, all.

It is a pleasure to acknowledge my wonderful family who have never been other than supportive. A heartfelt thank you goes to my parents who have always offered their unconditional love. Undoubtedly, I have learned from them the most important things of all. I would also like to thank my brothers, sister and sister-in-law, Jamie, Dean, Alana and Leanne, who now know more about Cervantes than they ever would have wished. Thank you for humouring me and for always giving me plenty to laugh about.

Finally, but by no means least, I would like to thank my husband, Rob, for his steadfast love and encouragement. His unfailing support and loud cheering are appreciated more than he knows. It is only fitting that this book is dedicated to him.

INTRODUCTION

~

Cervantes: Writing Drama On The Margins

'La libertad, Sancho, es uno de los más preciosos dones que a los hombres dieron los cielos'
Don Quijote, II, LVIII

Miguel de Cervantes (1547–1616) has long been considered a 'literary giant', an accolade attributed to him on account of his *magnus opus*, *Don Quijote de la Mancha*.[1] First published in 1605 and followed by a second volume in 1615, Cervantes's creation of *el ingenioso hidalgo* is credited with the birth of the modern novel and has achieved iconic status in Spanish cultural history.[2] In his lifetime, as today, the novel eclipsed the writer's broad range of work in verse, prose and drama; to the extent that, in relative terms, critical appraisal of Cervantes's other literary endeavours has been minimal.[3] In particular, his dramatic work received scant recognition and very few of his plays, and certainly none of his *comedias*, debuted in the Spanish *corrales*.[4] Cervantes took the unusual step of publishing the *Ocho comedias y ocho entremeses nuevos nunca representados* (Madrid, 1615), with a title which highlights this very fact.[5] The *Ocho comedias* were, in fact, generally overlooked until the twentieth-century and even then, the attention they attracted was negative.[6] Bruce Wardropper's assessment that: 'La crítica tradicional suele menospreciar o pasar por alto sus escritos extensos para escena',[7] is mild against Francisco Ynduráin's labelling of Cervantes's theatre as 'puro disparate'.[8] Cervantes's writings, of course, generally function as a kind of kaleidoscope in which his reader/spectator's gaze simultaneously settles on a host of variable perspectives via a prism in which 'truth' is always negotiable. It is, therefore, highly ironic that his dramatic works should be judged so resolutely inadequate and deficient.

Not until the middle of the twentieth-century was Cervantes's drama subject to any serious interrogation, although minor studies and editions of his work had been published in the early part of the century by authors/editors such as Cotarelo y Valledor and Schevill and Bonilla.[9] Joaquín Casalduero's pioneering study *Sentido y forma del teatro de Cervantes* (1951) paved the way for some re-evaluation of Cervantes's theatre, and coincided with a shift away from a historiographical and biographical approach towards an emphasis on textual and aesthetic concerns.[10] Over two decades would pass, however, before Cervantes's dramatic corpus received significant treatment in the form of Jean Canavaggio's *Cervantès dramaturge: un thèâtre à naître*.[11] In more recent years, Cervantistas such as Edward Friedman, Nicholas Spadaccini, Stanislav Zimic and Jesús González Maestro have contributed enormously to scholarship.[12] Nonetheless, their work on Cervantes's theatre occupies a small space in the field of Cervantine studies. One only has to compare the masses of published material on *Don Quijote* with studies on the author's drama to appreciate to what extent the novel's cult status has dominated (Cervantine dramatic studies are often limited to conference contributions, greatly overshadowed in the proceedings between copious pages dedicated to his prose).[13] However, lack of success in his own lifetime and a legacy of critical neglect should not impede investigation. As Carlos Arboleda has commented: 'La importancia de Cervantes como dramaturgo no se le ha reconocido lo suficientemente'.[14] This book aims to go some way towards recuperating the *Ocho comedias* and establishing the novelist's theatre as a crucial and significant part of the Cervantine, and Golden-Age, canon.

A key contributing factor in the general underestimation of Cervantes's drama has been a tendency to judge Cervantes vis-à-vis Lope de Vega. Relative to Lope's dramatic output and his highly successful and prolific career as a playwright, Cervantes is often found wanting. In fact, those commentators who have broached Cervantes's writings for the stage tend to focus on Cervantes's 'inability' to compete with Lope or to create theatre that fitted within the parameters of Lope's hugely popular *comedia nueva*. Although the dates of composition of Cervantes's *Ocho comedias* can only be approximate, it is clear that Cervantes wrote for the stage during two phases of his life; the decade beginning 1580 and again at the beginning of the seventeenth-century, preceding the publication of *Don Quijote II*.[15] It is within this latter phase that Cervantes encountered and clashed with Lope's newly fashionable drama. The dramatist himself explains his absence from the stage and Lope's subsequent monopoly:

> Tuve otras cosas en que ocuparme; dejé la pluma y las comedias, y entró luego el monstruo de naturaleza, el gran Lope de Vega y alzóse con la monarquía cómica. Avasalló y puso debajo de su juridición a todos los farsantes; llenó el mundo de comedias proprias [...] y todas, que es una de las mayores cosas que puede decirse, las ha visto representar o oído decir por lo menos que se han representado.[16]

Carroll Johnson draws attention to the two 'imágenes de violencia y discordia' which Cervantes uses to introduce Lope to his *lector* and which are often cited as indicative of Cervantes's contempt for Lope's *comedia* and the contentious relationship that existed between the men, both personally and professionally.[17]

Lope's poetics were concretised in his *Arte nuevo de hacer comedias en este tiempo* (1609) and transferred to the stage to popular acclaim. With this, a new national theatre was born in which Cervantes shared no part. Cervantes, in fact, was deeply concerned with the condition of the public stage at the beginning of the seventeenth-century.[18] The novelist was uneasy with the commercialism of a theatre which he felt had been compromised in terms of consumer demand and the fact that a playwright's work was packaged by theatre managers and directors to please the *vulgo* rather than to place more challenging demands on audience sensibilities. As Spadaccini notes: 'While Cervantes explicitly renounces the mediations of producers and actors and shows disdain for the "mass" audience of the public theater, Lope was to make all sorts of compromises for the benefit of that audience to ensure his plays a favourable reception'.[19] Lope's own dramatic treatise offers an ironic assertion of such a strategy: 'Que el vulgo con sus leyes establezca'.[20]

A running commentary charting Cervantes's ambiguous relationship with contemporary dramatic practise is evident throughout his work and highlights, in particular, his distaste for public theatre on the one hand and his intense desire to succeed as a playwright on the other. There are four main statements on drama in the Cervantine corpus: the conversation between the canon and priest in *Don Quijote I*; the dialogue between Comedia and Curiosidad in Act II of *El rufián dichoso*; the *Prólogo al lector* in the *Ocho comedias* and the *adjunta* to *Viaje del Parnaso*. The best known is found in chapter XLVIII of *Don Quijote I*. In his assessment of the dialogue between the *cura* and the *canónigo*, Friedman asserts that 'via the canon, Cervantes appears to degrade Lope by associating his plays with a vulgar public, ill-equipped to recognise dramatic excellence'.[21] The canon declares that he prefers plays 'que llevan traza y siguen la fábula como el arte pide no sirven sino para cuatro discretos que las entienden, y todos los demás se quedan ayunos de entender su artificio'.[22] The priest laments the fact that 'las comedias se han hecho mercadería vendible' which has reduced artistic credibility to the level of financial gain. One can only imagine how Lope might have reacted to Cervantes's very public attack. Nonetheless, Wardropper warns us of the danger of identifying Cervantes's views with those of the canon. For Wardropper, Cervantes's character:

> incarnates his dilemma with respect to the theater [. . .] His head may argue for the classical type of play, but his heart, rejecting the academic approach, seems to be with the productions of that "felicissimo ingenio destos reynos" whom the commentators identify with Lope.[23]

In fact, Wardropper's view would appear to be endorsed by one of Cervantes's own plays, *El rufián dichoso*, which adopts the dramatic model of Lope's *comedia de santos*. At the opening of Act II, allegorical figures Comedia and Curiosidad discuss the seventeenth-century Spanish stage. When questioned by Curiosidad concerning 'la causa por que dejas / de usar tus antiguos trajes' (ll. 1211–12), *comedia* responds:

> Los tiempos mudan las cosas
> y perficionan las artes,
> y añadir a lo inventado
> no es dificultad notable.
> Buena fui pasados tiempos,
> y en éstos, si los mirares,
> no soy mala, aunque desdigo
> de aquellos preceptos graves
> que me dieron y dejaron
> en sus obras admirables
> Séneca, Terencio y Plauto,
> y otros griegos que tú sabes.
> He dejado parte dellos,
> y he también guardado parte,
> porque lo quiere así el uso,
> que no se sujeta al arte (ll. 1229–44)

The dialogue is routinely cited as an example of Cervantes's acknowledgement (and perhaps appreciation) of current dramatic trends.[24] Jonathan Thacker, however, reminds us of the danger of isolating the dialogue from its context.[25] Following this line of enquiry, my own study of *El rufián dichoso* in Chapter Three of this book argues against those readings which purport acceptance of the *comedia nueva*.

In the *Adjunta al Parnaso* (1614), Cervantes expresses his uneasy relationship with theatre producers of the time. Pancracio asks Miguel (de Cervantes) why his plays have never been represented on stage, to which Miguel responds: 'Porque ni los autores me buscan, ni yo los voy a buscar a ellos'.[26] This attitude finds fuller expression in the dramatist's *prólogo*:

> volví a componer algunas comedias; pero no hallé pájaros en los nidos de antaño; quiero decir que no hallé autor que me las pidiese, puesto que sabían que las tenía, y así las arrinconé en un cofre y las consagré y condené al perpetuo silencio.[27]

After some years, however, Cervantes sold his *comedias* to a bookseller; thus, leaving it to posterity to judge their quality. Taken together, these statements clarify the reasons behind Cervantes's decision to redirect his theatre to a reader. There is, in fact, little evidence to suggest that his writings for the stage were originally and deliberately designated as private reading material; despite the fact that Spadaccini and Talens have argued that Cervantes directed his *comedias* to a private readership who would engage with the texts in a domain removed from the impositions of the public stage.[28] This is a persuasive argument but it ignores the fact that Cervantes wrote the *Ocho comedias* before they were rejected by theatre producers and that the decision to publish was taken subsequently. For that reason, Cory Reed's admonition that we should concentrate on Cervantes's decision to *print* his plays (not to *write* them) is significant.[29] In relation to the *Ocho entremeses*, Reed comments: 'Any discussion of Cervantes's interludes must therefore begin with the fact that they are in essence works of theatre, conceived in accordance with certain dramatic principles and conventions, and they must be analysed as such'.[30] Such a statement is entirely applicable to the *Ocho comedias* and will inform my own interpretation of the plays.

The stigma of the drama's status as *nunca representados* remains attached to the *comedias* and their lack of theatrical success has significantly contributed to the notion of Cervantes as a 'failed' dramatist. In a recent interview, the director of the *Compañía Nacional de Teatro Clásico de España*, Eduardo Vasco, justified the company's proclivity to stage Lope, Tirso or Calderón and to overlook Cervantes:

> [Cervantes] tiene una retórica mucho menos natural que la de Lope, mucho más personal; eso le hace ser un gran novelista, pero lo hace ser un autor para teatro que resulta muy correoso, [...] las comedias casi nunca se han montado porque son un mundo muy complejo. Lo mejor de sus comedias, ya te digo, es que las escribió Cervantes, pero como material teatral dejan mucho que desear.[31]

Although Vasco's comment pertains to a performative context, it is indicative of the fact that the importance of Cervantes's 'complex' theatre is generally qualified by its dissimilarity (and 'inferiority') to Lope de Vega's populist *comedia nueva*. Evaluation of Cervantes's drama as 'anti-Lope', created with the sole purpose of voicing the dramatist's preoccupation with Lope's theatrical domination, has resulted in a one dimensional argument that tends to prioritise what Cervantes's theatre does or, indeed, does not do within a very limited context. As Mercedes Alcalá Galán states: 'la experimentación artística y literaria en Cervantes en el caso de teatro siempre se juzga o como reacción contra la fórmula lopesca o como claudicación de los propios ideales estéticos con el fin de ganar el favor del público'.[32] Maestro condemns such a 'misplaced' methodology:

> Leer y ver su teatro como el resultado de una impotencia por parecerse o adaptarse al de otros dramaturgos de su época equivale a proponer una solución falsa a un problema igualmente falso [...] Cervantes nunca quiso imitar la *comedia nueva*, nunca quiso mimetizar el arte de ninguno de sus contemporáneos y, con toda probabilidad, al que menos de todos hubiera querido imitar sería a Lope de Vega. En el terreno teatral, Cervantes pretendió un imposible para su tiempo, pero no para la posteridad: triunfar en el teatro con un teatro alternativo a la *comedia nueva*.[33]

In other words, such analysis has ultimately limited itself to interpretations which underscore persistently ubiquitous anti-Lope aspects. This particular type of critical assessment is inevitably reductive, closing down rather than opening up lines of enquiry which could consider Cervantes's theatre on its own aesthetic terms and the wider socio-cultural concerns at stake. This book, then, while recognising and interrogating these 'anti-Lope' aspects of Cervantes's drama (relevant especially to the plays considered in Chapter One) aims to move beyond discussion of anti-*comedia* objectives to identify what, in fact, Cervantes's 'teatro alternativo' *promotes*.

Such an approach will be underpinned by an exploration of the theme of freedom in Cervantes's theatre. The playwright's traumatic experience as a captive in Algiers from 1575–1580 cannot be considered irrelevant to this.[34] As a man who understood what it was to be incarcerated and eventually liberated, Cervantes's writings explore the dialectic of captivity/freedom in self-consciously provocative contexts. As George Camamis comments: 'el cautiverio ha dejado huellas en toda su producción literaria'.[35] Cervantistas have generally acknowledged the pervasive presence of the theme in Cervantes's work. Luis Rosales, for instance, labelled freedom as 'el eje mismo del pensamiento cervantino'.[36] More recently, Melveena McKendrick has noted that the idea of liberty 'is one of the leitmotifs of Cervantes's entire work', and yet minimal attention has been paid as to how Cervantes's complex understanding of freedom finds literary expression in his drama.[37] Rosales's voluminous work on *Cervantes y la Libertad* makes only scant reference to *El rufián dichoso*, otherwise neglecting the *Ocho comedias*. Freedom, in fact, represents much more than just a motif or presence in the Cervantine canon. As Antonio Rey Hazas explains, it is an expression of Cervantes's aesthetics and poetics:

> Libertad, en definitiva, como poética del Quijote y de toda la obra cervantina, *como clave coherente de su quehacer artístico*, dentro y fuera de la novela, presente en los personajes, en el autor y en los lectores, obvia en la visión del mundo y en la concepción de la sociedad, en la teoría y en la práctica literarias, en el perspectivismo, la ironía y la relación vida/literatura (emphasis mine).[38]

This statement is especially resonant in light of the world into which the *Ocho comedias* were born; an environment typified by *desengaño*, a term which conveys 'the notion of the profound, almost existential, realization of the absolute vanity of human values and possessions, together with a realignment in the light of such a realization'.[39] Notwithstanding the darker veins of Renaissance experience which emerge even in some of the literature of the early sixteenth-century, there is no doubt that in relative terms, the early modern Spaniard was plunged into an inconstant and ambivalent world in which Spain was retreating from the world stage as global power and invincible empire. Maravall observes that the seventeenth-century was 'a long period of a profound social crisis'.[40] In fact, Spain faced problems of great magnitude on every level; economic crises, imperial retreat, ineffective and weak leadership under *Las*

Austrias and racial tensions, amongst others.⁴¹ Seventeenth-century Spain was, consequently, a profoundly disrupted society in which the individual has been considered an alienated, even a contradictory, subject; driven by a desire to reconstruct the unity and symmetry of the Renaissance which had ceded to unsettling instability.⁴² A difficult and complex relationship, therefore, existed at micro/macro level, between the individual Spanish subject and such a conflicted environment.⁴³

The specific issues facing Spain in the context of a more precarious power base and the collapse of the country's political-economic infrastructure coincided with a more widespread re-evaluation and questioning of the individual's place within a changing world.⁴⁴ Claude Lévi-Strauss comments that the interrogation of authority from a sceptical perspective was linked to discovery of the New World and produced radical rethinking.⁴⁵ Moreover, within such an environment, 'freedom was a multifaceted and often polemical concern in early modern Europe'.⁴⁶ In Spain, in fact, it was a problem that 'eclipsed all others in magnitude'.⁴⁷ Counter-Reformation ideology and theology contributed enormously to the debate as issues of free will, predestination and freedom of the individual reached fever pitch. A detailed discussion of this topic is clearly beyond the scope of this study; suffice it to say that contemporary ideology exercised tremendous influence in defining the limitations of individuality and human agency. Moreover, seventeenth-century Neostoicism encapsulated an attitude of resignation which focused on the individual's limited sphere of influence and inability to shape circumstances and events beyond his/her control.⁴⁸ This is particularly relevant within seventeenth-century Spain in which tensions between individual inclination and societal pressures to conform bred and festered.

The troubled realities of Golden-Age Spain found an outlet on both the dominant *corral* stage and Cervantes's dramatic imaginings. Within a broader project of articulating the complexities inherent in the Baroque subject, Cervantes offers a perverse response to the prevailing world view. Anne Cruz remarks that Cervantes's *entremeses* 'share with his other works a transgressive compulsion to exceed formal and aesthetic limits and challenge dominant ideology'.⁴⁹ This is precisely what occurs in his full length plays. For Cervantes, Lope de Vega's stage was an instrument of propaganda which ventriloquised the voice and values of the ruling classes and endorsed the socio-cultural/political infrastructure which underpinned early modern Spain.⁵⁰ In contrast, Cervantes's theatre would propagate alternative values: 'defensora de la herencia humanista, de la libertad y dignidad del individuo [...] su poética era la poética de la libertad'.⁵¹ Influenced by Erasmian Humanism, Cervantes was primarily concerned with freedom as it affected the individual.⁵² In fact, in the *Ocho comedias* it is the alienated individual who is positioned centre-stage, coerced, confined and confronted by a range of social pressures. Cervantes, therefore, creates a seditious theatre which subverts contemporary theatrical methodology, bringing to the fore individual selfhood as an entity in and of itself. As McKendrick comments, in Cervantes's world 'there is always the sense of a definable self to be discovered, cultivated, and adhered to in the face of the world's pressures'.[53] In fact, as we will see through interrogation of the theatrical strategies employed, Cervantes stages the self in various ways, but that these representations of individual, national and artistic selfhoods collectively signify a coherently formulated Cervantine aesthetic. It is the primary aim of this book to demonstrate that this is an aesthetic which represents a counter-perspective to contemporary Golden-Age drama.

My evaluation of the *Ocho comedias* will engage with a range of twentieth-century modes of thought insofar as they open up areas of investigation and illuminate Cervantes's dramatic practise. On ideas of role-play and metatheatre, fundamental to an investigation of theatrical strategies used by Cervantes, this study will be informed by studies offered by Hornby and Thacker.[54] On issues of self-fashioning as a 'manipulable, artful process', I will engage with Greenblatt.[55] Notions of performativity will be highlighted by theories advocated by Rokem and Butler.[56] Simerka's interpretation of Iser's phenomenological approach to reading will provide a broader application of reader-response theory which works in relation to dramatic performance.[57] Ultimately this is a spectator-oriented methodology, based upon an awareness of Cervantes's *comedias* as only fully realised in the context of the relationship to the *corral* audience he envisaged when he first wrote them.

This book is divided into three chapters. Existing scholarship on Cervantes's drama is, for the most part, fragmented, disparate and, on occasions, idiosyncratic. In order to accommodate this range of responses to individual plays and for my own contribution to be clear, it has been necessary to deal with literature reviews at the beginning of these sections. Chapter One examines those plays which are considered to be more directly influenced by Lope's formula: *La entretenida*, *El laberinto de amor* and *La casa de los celos y selvas de Ardenia*. It is my intention, however, to move beyond judgement of these plays as a reaction toward prevailing dramatic trends and, rather, to focus on what these plays disseminate in terms of Cervantine art and its representation of the repressed individual. In a review of E. Michael Gerli's appraisal of *El retablo de las maravillas* as an intertextual commentary on the state of contemporary drama, Friedman ponders: 'Despite the effectiveness of this reading, one may be left wondering how to interpret Cervantes's emulation of Lope in plays such as *El rufián dichoso*, *El laberinto de amor*, and *La entretenida*. The answer could be that structural similarities in fact mask ideological difference, and this issue would be worth exploring'.[58] Exploration of this 'difference' is at the forefront, therefore, of my analyses as I evaluate Cervantes's simultaneous deconstruction of Lope's theatre and promotion of his own art within the frame of his reconfiguration of seventeenth-century Spanish ideologies; especially with regard to societal infrastructure and the marginalisation of the contemporary woman. Illusion-breaking techniques are also foregrounded in this section in terms of how Cervantes exposes the inherent power and potential of the stage.

El gallardo español, *La gran sultana Doña Catalina de Oviedo* and *Los baños de Argel*, known usually as the *comedias de cautivos*, are the focus of Chapter Two. It is within these plays that the physical representation of freedom and slavery is most evident. Although these *comedias* are set in Oran, Constantinople and Algiers respectively, analysis will demonstrate that they remain Spain-centred. Spadaccini and Talens comment: 'The effervescence and continual change that traverse Spain, from imperial expansion to the bankruptcy of the state, serve not only as a historical and cultural frame but are also inscribed, analysed, and deconstructed through Cervantes's literary discourse'.[59] This undoubtedly applies to the *comedias de cautivos* in which Cervantes deconstructs a profoundly unsettling picture of the receiving world. Significant issues of national selfhood and identity come under scrutiny in these plays as Cervantes negotiates what it is to be Spanish in the seventeenth-century. By staging alternate subjectivities, Cervantes interrogates the realities of the socio-cultural and political infrastructure on which the early modern Spanish state is elusively and allusively founded. The dramatist dialogues with those discourses which precariously construct Spanish nationhood in order to critique and destabilise the 'absolutes' of Counter-Reformation Spain. As a result, the *corral* spectator is liberated from passive reception as these *comedias* both expose and counter-act the signifying systems at play within early modern Spain.

In the final chapter of the study, I will examine two plays which to date have not been connected: *El rufián dichoso* and *Pedro de Urdemalas*. I will argue that the *comedias* find a common point of reference through their *pícaro* protagonists. My analyses of these plays will discuss Cervantes's use, and subversion, of the picaresque genre. More significantly, this section demonstrates how Cervantes utilises the picaresque as a vehicle through which the machinations of the artistic process are exposed. Cervantes's engagement with the *ser/parecer* dialectic is particularly relevant here as the playwright portrays two protagonists who engage heavily with illusion but do not lose sight of their essential selves. Via Lugo and Pedro's ability to manipulate their circumstances, Cervantes comments on the far-reaching potential of dramatic art, especially within the context of audience reception. A heightened awareness of the individual's engagement with stringent social structures is expressed as Cervantes puts on stage two characters who freely determine their own path in life. Ultimately, Cervantes deals with art's relationship to/with life and, by implication, draws attention to his unorthodox poetics.

As a whole, this book underscores the autonomy of Cervantes's theatre and highlights the playwright's dissident conceptualisation of dramatic art within the context of the world which received it; an environment in which the individual experienced limited freedom. Christopher Caudwell has said:

> Liberty does seem to me the most important of all generalised goods — such as justice, beauty, truth — that come so easily to our lips. And yet when freedom is discussed a strange thing is to be noticed. These men — artists, careful of words, scientists, investigators of the entities denoted by words, philosophers scrupulous about the relations between words and entities — never define precisely what they mean by freedom.[60]

A compelling definition of freedom is not pinpointed or easily attained in the *Ocho comedias*. In fact, it may at times emerge in unsettling contradictions. For instance, *La entretenida* suggests that individual self-fulfilment can best be realised from within social role. The *comedias de cautivos*, on the other hand, rail against confinement in all its forms. Just as the issue of truth is subject to multi-perspectivism within Cervantes's writings, freedom is never encoded within the *comedias* in one single form. In the Cervantine prism, it is refracted and dispersed in diverse ways; a strategy which provokes dynamic and active audience participation. As such, Cervantes's staging of freedom renders a multi-faceted perspective from which to perceive and engage with the conflicts and contradictions which inform the Spanish Baroque epoch.

Judged in relation to our own twenty-first century postmodern sensibilities, Cervantes does not promote freedom in radical terms, but he does challenge the systems and authorities of his own day to produce a re-conception, a counter-perspective, of early modern Spanish ideologies and their artistic imaginings. Ultimately, it is my intention to bring Cervantes the dramatist 'in from the margins' and to establish his alternative dramatic voice as one which should not be overlooked, or silenced.

Notes to the Introduction

1. See Melveena McKendrick, *Cervantes* (Boston: Little, Brown, 1980), p. 7.
2. Miguel de Cervantes, *Don Quijote de la Mancha*, ed. by Francisco Rico (Madrid: Alfaguara, 2004).
3. Major works in these genres include: *La Galatea*, ed. by Juan Bautista Avalle-Arce (Madrid: Espasa-Calpe, 1961); *Viaje del Parnaso*, ed. by Vicente Gaos (Madrid: Castalia, 1973); *Novelas ejemplares*, ed. by Harry Sieber (Madrid: Cátedra, 1980); *Los trabajos de Persiles y Sigismunda*, ed. by Juan Bautista Avalle-Arce (Madrid: Castalia, 1969); *La Numancia*, ed. by Robert Marrast (Madrid: Cátedra, 1989).
4. In the prologue to the *Ocho comedias*, Cervantes remarks that *Los tratos de Argel*, *La destruición de Numancia* and *La batalla naval* were performed in Madrid. See *Prólogo al lector* in *Teatro completo*, ed. by Florencio Sevilla Arroyo and Antonio Rey Hazas (Barcelona: Planeta, 1987), p. 9. *La batalla naval*, which is also mentioned in the *Adjunta al Parnaso*, is now lost.
5. The *Ocho comedias* were first published in Madrid, 1615 by the 'viuda de Alonso Martín'. Cervantes's *entremeses* have received more extensive treatment than the *comedias*.
6. Jonathan Thacker observes: 'In spite of recent spirited arguments to the contrary, readers

of the past two centuries have tended to deem the plays failures'. See 'Cervantes, Tirso de Molina, and the First Generation', in *A Companion to Golden Age Theatre* (Woodbridge: Tamesis, 2007), p. 57.

7. Bruce Wardropper, 'Comedias', in *Suma cervantina*, ed. by J. B. Avalle-Arce and E. C. Riley (London: Tamesis, 1973), p. 147.
8. Francisco Ynduráin, ed., *Obras dramáticas de Miguel de Cervantes* (Madrid: Biblioteca de Autores Españoles, 1962), p. xxxvii. See also Robert Marrast, *Miguel de Cervantès: Dramaturge* (Paris: L'Arche, 1957).
9. Armando Cotarelo y Valledor, *El teatro de Cervantes* (Madrid: Revista de Archivos, Bibliotecas y Museos, 1915) and *Comedias y Entremeses*, ed. by Rodolfo Schevill and Adolfo Bonilla (Madrid: Impr. de B. Rodríguez, 1915-22). See also Ángel Valbuena Prat, 'Las ocho comedias de Cervantes', in *Homenaje a Cervantes*, ed. by Francisco Sánchez-Castañer (Valencia: Mediterráneo, 1950), pp. 257-66 and Bruce Wardropper, 'Cervantes' Theory of the Drama', *Modern Philology*, 52 (1955), 217-21.
10. Joaquín Casalduero, *Sentido y forma del teatro de Cervantes* (Madrid: Aguilar, 1951). When the work was printed again in 1966 E. C. Riley said that Casalduero's work was 'still the most complete and important assessment of Cervantes's theatre since Cotarelo's ancient study'. See *Bulletin of Hispanic Studies*, 45 (1968), p. 45.
11. Jean Canavaggio, *Cervantès dramaturge: un théâtre à naître* (Paris: Presses Universitaires de France, 1977).
12. Edward H. Friedman, *The Unifying Concept: Approaches to the Structure of Cervantes' Comedias* (York, South Carolina: Spanish Literature Publications Company, 1981); Nicholas Spadaccini, 'Cervantes and the Spanish comedia', in *Ideologies and Literature. Plays and Playhouses in Imperial Decadence*, ed. by Anthony Zahareas (Minneapolis: Institute of Ideologies and Literature, 1985), pp. 53-67; Stanislav Zimic, *El teatro de Cervantes* (Madrid: Castalia, 1992) and Jesús G. Maestro, *La escena imaginaria: poética del teatro de Miguel de Cervantes* (Madrid; Frankfurt: Iberoamericana-Vervuert, 2000).
13. For example, Manuel Criado de Val, ed., *Cervantes: su obra y su mundo. Actas del I Congreso Internacional sobre Cervantes* (Madrid: Edi-6, 1981) and Antonio Bernat Vistarini, ed., *Actas del Tercer Congreso Internacional de la Asociación de Cervantistas* (Palma: Universitat de Illes Balears, 1998).
14. Carlos Arturo Arboleda, *Teoría y formas del Metateatro en Cervantes* (Salamanca: Universidad de Salamanca, 1991), p. 85. Melveena McKendrick remarks: 'The fact that theatrical success eluded Cervantes does not mean we can afford to ignore his theatrical writing'. See 'Writings for the stage', in *The Cambridge Companion to Cervantes*, ed. by Anthony J. Cascardi (Cambridge: Cambridge University Press, 2002), pp. 131-59 (p. 132).
15. Cervantes does not make clear when he wrote the *Ocho comedias*. See M. A. Buchanan, 'The works of Cervantes and their dates of composition', *Transactions of the Royal Society of Canada*, 32 (1938), 23-39.
16. Miguel de Cervantes, *Teatro completo*, ed. by Florencio Sevilla Arroyo and Antonio Rey Hazas (Barcelona: Planeta, 1987), p. 10. All quotes and citations from the *Ocho comedias y ocho entremeses nuevos nunca representados* in this study are taken from this edition. Where emphasis has been added to these, this is indicated with italics.
17. Carroll B. Johnson, 'El arte viejo de hacer teatro: Lope de Rueda, Lope de Vega y Cervantes', *Cuadernos de Filología*, 3 (1981), 247-59 (p. 256).
18. For instance, see Antonio Rey Hazas, 'Cervantes y Lope de Vega', in *Poética de la libertad y otras claves cervantinas* (Madrid: Ediciones Eneida, 2005), pp. 61-82. Cervantes makes plain his abiding interest in the theatre throughout his work. José María Díez Borque comments that: 'Aunque creador de la novela moderna, Cervantes era un hombre de teatro, preocupado, y aun obsesionado, por él'. 'La historia del teatro según Cervantes', in

Cervantes y la puesta en escena de la sociedad de su tiempo (Actas del Coloquio de Montreal, 1997), ed. by Catherine Poupeney Hart, Alfredo Hermenegildo and César Oliva (Murcia: Universidad de Murcia, 1999), pp. 17–53 (p. 18).
19. Spadaccini, 'Cervantes and the Spanish comedia', p. 55.
20. Lope de Vega, *El arte nuevo de hacer comedias en este tiempo*, ed. by Juana de José Prades (Madrid: Consejo Superior de Investigaciones Científicas, 1971).
21. Friedman, 'An Archetype and its modifications: Cervantes's dramatic theory and practice', *The American Hispanist*, 15 (1978), 9–11 (p. 9).
22. Miguel de Cervantes, *Don Quijote de la Mancha*, ed. by Francisco Rico (Madrid: Alfaguara, 2004), pp. 493–94. All citations from the novel are taken from this edition.
23. Wardropper, 'Cervantes' Theory of the Drama', p. 221.
24. For instance, McKendrick writes: 'By the time he realized that Lope's national drama was indeed a new art form rapidly achieving status and respectability, and acknowledged that art must change with the times, it was too late'. See 'Writings for the stage', p. 131.
25. Thacker, 'La figura de la comedia en *El rufián dichoso* de Cervantes', in *La comedia de santos*, ed. by Felipe B. Pedraza Jiménez and Almudena García González (Almagro: Universidad de Castilla-La Mancha, 2008), pp. 121–34 (p. 122).
26. Cervantes, *Poesías Completas, I. Viaje del Parnaso y Adjunta al Parnaso*, ed. by Vicente Gaos (Madrid: Castalia, 1973), p. 183.
27. Cervantes, *Teatro completo*, pp. 11–12.
28. See Spadaccini, 'Cervantes and the Spanish comedia'. Jenaro Talens argues: '[Reading] implies a necessary active role that contradicts that of the passive *vulgo* produced and generalized by Lope's model of *comedia nueva*. For that reason, Cervantes turns to the print media'. See 'Narrating Theatricality', in *Ideologies and Literature. Plays and Playhouses in Imperial Decadence*, p. 97.
29. Cory A. Reed, 'Cervantes and the Novelization of Drama: Tradition and Innovation in the *Entremeses*', *Cervantes*, 11 (1991), 61–86 (p. 64). Anne Cruz concurs with Reed's argument and comments that: 'Spadaccini seems to accept too readily that Cervantes had lost interest in staging his *comedias* and *entremeses* and decided to publish them instead'. 'Deceit, Desire, and the Limits of Subversion in Cervantes's Interludes', *Cervantes*, 14 (1994), 119–36 (p. 122).
30. Reed, 'Cervantes and the Novelization of Drama', pp. 64–65. John J. Allen's work on the structural composition of the *comedias* confirms the plays as texts designated for performance. A study of the playwright's *acotaciones* leads Allen to conclude: 'It is clear that Cervantes' plays were not written for a reader, but for the stage'. See 'Some aspects of the staging of Cervantes's play', *Crítica Hispánica*, 9 (1989), 7–16 (p. 9).
31. An interview by Alejandro González Puche in *Blog Theatrica*; Madrid, 24th October 2007. See <http://parnaseo2.uv.es/blogtheatrica/?p=30>. *Los baños de Argel*, *La gran sultana*, *Pedro de Urdemalas* and *La entretenida* have been staged within the latter half of the last century.
32. Mercedes Alcalá Galán, '"Dios te dé salud y a mí paciencia". Teoría del teatro en Cervantes', in *La media semana del jardincito: Cervantes y la reescritura de los códigos*, ed. by José María Manuel Morán (Padova: Unipress, 2002), pp. 255–75 (p. 271).
33. Jesús González Maestro, 'El triunfo de la heterodoxia. El teatro de Cervantes y la literatura europea', *Theatralia: Revista de Teoría del Teatro*, 5 (2003), 19–48 (p. 20).
34. In September 1575, Cervantes, who had fought and sustained injuries as a solider in the battle of Lepanto in 1571, set sail from Naples to Spain on *El Sol*. The galley was captured by Barbary pirates and Cervantes, along with other Spaniards including his brother, Rodrigo, was taken prisoner. He spent five years enslaved in North African captivity until he was eventually ransomed by a Trinitarian friar, Juan Gil and returned to his homeland in 1580. See William Byron, *Cervantes: A Biography* (London: Cassell, 1979); Jean

Canavaggio, *Cervantes* (Madrid: Espasa Calpe, 1987); Donald McCrory, *No Ordinary Man: The Life and Times of Miguel de Cervantes* (London: Peter Owen, 1999).

35. George Camamis, *Estudios sobre el cautiverio en el Siglo de Oro* (Madrid: Gredos, 1977), p. 51.
36. Luis Rosales, *Cervantes y la Libertad*, 2 vols (Madrid: Instituto de Cooperación Iberoamericana, 1985), p. 33.
37. McKendrick, 'Writings for the Stage', p. 143.
38. See blurb of Rey Hazas's *Poética de la libertad*.
39. Jeremy Robbins, *The Challenges of Uncertainty: An Introduction to Seventeenth-Century Spanish Literature* (London: Duckworth, 1998), p. 17.
40. José Antonio Maravall, *Culture of the Baroque: Analysis of a Historical Structure* (Manchester: Manchester University Press, 1986), p. 19. Maravall's analysis of the turbulent socio-political backdrop to Baroque literature points particularly to events such as the unsuccessful wars with England and France, the rebellions in the Netherlands and Aragon, the 1588 defeat of the *Armada 'Invincible'*, the 1596 bankruptcy and the plague of 1600.
41. For a fuller analysis of the period in general see J. H. Elliott, *Imperial Spain 1469–1716* (London: Edward Arnold Publishers, 1963). Also see Henry Kamen, *Spain 1469–1714: A Society of Conflict* (Harlow: Longman, 1991).
42. George Mariscal, *Contradictory Subjects: Quevedo, Cervantes and Seventeenth-Century Spanish Culture* (Ithaca; London: Cornell University Press, 1991).
43. For a recent example of analysis of literary texts in this context see, for instance, David R. Castillo and Massimo Lollini, eds., *Reason and Its Others. Italy, Spain and the New World* (Tennessee: Vanderbilt University Press, 2006). In particular, see Part Two 'Of Houses and Cities: Early Modern Spaces and the Aporias of Baroque Reason' which discusses crises of identity and notions of containment and transgression in texts such as *La destrucción de Numancia* and the *Novelas ejemplares*, as well as other non-Cervantine texts.
44. According to McKendrick, some of the topics which were questioned and negotiated by the early modern Spaniard include: the state of Spain, kingship, absolutism, reason of state, racial purity, social mobility and honour. See *Playing the King: Lope de Vega and the Limits of Conformity* (London: Tamesis, 2000), p. 4.
45. Claude Lévi-Strauss, *Tristes Tropiques*, translated by John and Doreen Weightman (New York: Atheneum, 1979), p. 102.
46. David A. Boruchoff, 'Free Will, the Picaresque, and the Exemplarity of Cervantes's *Novelas ejemplares*', *Modern Language Notes*, 124 (2009), 372–403 (p. 372).
47. Henry W. Sullivan, *Tirso de Molina & the Drama of the Counter-Reformation* (Amsterdam: Editions Rodopi, 1981), p. 10.
48. See Robbins, *The Challenges of Uncertainty*, pp. 18–19. See also Robbins's more recent study which traces the development and impact of key concepts such as Scepticism and Stoicism on early modern Spanish thought and culture. *Arts of Perception: The Epistemological Mentality of the Spanish Baroque, 1580–1720* (New York: Routledge, 2007).
49. Cruz, 'Deceit, Desire, and the Limits of Subversion', p. 122.
50. Maravall's thesis, which views the *comedia* as a form of propaganda which served to reinforce existing order, has been significantly challenged since its publication in 1972. Postmodern critics draw attention to the dangers in 'assuming' a monolithic audience, as Maravall can be said to do. Recent trends in scholarship take into consideration a range of factors which produced 'meaning' and contributed to dramatic production. See, for example, José A. Madrigal, ed., *New Historicism and the Comedia: Poetics, Politics and Praxis* (Boulder, Colorado: Society of Spanish and Spanish-America Studies, 1997).
51. Rey Hazas, *Poética de la libertad*, p. 74.

52. See McKendrick, 'Writings for the stage', p. 135 and Ruth El Saffar, 'Voces marginales y la visión del ser cervantino', *Anthropos*, 98–99 (1989), 59–62 (p. 62). Alban Forcione's work is significant in this regard. His study of four of the exemplary novels questions how their vision of human freedom has been shaped by Erasmus. See *Cervantes and the Humanist Vision: A Study of Four Exemplary Novels* (Princeton: Princeton University Press, 1982). Forcione describes how Cervantes powerfully experienced Erasmism during his formative years and labels the playwright Erasmus's 'greatest literary disciple', p. 20.
53. McKendrick, 'Writings for the Stage', p. 136.
54. Richard Hornby, *Drama, Metadrama and Perception* (Lewisburg, Pennsylvania: Bucknell University Press, 1986); Jonathan Thacker, *Role-Play and the World as Stage in the Comedia* (Liverpool: Liverpool University Press, 2002).
55. Stephen Greenblatt, *Renaissance Self-Fashioning: From More to Shakespeare* (Chicago; London: University of Chicago Press, 1980), p. 2.
56. Freddie Rokem, *Performing History: Theatrical Representations of the Past in Contemporary Theatre* (Iowa: University of Iowa Press, 2000); Judith Butler, *Gender Trouble and the Subversion of Identity* (London: Routledge, 1999).
57. Barbara Simerka, 'Early Modern Skepticism and Unbelief and the Demystification of Providential Ideology in *El burlador de Sevilla*', *Gestos*, 23 (1997), 39–66; Wolfgang Iser, 'The Reading Process: A Phenomenological Approach', *New Literary History*, 3 (1972), 279–99.
58. E. Michael Gerli, *Refiguring Authority: Reading, Writing, and Rewriting in Cervantes* (Lexington: University of Kentucky Press, 1995). Friedman's review can be found in *Modern Philology*, 95 (1998), 540–43 (pp. 542–43).
59. Nicholas Spadaccini and Jenaro Talens, *Through the Shattering Glass: Cervantes and the Self-Made World* (London; Minneapolis: University of Minnesota Press, 1993), p. xii.
60. Christopher Caudwell, 'Liberty. A study in bourgeois illusion', in *Studies in a Dying Culture* (London: John Lane, 1938), pp. 193–94.

CHAPTER 1

Encuentro con Lope en el Camino

'Tengo libre condición, y no gusto de sujetarme'
Don Quijote, I, XIV

Canavaggio has commented that: 'No se puede hablar de Cervantes sin encontrar a Lope en el camino', a view substantiated by the fact that critical attention concerning Cervantes's *Ocho comedias* has prioritised the playwright's unease with Lope's highly popular theatre.[1] Canavaggio's observation, however, is particularly reflective of studies of *La entretenida*, *El laberinto de amor* and *La casa de los celos*. Each of these plays has been identified as a Cervantine reaction to dominant contemporary theatrical practise and all have been subject to analysis vis-à-vis Lope to varying degrees. This is especially true of *El laberinto de amor* and *La entretenida* and is an entirely valid approach. Both plays demonstrate Cervantes's blatant engagement with the commercially successful *comedia nueva* in order to both utilise and undermine Lope's crowd-pulling *capa y espada* formula. As Friedman notes: '*El laberinto de amor* may be seen as the complication of a model, and his [Cervantes] *La entretenida* as the deflation or parody of a model'.[2] *La casa de los celos* has traditionally resisted comparison with Lope's theatre and is clearly a less striking example of the playwright's dialogue with prevailing dramatic trends.[3] However, Marcella Trambaioli has recently demonstrated that *La casa* was constructed 'con la intención de subvertir varios hitos del universo literario lopeveguesco de la primera época, y para afirmar, al mismo tiempo, su personal interpretación de los comunes referentes ariostescos y, más en general, literarios'.[4] For the purposes of this chapter, these three plays will be considered dialogical works, and evidence of Cervantes's engagement with the theatrical model promoted by Lope de Vega.

Analysis of *La entretenida*, *El laberinto* and *La casa de los celos* will focus especially on aesthetic and ontological issues. As highlighted in the Introduction, the Baroque subject has been recently analysed as a repository of conflicted feelings of alienation and disillusionment. The plays under investigation explore the individual's relationship with the world in terms of identity and freedom. As such, the restrictions and confinement faced by marginal groups is especially emphasised. In this chapter, an interrogation of the theatrical strategies used by the dramatist to highlight notions of individuality will broach questions concerning Cervantes's depiction of art as a powerful device with limitless potential for exploitation. This line of enquiry will explore how illusion is perpetually undermined on the Cervantine stage and consider how this bears implications for the relationship between the stage and the consumer. Ultimately this section aims to demonstrate that *La entretenida*, *El laberinto de amor* and *La casa de los celos* conceptualise Cervantes's own perception of theatre. The metastrategies which the dramatist employs inevitably involve a decidedly antagonistic dialogue with the *comedia nueva*. Nevertheless, as we will see, such an approach opens up constructively to reveal how these plays function as powerfully positive statements of Cervantine drama itself.

1.1 '¿Todo aquesto es burla?': Shattering the Spectacle and Sustaining the Self in *La entretenida*

More than any of Cervantes's plays *La entretenida* showcases his engagement with the fundamentals of the *comedia nueva*, in terms of structure, theme and form, in a manner which deliberately derides the formula. Scholarly analysis has tended to focus on two facets of the drama which underpin this line of enquiry: on the one hand role-play and the metatheatrical elements of the drama; on the other the play as parody and the evaluation of its parodic strategies.

Friedman, Cubero, Thacker and Kartchner exemplify the former approach and have interrogated the metadramatic facets of the comedy to produce readings which expose the drama as a self-reflexive construct intent on drawing the spectator's attention to its artifice.[5] These notions serve to tease out conclusions which highlight the play as theatre about theatre, and in particular, theatre about Lope's theatre. Friedman's focus on role-play provokes pertinent questions which concern the self-consciousness of the drama but is interestingly situated within T. A. O'Connor's provocative argument 'Is the Spanish Comedia a Metatheater?'.[6] According to Friedman the failure of role-play in *La entretenida* highlights the merit of O'Connor's question. Thacker, in his discussion of social roles and social justice, draws attention to Friedman's argument:

> Friedman is asserting that individuals who respect their social roles and try to play them, even if side-tracked by the need to invent a fiction, will receive society's blessings in the fulfilment of their desires, while those who express selves, who are ruled by the will and see social rules as an impediment [...] will be frustrated.[7]

In terms of the latter approach, that is, the play as parody, *La entretenida* is often studied with reference to *El laberinto de amor*. Casalduero comments that *La entretenida*'s position within the volume of *Ocho comedias* is strategically significant: 'en la colección colocada inmediatamente después del *Laberinto*, tenemos un efecto de contraste — buscado y querido por el autor'.⁸ *El laberinto* portrays three women determined to exercise their discriminate capacity to choose husbands and outwit the restrictive authority which controls their lives. *La entretenida* also sees its characters pursue love interests and employ the strategies utilised by the heroines of *El laberinto*, but the female protagonists of *La entretenida* fail at every turn. Friedman remarks that in the world of literary creation: 'anti-type is as certain to follow type as the night the day [. . .] To break rules, one must be conscious of the rules; to invent an anti-type, one must acknowledge the conventions of a prototype'.⁹ It is this juxtaposition of imitation and deflation, in particular, which has initiated an appraisal of *La entretenida*'s function as a parody of Lopean comedy. The drama's use of parodic strategies operates on the premise of Margaret A. Rose's general definition of parody as 'the comic refunctioning of preformed linguistic or artistic material'.¹⁰ For *La entretenida*, this 'refunctioning' works as a destabiliser and an agent of revisionism which calls the *comedia nueva*'s formula into question and in Friedman's opinion 'deconstructs Lope, crafts a "Cervantine" play, and inscribes his [Cervantes] predicament into the text'.¹¹

Friedman's reading of the play also takes into account Cervantes's angst and frustration in contending with Lope's theatrical monopoly. The critic's engagement with Lope's model argues that the failures and frustrations of *La entretenida*'s characters are reflective of Cervantes's personal and professional predicament which causes life and art to merge in the work. Cervantes's biographical circumstances are also a feature of studies by Zimic and López Alfonso: both scrutinise how the playwright undermines and subverts typical elements of the *comedia*.¹² The most obvious example is the play's lack of matrimonial closure; a device which critics view as key to unlocking the play's parodic purpose.¹³ George Mariscal, on the other hand, explores the social aspects of Cervantes's theatre via the issues of class and gender and evaluates *La entretenida*'s non-ending as a refusal to establish order and thus resist social and literary control.¹⁴

Parodic strategies and the notion of an active and informed reader are undoubtedly interdependent.¹⁵ This mutually supporting relationship raises issues of reception. Rose notes that:

> Parody can play upon the expectations of an imagined reader or recipient in the construction of its parody. In this sense the discussion of the reader and parody has to be concerned not only with the external reader's reception or recognition of a parody, but with the parody's own internal evocation of the expectations of the reader.¹⁶

Despite emphasis on parody by critics of *La entretenida*, no explicit attention has been paid to readership and/or audience reception. Rose states that there are two models of communication within the role played by the reader in the reception of parody:

The first of these is between the parodist and the author of the parodied text, and the second between the parodist and the reader of the parody, who may also be assumed to be a reader of the parodied text in either its original and/or its parodied form in the parody of which they are a reader.[17]

It is this latter method of communication which has escaped critical attention. As part of a system of literature, *La entretenida* was intended for reception by an audience. It is pertinent to recall at this point that Cervantes's plays were published rather than performed. The notion of 'readership' is, therefore, relevant and important, but it should not distract from the fact that Cervantes wrote *La entretenida* with a theatre audience in mind, even though a contemporary reader could only have imagined the drama as a staged performance.[18] Although the implications for reception of visual and textual mediums represent a substantial disparity of experience and effect, they both connote a method of transmitting signs to which their receiver is subjected. In the context of the play in question, an audience would have engaged with the drama in order to form expectations and meaning and would have determined their interpretation through the experience of watching the drama.

This argument reflects Hans Jauss's theory of reception which involves viewing literature from the perspective of an active reader or consumer.[19] Jauss proposes that literature should be treated as a dialectical process of production and reception. He states that: 'Literature and art only obtain a history that has the character of a process when the succession of works is mediated not only through the producing subject but also through the consuming subject — through the interaction of author and public'.[20] Wolfgang Iser, one of the major proponents of reader-response theory, also proposes a focus on the role of the consumer in the production of textual meaning. Iser advocates a reader-oriented approach which 'lays full stress on the idea that, in considering a literary work, one must take into account not only the actual text but also, and in equal measure, the actions involved in responding to that text'.[21] Barbara Simerka's adaptation of Iser for Spanish Golden-Age theatre significantly broadens his entirely literary reception-oriented focus. Simerka advocates an approach which is fully informed by the historical, social and intellectual norms which shaped the thinking and world view of a seventeenth-century audience and observes that such a perspective provides a materialist sociology of reception.[22] Simerka's focus, therefore, supplements Iser by including the significant non-literary discourses in circulation and considers how these too would impact upon the audience's experience of the dramatic work. Simerka's more 'open' model allows for an interrogation of *La entretenida*, informed by the notion of an 'implied audience', that recovers potential responses towards the play that are inclusive of contemporary socio-cultural and extra-textual anxieties.

Such a perspective is particularly significant in light of the fact that *La entretenida*'s plot and themes explicitly foreground the plight of the individual, prioritising notions of individuality and autonomy but within the context of the restrictions — both aesthetic and socio-cultural — that the characters of the *capa y espada* face. My analysis of the play will, therefore, be informed by this complex representation of freedom. One aspect of my study will concern the presentation of women in the drama, specifically narrowing our focus to one of the female protagonists who represents a departure from the conventional portrayal of women of the time. While other characters in the play seek to fashion selves and indulge in role-play to do so, the character of Marcela Osorio does not assume roles nor invent fictions; rather she exemplifies the capacity of the individual to remain true to self. However, this stable core of 'self' is never entirely at variance with social codification and is paradoxically never performed as Marcela's interventions are unconventionally indirect. She resourcefully articulates subjectivity by means of a letter which literally takes her place on stage. Stephen Greenblatt's theory that in the Renaissance 'there appears to be an increased self-consciousness about the fashioning of human identity as a manipulable, artful process' may certainly apply to many of the characters in *La entretenida* such as Cristina, Cardenio and Torrente.[23] However, it is reversed in the portrayal of Marcela who neither negotiates her identity, nor compromises it, in order that she might express her opinion and exercise judgment regarding potential suitors. While she represents the struggle of the seventeenth-century subject in her attempt to reconcile desire with social stipulations; Marcela appropriates her goal without relying on orthodox *mujer varonil* techniques.

The second part of my analysis examines the interlude of Act III and explores how, via the issue of class, the drama subverts conventional strategies of role-play. The actors, who indulge in role-play and are fully aware of its vast potential, are unable to self-fashion or successfully play another role outside of their own. Rather, the *entremés* only serves to emphasise the character's 'natural' identities; their failure ironically stressing their individuality. These 'natural' roles are socially conditioned and connote the character's rank and position in society. By means of the interlude, Cervantes exposes the impossibility of ascending or altering one's designated social duty. Thus, the *entremés* comments ironically on the *comedia nueva*'s tendency to facilitate social mobility; whilst it also allows an audience to glimpse the possibilities when the individuality of the subject comes to the fore. Finally, I will examine the resolution of *La entretenida* which has long been considered a generic inversion of the *comedia nueva*'s formulaic closure. However, by developing Catherine Connor's argument concerning marriage as 'intrinsically social in terms of its roots and its performance', my interrogation of the resolution will take into account the implications of implied audience response in the context of the significance of marriage for the seventeenth-century spectator.[24] Cervantes's relationship with the public theatre and his evaluation of dramatic art in general finds particularly powerful expression in this play. *La entretenida*'s subversive exploitation of established *comedia* conventions prompts the spectator to call them, and the world which receives them unproblematically, into question.

Seeing Through the Mujer Varonil

Friedman observes that the failure of the female characters of *La entretenida* undermines 'a fundamental component of Lope's comedies: the highlighting of the confident, resourceful, and feisty woman'.[25] The dynamic, determined woman was far more likely to appear in comedy than in serious drama as 'comedy creates a new, and naturally ironic, dominant, which includes a particular type of female protagonist'.[26] McKendrick's study on 'types' of women on the Golden-Age stage has delineated the categories into which various female depictions fall; establishing the term and category of *mujer varonil* which denotes an 'ironic, dominant' woman most frequently seen in the *comedia*.[27] She explains *mujer varonil* as meaning the woman who:

> departs in any significant way from the feminine norm of the sixteenth and seventeenth centuries. She can take the form of the *mujer esquiva* who shuns love and marriage, the learned woman, the career woman, the female bandit, the female leader and warrior, the usurper of man's social role, the woman who wears masculine dress, or the one who indulges in masculine pursuits.[28]

Notions of social inequality and gender difference were, of course, perpetually exploited in Golden-Age theatre. Seventeenth-century patriarchy functioned as a structuring apparatus which controlled differences between male/female and husband/wife. Biological differences between the sexes were translated into codes of behaviour which determined women as subject to men. Woman was mediated by society in terms of her conduct, speech and the 'space' she could inhabit. Mary Beth Rose sums up the Renaissance ideal of womanhood as 'subordination and obedience, modesty, chastity, shyness, gentleness, innocence and silence'.[29] The ideal male construct was noble, brave, a protector of his own sexual property, of pure blood and good reputation. Gender, then, determined one's relationship with the world and the *comedia* enjoyed toying with established conventions by often depicting powerful women who departed from the contemporary Spanish norm. Women such as Antiopía and Deyanira in Lope's *Las mujeres sin hombres*, Rosaura in Calderón's *La vida es sueño* and Cervantes's Julia, Porcia and Rosamira in *El laberinto de amor* exemplify female dynamism as they perform masculinity to achieve a favourable outcome which potentially challenges and destabilises authority.

Cervantes's empathetic attitude toward women, love and marriage is prominent throughout his work and especially prevalent in the *Novelas ejemplares*. McKendrick notes that Cervantes manifests an 'acute awareness of the injustice of the accepted attitudes that governed relations between the sexes',[30] an analysis which is shared by critics such as Sara A. Taddeo.[31] Certainly, he is responsible for the creation of strong female characters such as the militant Marfisa in *La casa de los celos* who claims that she is 'más varón en las obras / que mujer en el semblante' (III. 2203-04) and Marcela in the *Quijote* who asserts her right to marry or not as she chooses. A prevalent motif in the corpus of the dramatist's work is the enhanced linguistic agency of the female characters. Characters such as Catalina in *La gran sultana* exhibit how Cervantes permits his female protagonists to manipulate language to ensure that their voices are not subsumed by ruling authority. Women, therefore, emerge as articulate individuals in their own right and his theatre, in particular, displays a consciousness of the marginal status imposed upon them. Nevertheless, Cervantes does not hesitate to depict an anti-heroine in *El casamiento engañoso*, nor does he shy away from portraying women who are questionable in terms of integrity and honour, such as the *dueña* in *El celoso extremeño*. Moreover, although the predicament of the seventeenth-century Spanish woman comes under scrutiny in the play, Cervantes's stance is by no means radical. Cervantes responded to the fact that women forged futures within the remit of what was socially and culturally available and, therefore, usually married and had children. Connor argues that the married state in early modern Spain was:

> the most commonly desired one for most women because it was the legal structure offering the greatest potential for economic, socio-cultural and political security. It still was, in short, the only social medium, although a traditional and patriarchal one, in which they might have hoped to improve their lives and, eventually, those of their daughters. Not only did married women prosper more decisively than un-marrieds, but society flourished when couples were able to marry, form households, produce and reproduce.[32]

The fundamental role of the married woman finds artistic expression in Cervantes's drama through the idea that woman will fulfil her role in society better if she is permitted to choose her own husband. It is precisely in this regard that Cervantes's women characters in *La entretenida* deviate significantly from the model typically presented in both the comedies and *capa y espadas* of the time. The dramatist's recognition of the legitimacy of a woman's need to forge her own relationship with the opposite sex is key to understanding his unconventional representation of femininity. Cervantes upholds a woman's right to discriminate, but she should be allowed to seek and attain that which is possible and available within the confines of society. His depiction of women, therefore, differs from that of *comedias* such as Lope's *La dama boba* in which the female protagonist triumphs based on the violation of patriarchal law and social protocol. Finea abandons the fiancé chosen by her father and hides in an attic with another man without destroying family honour. She also breaks both her engagement and her father's word with no legal repercussions. Cervantes's women characters, in contrast, neither create nor inhabit such an idealistic environment. They represent the reality of the limited possibilities for the seventeenth-century woman and attest to the fact that they have negligible control over their destinies.

It is highly significant that the female characters of *La entretenida* are neither free nor forward thinking. They seem not to engage with the norms of the day intelligently nor shrewdly in order to overturn them, insofar as it suits their personal circumstances. They do not manipulate resources readily available to them, such as language (or silence as in *El laberinto*) and ultimately, their desires are thwarted and frustrated. Notably, unlike the heroines of *El laberinto*, the women of *La entretenida* are, for the most part, unsympathetic characters and their failure to arrange marriages does not provoke any great degree of empathy. Even the predicament of Marcela Osorio, who is reduced to the metaphor of a caged animal, does not incite an intensity of response as she never appears on stage. She represents a contrast to Lope's Marcela in *El perro del hortelano* who is a witness to the on-off relationship between the countess of Belflor and her scribe, Teodoro. Although Lope's Marcela is granted a stage presence, her voice is often quashed by others and eventually subsumed by Diana who denies Marcela the man whom she loves. She scarcely speaks but her few words eloquently express her exasperation. Lope contrasts Marcela's silence and her physical presence in order to heighten audience perception of the unjust treatment that she receives. Ultimately, Marcela underscores the conventional interpretation of the compliant female, subject to the rule of the men in her life. We shall see in this chapter that although Marcela Osorio is both silent and absent, she is a much more unorthodox character. She may not invoke audience sympathies until the closing scene of *La entretenida*, but she manages to undermine the boundaries imposed upon her in order to 'articulate' her desires and determine her future. Marcela Osorio is, therefore, not restricted by literary codes which would render her conformist to prevailing authority and secondary to the play's main events.

Thacker remarks that women on the Golden-Age stage often found themselves in hopeless situations which required desperate measures: 'The partial solution that female characters tend to stumble across in times of desperation is to abandon their social role temporarily, and *act*'.[33] In *La entretenida* only Marcela Osorio can be described as being in a 'desperate situation' and as she is never on stage, she cannot be said to 'act', but rather resorts to letter-writing to achieve her goals. Moreover, Marcela Almendárez, as we shall see, usually finds herself as a passive participant of someone else's fiction and fails to mobilise her own resources to make any substantial difference to her situation. Cristina, a *fregona*, has social aspirations which paint her as selfish and capricious. She is also portrayed as flirtatious and a suggestion of promiscuity further taints her character. Although *La entretenida*'s depiction of woman may subvert the conventional Spanish portrayal of the active, resourceful and shrewd *mujer varonil*, it is evident that such a strategy not only affirms the drama's parodic purpose, but has the added affect of creating distance between *La entretenida* and the dramatist's own *capa y espada*, *El laberinto de amor*. Casalduero remarks that:

> *El laberinto de amor* nos trasladaba a un mundo de fantasía, con sus duques y princesas y disfraces, sus juicios de Dios, sus cárceles, sus amores; tiene la alegría de tantas altas damas hermosas cogidas en la madeja del amor, que deliciosamente enredan y felizmente consiguen desenredar.[34]

El laberinto conveys a utopian environment where characters achieve success in spite of the dictatorial nature of established norms. *La entretenida*, on the other hand, grounds us in a world characterised by failure and frustration which is not easily overcome. A decidedly parodic relationship, therefore, does exist between Cervantes's own *capa y espada* and his deflation of Lope's successful formula. However, how might a seventeenth-century spectator experience and respond to this construction and juxtaposition of type and anti-type? Perhaps an answer lies in a closer look at Marcela Osorio who assumes a role of seminal importance in Cervantes's intentions to deconstruct Lope's model and yet, to date, no sustained study has been offered on Marcela. My own analysis of Marcela Osorio aims to determine the implications of Cervantes's parodic depiction of the *mujer varonil* for a contemporary spectator. As we shall see, Marcela is a vehicle through which the audience are challenged to look beyond the appearances of the stage and observe the very apparatus that makes it function.

Marcela Osorio

Confined by her father to a monastery lest she attempt to choose her own husband, Marcela Osorio represents the attitude to woman exercised by patriarchy. Her father, Don Pedro, has chosen Don Antonio as her husband irrespective of any opinion his daughter would have. Marcela is subject to her father's authority and is hidden away from the world. She can be likened to Leonora in *El celoso extremeño* whose husband, Carrizales, constructs impenetrable walls around his wife to prevent her from coming into contact with any male. The circumstances of both women embody their positions as subservient to an obdurate patriarchally-structured society. Marriage, rather than operating on the premise of love, represented business-like negotiations, which according to James Casey, involved a 'weighing up on each side of a variety of factors: geographical location of the family, wealth, honour, influence exerted by intermediaries'.[35] As an aristocratic woman in her father's household, Marcela is a bargaining chip who possesses no sense of entitlement to make a decision which would affect her own life and her family. Her confinement directly mirrors the plight of Rosamira, Porcia and Julia in *El laberinto* and Margarita in *El gallardo español*, who are subject to a father's rule and forbidden to resist the system into which they have been born. However, Marcela is a much more passive object than these women and, therefore, more easily subdued by her father's restrictions. Her 'silencing' makes her not unlike the female protagonists of *El burlador de Sevilla*, who are linguistically overpowered by Don Juan, but her invisibility allows her to assume a more radical role in the drama. For Cervantes not only denies Marcela a voice, but a physical presence; and it is this dramatic device which allows the playwright to foreground the plight of a character who is, in fact, literally located at the periphery. Moreover, she provides ample opportunity to toy with audience expectations.

Marcela is made known to the audience only through passing reference by others and mainly by her suitors. For the spectator she occupies little space in the central plot, but in fact, plays a much more significant role than has often been recognised. She is forcefully re-introduced in Act III, but until this point, Marcela Osorio has only ever existed in the language of others, and an audience would have reason to doubt that she exists at all. This is compounded by the fact that the 'other' Marcela [Almendárez] learns that her brother, Don Antonio, is in love with a woman named Marcela and presuming it to be herself, believes that he is guilty of an incestuous attachment:

> Marcela: ¿Siquiera no me dirás / el nombre desa tu dama?
> D.Antonio: Como te llamas, se llama.
> Marcela: ¿Como yo?
> D.Antonio: Y aun tiene más: / que se te parece mucho.
> Marcela: [*Aparte.*] ¡Válame Dios! ¿Qué es aquesto? / ¿Si es amor éste de incesto?
>
> (I. 181–86)

Antonio and Marcela's dialogue is determined and destabilised by the fact that the name 'Marcela' has different connotations for each sibling; Antonio refers to Marcela Osorio while his sister immediately thinks of herself. Therefore, 'Marcela' is a sign which does not signify a concrete reality and lends itself to the creation of an incest motif which, in actual fact, has no substance. Marcela believes that Antonio's use of 'her' name in this context connotes a shift in their relationship and signifies a more personal and intimate attachment. Traugott and Pratt argue that: 'In performance, transitions in naming are often difficult, for they mean changing not just a habit, but a whole set of social assumptions that goes along with naming'.[36] This conversation, then, redefines the parameters of Marcela's relationship with her brother for her and the audience and substitutes on-stage reality with a fiction; thereby demonstrating the capacity of the stage to fabricate illusion upon illusion.

Cervantes's comic use of the incest motif in *La entretenida* not only characterises Marcela Almendárez as essentially egotistical, but suggests to the spectator that Don Antonio's 'Marcela' may, in fact, be his sister, bearing in mind that

Marcela Osorio has never materialised. Moreover, in a society governed by rigid rules of discourse, it is entirely plausible that a character might speak indirectly as a means to direct communication.[37] On a more significant note, the suggestion of an illicit relationship bares consequence for an audience who had strict ideas of moral conduct. Seventeenth-century Spanish theatre was, of course, also subject to frequent demands for decorum by the powerful control of the church.[38] As Duncan Moir remarks: 'Perhaps the most important of the classical doctrines is that of literary decorum — seemliness and appropriateness in all things, in characterization, actions, saying, style'.[39] Indecorous conduct features heavily in the plot of *El castigo sin venganza* which sees a pseudo-incestuous relationship between a duchess and her step-son. The audience is clearly led to reflect on how Casandra's distorted ideals represent a deviation from Christian respectability and are incompatible with the standard of behaviour demanded from a member of the aristocracy. Although *El castigo sin venganza* was published much later than the *Ocho comedias* (1631) a contemporary audience would have been familiar with other 'incest' plays such as Lope's *El vaquero de Moraña* (1603) and *La fianza satisfecha* (1612). Therefore, for an audience familiar with motifs of incest in the *comedia*, a brother-sister relationship is not beyond the bounds of possibility, especially when expounded by a phantasmal character and within the contrived context of mistaken identity. However, the suggestion of anything illicit in *La entretenida* is effectively still-born and cleared up without complication in the middle of Act II. Furthermore, Marcela Osorio's letter heralds her existence and definitively quashes the incest motif. As a digression from appropriate and seemly behaviour, Cervantes manipulates the implications of an incestuous attachment in order to expose it for what it is — a theatrical device capable of shocking an audience and arousing, at least for a time, the spectator's interest. A *comedia* audience is compelled to await a resolution which will restore order, harmony and decorous values. Thus, when no immoral liaison transpires and Marcela features in the final act as a resourceful individual capable of undermining her father's authority and creates a sub-plot which becomes inextricably linked with a more central plotline, the audience is aware that their expectations have been utterly subverted. Iser remarks: 'literary texts are full of unexpected twists and turns, and frustration of expectations. Even in the simplest story there is bound to be some kind of blockage, if only for the fact that no tale can ever be told in its entirety'.[40] The audience has effectively been duped and Cervantes grants his spectator cause to note their position as receivers of an influential and manipulable art form.

It transpires that Marcela has mobilised her limited resources to counter-act her father's attempt to smother her voice and prevent her from choosing her own husband. She has written a letter to Don Ambrosio declaring her love for him: 'Ya Marcela ha parecido, / y con esa letra y firma / todos mis bienes confirma; / ya, cual veis, soy su marido' (III. 2748–51). Action in the Golden-Age *comedia* often evolves from both spoken and written language. The impact and consequences of Marcela Osorio's written speech act in *La entretenida*, however, presents a stark contrast to female characters in the *comedia nueva* who access authority via writing, but find that this access is limited. Emilie Bergmann's study of the female protagonist, Estrella, in *La estrella de Sevilla* concludes that while reading and writing in several *comedia* texts 'enable women to choose some aspects of their lives; a woman is written upon in *La estrella de Sevilla* and is left only with the choice to accept with dignity the disaster that writing imposes upon her'.[41] As we shall see, in *La entretenida* Marcela's letter replaces her on stage and literally becomes an actor which writes her fate. Her words are designated a role of their own which is instrumental in re-writing the intentions of her father.

Marcela's plight and unfortunate circumstances are highlighted by a speech (III. 2772–95) in which her father uses the analogy of a shackled animal: 'una niña a quien apenas / el sol ni el viento han tocado; / un armiño aprisionado / con religiosas cadenas; / una que son sus cuidados / de simple y tierna doncella; / y ofrezco en dote con ella / de renta dos mil ducados' (III. 2788–95). Mariscal observes that the imagery of the ermine signifies whiteness and purity and also marks the aristocratic character of the female: 'In the image of the ermine the deep structure of aristocratic masculine desire — that women protect the family bloodline at all cost — is transferred to the female and subsequently presented to her as if it were her own'.[42] These sentiments are echoed by Ocaña in Act I who reflects that: 'La mujer ha de ser buena, / y parecerlo, que es más' (I. 81–82). A woman's value, therefore, hinges not only on her submissiveness to the dominant structure of which she is a part, but also her ability to project this image in public. In Marcela's case, this value is economic, reductive and objectifying. She is an object of exchange that must retain integrity and honour lest she taint her father's reputation. At this point the audience, unlike Don Pedro, is privy to the fact that Marcela has arranged for a marriage with a suitor of her own choice, and thus the father's display of disapproval provokes a sense of empathy and alignment with the daughter. The older man's tirade when it is revealed that his daughter has wilfully disobeyed him — '¡Hijas inobedientes, / que al curso de los años / anticipáis el gusto, / destrúyaos Dios, los Cielos os maldigan!' (III. 2848–51) — highlights Marcela's role as emblematic of all women. His discourse is a conventional reaffirmation that woman is subservient to male authority and responsible for upholding male honour even within the restricted context of what was possible for the seventeenth-century woman. While Marcela's desires are natural, they are also respectable, given that she has arranged a marriage with an entirely suitable nobleman; a union which will in no way compromise the social standing or moral integrity of the Osorio family.[43] Cervantes, therefore, uses her plight as a vehicle to exemplify the individual's right to free choice and the fact that this need not threaten prevailing social structures. This could compel some level of interrogation by the spectator of his, or indeed *her*, own place in this society, for Marcela functions, as Iser would have it, as a 'gap' in the play. Iser states that 'whenever we are led off in unexpected directions, the opportunity is given to us to bring into play our own faculty for establishing connections — for filling in the gaps left by the text itself'.[44] In *La entretenida*, Marcela is a material 'gap' and the receiver is compelled to respond dynamically and to establish the connection between her and the restrictive parameters of the social system into which both she and the receiver have been born.

Marcela's degradation is further intensified by Don Antonio's response to the situation which echoes her father's diatribe and expresses his unease with Marcela's active role in the public sphere. It is worth noting that the idea of a 'public sphere' has not been fully conceptualised in relation to the early modern period.[45] With specific reference to the socio-political context of seventeenth-century Spain, William Childers has provocatively challenged Jürgen Habermas's theory of the public sphere, which privileges the Enlightenment as the moment when the modern world came into being.[46] Childers's engagement with Habermas's theory 'uses discursive practices in Hapsburg Spain to exemplify an alternative model of the public sphere' and highlights the Baroque as 'a distinctive modernity' which challenges 'the equation of the modern with post-Enlightenment reason'.[47] Childers states that:

> In the Baroque a full-fledged public sphere takes place, in which individuals and groups attain political agency without the transparency of rational debate or any pretence of equal participation. Its prominent features include asymmetrical access, distortion of public discourses due to their hidden or partially hidden relations to power, and internal divisions between "modern" and "archaic" practices. Rather than an idealised, timeless abstraction, the public sphere of the Baroque is a hybrid, compromise formation, made up of a blending of earlier and later practices, technologies, and social structures.[48]

In a hierarchically-structured society, the ruling classes of seventeenth-century Spain were privileged with inherited status, power and wealth. Such resources served as regulatory devices which prevented disruption in the community whilst doubly maintaining and propagating established political and social structures rather than serving to facilitate a space in which individuals and groups could discuss matters of mutual interest or allow for agreement and difference of opinion.

Marcela has, in fact, contracted a *cédula* with Don Ambrosio, provoking Don Antonio to say: 'Doncella de escritorios, / de públicas audiencias, / de pruebas y testigos, / no es para mí' (III. 2860–03). Bergmann observes that: 'women's legal status excluded them from contractual agreements. In addition, when women wrote, even their poetry and fiction was restricted to an audience of immediate family and friends, with rare and significant exceptions'.[49] In this environment, a woman functioned as an object of exchange between patriarchal groups and her social value, therefore, depended on public conformity to an image which upheld her family's name and honour. Marcela's letter, then, represents a public defiance of convention and is an external manifestation of inner determination and society's inability to curb her. It breaches the divide between private and public and symbolises in rational terms Marcela's right to choose her own husband. Marcela's ownership of the letter, therefore, allows her to appropriate a space and discourse from which she is usually excluded. Her incarceration is symbolic of the marginalised individual's place in a society which implements repressive structures in order to prohibit and prevent the production or circulation of discourse contrary to its own. Marcela, then, is not only emblematic of all women, but of all marginalised groups. Cervantes highlights the contradictory and conflicted position of those in this situation. On the one hand, the individual must adhere to established standards so as to ensure the successful management of social edifice, but on the other, must not seek ways in which to improve social performance lest punishment is meted out for deviant conduct.

Cervantes reinforces the constraints of patriarchy by displaying the dominant attitude twice over via the men who control Marcela's life — her father and suitor. However, Marcela's defiant response doubly inscribes her predicament into the text; the intrinsic written letter subsequently becomes an integral part of the final act. Marcela writes a letter in order to get beyond the confines of the monastery's walls, but also to transcend her father's will. In this way, she literally becomes the author of her life and destiny. Although her father wields the authority to imprison Marcela, his power over her internal resolve is severely limited. Cervantes thereby foregrounds the power of the written word in the mind of the audience, within an aesthetic frame in which the marriage of Marcela Osorio is the only feasible resolution for a spectator heavily influenced by the *comedia nueva*'s penchant for matrimonial closure, however contrived it may be.[50] As an unseen 'on-stage' author manipulating the course of events, Marcela mirrors the role of the unseen 'off-stage' dramatist. She illustrates his ability to frustrate, fulfil or shatter the expectations of the audience. The mechanisms of the stage are exposed through the combined machinations of the internal author, Marcela and the external author, Cervantes who both have negotiated audience conjecture. Robert Phiddian uses the metaphor of 'writing under erasure' to explain the effect that a parody of the generic formula would produce:

> All parody refunctions pre-existing text(s) and/or discourses, so it can be said that these verbal structures are called to the readers' minds and then placed under erasure. A necessary modification of the original idea is that we must allow the act of erasure to operate critically rather than as merely neutral cancellation of its object. Parodic erasure disfigures its pre-texts in various ways that seek to guide our re-evaluation or re-figuration of them.[51]

The 'disfiguring' of *comedia* conventions in *La entretenida* forces a recognition of its 're-figured' signs on the part of the audience which must, therefore, question and evaluate their own role in the theatre as receivers of manipulative dramatic devices. Moreover, it is highly significant that Cervantes's dramatic 'self-fashioning' takes the form of a silent (or silenced) marginal female. Marcela's peripheral social position reflects Cervantes's anxieties regarding the negligible status of his own voice. Unlike Lope, who often places himself centre-stage in the guise of the character Belardo, Cervantes forges a voice in a marginal female. But this alignment with Marcela goes beyond the expression of authorial anxiety. Just as Marcela utilises the written word to counter-act the unjust restrictions imposed upon her, Cervantes creates a theatre (which was also eventually directed at a reading public) that contends with the contemporary Spanish stage.

Of course, the very notion of Marcela as a powerful woman with the linguistic legerdemain to articulate her desires is undermined to some degree by her non-appearance; the fact that she is never allowed to fully fulfill the role of the *mujer varonil* reducing the impact that her dynamic persona could exert on stage. However, this 'conspicuous by absence' strategy serves as an emphatic function to underscore the injustice of the situation. Frustration which arises from not seeing Marcela, or knowing that she even exists or if she does, whether or not she will marry, causes an audience to look in other directions. Iser quotes B. Ritchie:

> Frustration blocks or checks activity. It necessitates new orientation for our activity, if we are to escape the *cul de sac* [...] surprise merely causes a temporary cessation of the exploratory phase of the experience, and a recourse to intense contemplation and scrutiny.[52]

The spectator of Cervantes's play might well be oriented towards scrutiny of his/her own expectations of a conclusion in which the unseen protagonist would secure her desire. By subverting the expectations of the spectator Cervantes advocates a redefinition of the female typical to the seventeenth-century stage. His portrayal of Marcela shatters superficial stereotypes of the obligatory *mujer varonil* who becomes whatever she needs to be in order to reap maximum gain from her situation. Cervantes proposes an alternative view by crafting a woman who utilises her inner strength to facilitate the shift from passive object to active subject. In this respect, Marcela's non-appearance is a positive strategem. By not changing before our eyes, Marcela is liberated from literary traditions which would demand conformance to what had become on stage a female construct. The dramatist underscores the fact that the stock character is afforded a very limited space and that her purpose is to conform. For Cervantes, the *mujer varonil* shatters any sense of mimetic representation and is no 'freer' than the seventeenth-century female theatre-goer. Furthermore, by divesting the female character of the illusions created on/by the stage, the audience is compelled to see her as a creation for the stage, also. Cervantes discredits the superficiality of stage-managed effects and his portrayal of Marcela, 'constructed' through the words of others, prioritises intellectual engagement over entertaining spectacle 'para que gente ignorante se admire y venga a la comedia'.

According to McKendrick, the *mujer varonil* 'contains the requisite Baroque tension: the tension between the reality of woman's position and her illusions, emotional needs and desires'.[53] This tension undergoes a symbolic transformation in Cervantes's drama — where it is the letter which exists within a real and legal context. In fact, the letter has a more mimetic function than the *mujer varonil* which 'is not what she seems to be nor what she is expected to be. Either her sex hides her masculine characteristics or her masculine characteristics (clothes, actions) hide her sex. In other words, the reality she seems to present is an illusion'.[54] Cervantes's (non)-representation of Marcela strips away the layers which mask the illusion and exposes the deception for what it is. In this play it suits Cervantes's purpose not to present the *mujer varonil* as a manifestation of the possibilities available to the seventeenth-century woman. This allows him to convey that this stock characterisation has no bearing on contemporary social realities. Viewed in this way, Marcela is not only a distortion of the typical *mujer varonil*, but of the *capa y espada* genre as a whole.

The Interlude: Play on Play

The highly comic interlude of Act III, performed by the servants of Don Antonio's household, represents one of the most engaging and complex aspects of Cervantes's text. Multilayered in its dramatic function, the interlude produces a lull in the play in which the dramatist disrupts the *capa y espada* formula in order to achieve distance from it and craft a play which, as we shall see, is distinctly Cervantine. In this play within the play, Cervantes inscribes the audience's position as consumer and receiver directly into the text. The audience is thus positively 'estranged' and allowed to appraise their function and that of the actors on stage from a critical distance. Thacker observes that: 'A play presents trained actors who have learned and studied their parts, mimicking us, the actors who extemporize with the aid of the myriad and usually unwritten social guidelines — the structures that support our interactive role-playing and mutual comprehension'.[55] The interlude, therefore, presents fictitious characters that mimic the behaviour of accepted social categories and beings which serves to inform our understanding of the character's public reality and emphasises the 'techniques by which everyday persons sustain their real social situations'.[56]

As the interlude is written and directed by servants for their masters (in which the servants literally take centre stage) social structure and order is made much less certain for the spectator. This is the case in *La entretenida* as a whole, as illustrated, for example, in the episode in which Cardenio and Torrente disguise themselves as Don Silvestre and his servant and successfully cast Don Antonio and Marcela as their unsuspecting audience. The servants are instrumental in securing permission for the staging of their interlude by preying on the good humour of Don Antonio, who has gained Don Pedro's consent to marry his daughter Marcela Osorio. Cristina, a *fregona*, manipulates Marcela Almendárez, Don Antonio's sister, to ventriloquise her desire to produce a play: 'En nombre de Cristina, / os pido deis licencia / para que aquesta noche / os hagan una fiesta los de casa; / Muñoz y Dorotea, / Torrente con Ocaña' (III. 2018-23). The dichotomy of social relations is stressed with the onus firmly placed on the nobleman to affirm his approval. Cristina's desire to organise a diversion from the tedium and hardship of everyday life serves to solidify audience speculation that the lower class is subject to poor treatment, a perception which is encoded throughout the text. This notion is emphasised by Don Antonio's warning to his kitchen maid: 'El término decente / de honestidad se guarde, / Cristina' (III. 2046-48). This charge implicitly insinuates that Cristina, as a member of the subordinate class, lacks morals and an understanding of what constitutes good taste. As Mariscal notes, the association of the lower class with a deficiency of moral values and probity is 'symptomatic of the ways in which, for early modern Spanish culture, a discourse of morality often masked questions of exploitation, status and class divisions'.[57] What effect, then, might Don Antonio's insinuation have on a contemporary audience? The spectator, participating in what Iser labels the 'process of recreation', is given cause to reflect back on Cristina's dialogue at the opening of Act II which catalogues the relationship between a servant and her mistress:[58]

> Pero, ya que falte
> este detrimento,
> sobran los del ama,
> que no tienen cuento:
> "Ven acá, suciona.
> ¿Dónde está el pañuelo?
> La escoba te hurtaron
> y un plato pequeño.
> Buen salario ganas;
> dél pagarme pienso,
> porque despabiles
> los ojos y el seso.
> Vas y nunca vuelves,
> y tienes bureo
> con Sancho en la calle,
> con Mingo y con Pedro.
> Eres, en fin, pu...
> El 'ta' diré quedo,
> porque de cristiana
> sabes que me precio" (II. 1024-43)

Don Antonio's command, juxtaposed against the backdrop of Cristina's incessant complaints of her lowly, and hence, exploited position serves to exemplify the precarious, illusory ground on which the discourse of honour rested. For a seventeenth-century audience, the fragile nature of such a code is emphasised. However, Cristina's tirade cannot be considered as an unproblematic denunciation of the entitlements afforded to the aristocracy as she desperately covets upward mobility. She rejects Ocaña due to his social position as a lackey: 'De tus malas intenciones / agora se vee el exceso; / agora se echa de ver / que eres loco y laca' (I. 39–42) and relishes her own position as the object of affection of no less than three men. She imagines herself as a lady pursued by three suitors whose choice must be predicated on the basis of social mobility. The obsession with reputation and honour is, then, revealed to be so pervasive that it permeates all roles and ranks. Cristina represents for the audience, a 'contradictory subject' who would denigrate the aristocratic world to which she is subordinate and yet act out the patriarchal structures which are designated to control social order.[59] The maid's incongruous position exposes the societal conditioning of which she has been a part and emphasises the individual's struggle to reconcile self and social fulfillment with their allotted role in life.

Cristina's position as a common kitchen maid is compounded by the laments of other servants such as Ocaña who feels undervalued and unappreciated: 'A nadie se le trasluce, / por más que yo lo procuro, / el ingenio lucio y puro / que en este lacayo luce' (I. 613–16). The *entremés*, therefore, presents an opportunity for the lower classes to escape the restrictions that inform their lives. The world of class division is, in fact, turned upside down by the interlude, much in the same way the *comedia* often allowed servants to play out their roles in excess of the boundaries which delineated their function, even permitting some to 'attain' nobility.[60] By constituting the audience of the play, Don Antonio, Don Francisco and Marcela, are forced to occupy a relatively more passive role than their natural roles allow. Now the servants can engage with the theatricality of life and exploit it to enjoy the freedom which their drama offers. Hornby reflects on the significance of role-play in the theatre:

> performers and audience members are in a sense 'actors' in the theatrical experience, dropping their regular identities and trying out new ones. This is valuable for both the individual and society. Just as the individual must revise his identity at crucial times throughout his lifetime, so too must a dynamic society frequently revise the way in which it wants its members to play roles.[61]

By staging their own performance, the servants are temporarily permitted to leave their roles and exercise a new sense of self which knows no limits.

However, although the interlude serves to elucidate aspects of the social lives of the characters, it also demonstrates their inability to shun their social roles, thereby operating as a subtle agent of societal destabilisation. The aristocracy, who usually engage with social roles characterised by the freedom which these roles inherently permit, are now subject to their servants and thus, acted upon. Moreover, the interlude is an accumulation of persistent role-playing throughout *La entretenida* and serves to reverse the rigid hierarchal edifice of seventeenth-century Spanish life, thus undermining the structure, albeit temporarily. Butler labels this effect 'subversive repetition' and suggests that practices of repetition which permeate and shape culture and dictate social norms, can be turned back on themselves, and subsequently contest the very 'truths' or 'natural facts' such practices establish.[62] As the players draw their masters into their fiction, Cervantes utilises the power of the visual medium to prompt an audience to reflect on the fact that the servants are literally upstaging their noble counterparts and that they act, and function, independently of their employers. This contrasts greatly with the *comedia nueva* which sees its servants copying and emulating the behaviour of their masters and often playing second fiddle to the whims of the aristocracy. The dramatist, therefore, shatters superficial *comedia* stereotypes, whilst also calling into question the fragile roles which are so readily abandoned and embraced by lower and upper class alike.

Nonetheless, the players' stage roles also function ironically as devices which merely serve to emphasise the reality of their social circumstances. By performing for their masters, they re-represent their roles as servants who administer to the needs of the individuals to whom they are subservient. In this case, they are diversions and entertainment for the Almendárez family and their friend, Don Francisco. This is further compounded by the fact that the servants do not change their names or their occupations for the purposes of their drama. The stage directions read: '*Salen Dorotea y Cristina como fregonas*' (III. 2249). Naming is here, and throughout Cervantes's work, synonymous with identity.[63] This suggests to the spectator that just as the interlude constitutes an extra illusory layer in the fabric of the play, the active identities assumed by the servants within it, are equally artificial and cannot disguise who they are as individuals. Identity is, therefore, not 'worn' externally but represents a stable core. However, this is not solely an issue of class but pertains to the role in life which each individual has been given. This is exemplified through the failure of each character to control their lives because they deviate from the role intended for them. As Friedman states: 'Because their roles are not genuine, those who play roles in *La entretenida* are destined to fail'.[64] The players of both the *entremés* and the play as a whole are motivated by self-interest to negate the social roles which are appropriate to their position. Donald Larson observes that Golden-Age comedy reveals that each individual has a particular role to play:

> for each person on earth there is one role which he can most appropriately play, that all other roles are in various degrees inappropriate, and that happiness and genuineness stem from the assumption of that peculiarly apposite role to which one has been, in a sense, predestined.[65]

La entretenida's characters fail, then, because their misguided attempts to forge new social roles shatter societal harmony.

The notion of a 'predestined' role and its associated happiness is accentuated by Marcela's closing words: 'Yo quedaré en mi entereza, / no procurando imposibles, / sino casos convenibles / a nuestra naturaleza.' (III. 3076–79). In the symbolic theatre space of the interlude, Cervantes foregrounds the *comedia nueva*'s tendency to exploit role-play as a means to escape obligations and undermine social edifice through developing an identity other than that already allotted by society. Robbins comments that:

> Baroque theatre presents no clear division between the individual and society, between the body and the body politic. The individual is conceived of as a social entity, and playwrights dramatize the alarming way in which the body is never autonomous but, rather, a space defined by the multiple and conflicting discourses of sex, religion, politics and power.[66]

La entretenida subverts this notion by representing the fact that inflexible and austere hierarchical structures may compel the subject to act out of their role in order to seize an identity, but this 'acting out' is ultimately futile. Cervantes's response, therefore, to the Baroque world view of 'identity as projected and constituted by its public role' is a seditious one.[67] By highlighting the redundant nature of the character's role-playing, the dramatist calls attention to their intrinsic individuality; rejection of classification based on their societal function.[68] In this way, Cervantes engages with the compulsive contemporary obsession with, and tension between, *ser* and *parecer*. By exposing their adopted roles as illusion-making devices which have little bearing on reality, the concept of *parecer* is paradoxically granted no sense of legitimacy in this theatre.[69] This is a blatant inversion of the *theatrum mundi* motif which painted life as inherently theatrical. Cervantes deliberately deflates dramatic tension by denying a potential conflict between self and society; the interlude's characters are represented as self-consciously satisfied and stable rather than as excluded individuals seeking a sense of belonging.[70]

The comic farce is brought quickly to an end by an *alguacil*. On a superficial level, the appearance of the *alguacil* adheres to *comedia* conventions which typically see a person in position of authority fulfil a *deus ex machina* function. Closing scenes in a *tragedia* often feature kings (such as in Calderón's *El alcalde de Zalamea*), members of the aristocracy and law-enforcers who act as devices which restore social harmony and verify the ending of the play. These characters are representative of the *comedia*'s tendency to resolve loose ends hastily and subsume the dissident nature of the play by slotting its characters back into their social role. An audience expects, therefore, that the *alguacil* will affirm the lowly and lofty positions of the servants and their masters, respectively. However, upon seeing that the *entremés* is a *comedia* rather than a *tragedia*, the *alguacil* promptly exits, observing that his presence is superfluous: 'De que todo sea comedia, / y no tragedia, me alegro, / y así, a mi ronda, señores, / con vuestra licencia, vuelvo' (III. 2496–99). By drawing attention to the genre in which the interlude and the play as a whole belongs, the audience is made aware of its comedic value and purpose. The observation, then, stresses the procedures which give comedy its identity.[71] It highlights the events of the *entremés*, such as Ocaña and Torrente's fight, as conventional comic devices and underscores how an audience should respond to the diversion. The *alguacil*'s intervention breaks the theatrical frame and highlights the symbolic nature of this theatre within the theatre. It not only unmasks the routine and contrived manner in which the *comedia* frequently ends, but makes manifest the audience's dependence on a conclusion which settles all complications neatly.

Unsettling Conclusions

As has been established, the unresolved ending of *La entretenida* is generally interpreted as Cervantes's attempt to parody conventional Golden-Age practices. Many *comedia* texts engineer a sense of resolution in the closing scene by tying up loose ends which result from the implicitly subversive aspects of the preceding acts. Northrop Frye engages with the notion of closure in Renaissance comedy in his exposition of the three stages of a play: the 'old' society that imposes rules which are antagonistic to the desires of the hero or heroine; loss of identity and consequent confusion; and the resolution of confusion and discovery of identity via the institution of marriage.[72] Many Golden-Age female characters are conceded marriage as a victory (of sorts), such as Diana in Lope's *El perro del hortelano*, Finea and Nise in *La dama boba*, Rosaura in Calderón's *La vida es sueño* and Cervantes's own heroines in *El laberinto*, to name but a few. Marriage signals the containment of chaos and disorder, the restoration of harmony and heralds the establishment of new family units. Connor observes that: 'For the spectators of any culture, weddings are extremely important sociocultural markers of change, transition, and new foundations in the lives of individuals and their immediate societies'.[73] *La entretenida*, however, not only deviates from the routine formula but self-consciously underscores this deviation: 'Desta verdad conocida / pido me den testimonio: / que acaba sin matrimonio / la comedia entretenida' (III. 3084–87). Cervantes has no reason to accommodate the convention as social order is never overtly disrupted nor threatened in *La entretenida*. The drama's final scene functions, as Iser would have it, as a 'component part' which builds on perspectives already established throughout.[74] Cervantes's criticism of the contrived manner of many *comedia* endings is incontrovertible. However, *La entretenida*'s own parodic finale also introduces a new sense of frustration about a plot which has undergone no progression from the opening scene. The stationary nature of the text may motivate an audience to call into question the theatrical experience. Moreover, what is really at stake with regards to a play ending in marriage is, as Connor points out 'the closure reached by individual spectators as they attempt to make meaning of the events of the entire play within the frameworks of their own life experiences'.[75] Cervantes's spectator understands marriage as the establishment of a new family unit and reconciliation with patriarchy. *La entretenida*, then, undermines, both socially and artistically, propagandistic elements of the institution.

The play begins with the promise of marriage and closes with a very vague sense of possible future unions. An audience can only suppose that Marcela Osorio will marry Don Ambrosio as the text does not indicate that she will obtain her father's permission. Marcela Almendárez's marriage depends on Clavijo acquiring papal dispensation from Rome and Cristina can only hope that one day she will find love. These expressions of hope represent perfunctory concessions. As future events which may or may not occur, they are located outside the theatrical frame and provide an incomplete resolution based on the elusiveness of speculation. As discussed, frustration of audience expectations tends to direct attention elsewhere. The absence of a concrete conclusion may compel the spectator to focus on the events that have preceded the final scene; to engage with the conduct of the characters through which crucial issues have been raised, such as notions of individual autonomy and the subject's relationship to, and with, oppressive social structures. Cervantes's theatre, then, diverges greatly from that of Lope's where concepts of individuality and characterisation are acknowledged by the author as secondary to plot.[76] While Cervantes's *La entretenida* concentrates on the consequences of individual behaviour, Lope manipulates conventions to ensure that any social impediments, such as rank and lineage, are deftly removed. The *comedia nueva* often crafted plays which see persons from lowly backgrounds experience an anagnorisis which reveals them as members of the aristocracy and permits a union that had once been deemed economically and socially impossible. This is, of course, also the case in Cervantes's *Pedro de Urdemalas* and *La gitanilla* but, significantly, the conversion to nobleperson does not occur as any sort of fortuitous coincidence.[77] In Lope's *El perro del hortelano*, however, Teodoro concocts a scheme through which his achievement of social mobility is fraudulent. This contrast demonstrates how Cervantes's drama and Lope's *comedia nueva* differ. *La entretenida* confirms that Cervantes is not interested in solutions to problems which plainly violate rules of verisimilitude. The collective failure of the play paradoxically affirms the artificiality of the theatrical space and the misuse of art. The dramatist, in fact, denounces art which raises false hopes and causes people to aspire to impossible levels, such as changing rank: 'Hay poetas tan divinos, / de poder tan singular, / que puedan títulos dar / como condes palatinos; / y aun, si lo toman despacio, / en tiempo y caso oportuno, / no habrá lacayo ninguno / que no casen en palacio / con doncellas de la reina' (I. 625–33). The playwright posits an alternate view of the *comedia*'s so-called 'reflection' of life by denying his characters and his audience any sense of fulfilment.⁷⁸ With reference to stage-managed effects, Spadaccini remarks that: 'The power of the medium is deemed to be extraordinary because the audience of the playhouse does not reflect upon or see through its illusion-making devices'.⁷⁹ Cervantes crafts plotlines such as that of the absent Marcela and ends his play without marriage to force an audience to do precisely that, to 'see through' the dramatic art and to engage with theatre for what it is, a system of representation. The resolution, then, challenges a public who were, in Cervantes's opinion, unprepared and unwilling to interrogate the machinations of the stage.

This censure of the *comedia nueva*, and those who slavishly adhered to its model, also provokes the contemporary spectator to re-evaluate the way in which they engage with the messages of the stage. *La entretenida* ruptures, shifts and controls response in order to fabricate a play which resembles a Lopean *comedia* on a superficial level, but rigorously breaks the mould ideologically and artistically. The dramatist's prime focus is the subject's experience of a world in which natural inclinations and the demands of society appear to function antagonistically. Marcela's non-appearance paradoxically highlights the impossibility of autonomy for the seventeenth-century woman. It also brings sharply into focus the contradictions of the Baroque epoch. Like the three heroines of *El laberinto*, Marcela represents a threat to the very system that her role as wife will sustain. The society depicted by Cervantes in *La entretenida* is one that is caught in a vicious circle. The interlude, as a play within a play, dramatises the individual's compulsion to act outside of his/her own role in order to forge a new identity, whilst also demonstrating the redundancy of such behaviour. Moreover, it advocates that individual self-fulfillment can be realised without radical social mobility. It would appear, then, that Cervantes is more of a pragmatist than Lope; promoting freedom within the limits of what is possible.

1.2 Expressive Selves in *El laberinto de amor*

In the convoluted world of Cervantes's *El laberinto de amor*, the reader/spectator is invited to negotiate a tangled web of deception, transformation and mistaken identity. The plot is often dense with complex situations and it is often difficult to foresee how, or if, the drama's characters will succeed in surmounting the obstacles which impede their exit from the maze. In fact, it is precisely because of its plot confusions that *El laberinto* has provoked minimal critical attention.⁸⁰ Those commentators who have broached the play have judged it harshly. Yndurráin asserts: 'Cuando se quiera tomar el pulso a Cervantes como crítico de sí mismo [. . .] no debe olvidarse que escribió *El laberinto de amor* y *La casa de los celos*, y lo que es más grave, que las mandó a la imprenta'.⁸¹ I would suggest that analysis of this type has failed to contextualise the play in relation to its title which clearly expresses and anticipates the confusion which we will encounter. Zimic rebuffs those who condemn the play for its inherent confusion: 'Es cómico y, a la vez, penosamente irónico que se reproche al artista la eficacia en la representación de lo que específicamente quiere representar'.[82] In a perverse sense, critical indignation is a tribute to Cervantes's skill in creating a labyrinth through which his characters and his audience must both pass in order to better understand the complexities at work in this *capa y espada*.

El laberinto de amor chiefly deals with the theme of identity and, like *La entretenida*, dramatises the antagonism between natural inclination and rigid social authority, exploring how this tension manifests itself in the lives of three young women, Rosamira, Julia and Porcia, who are determined to wield control over their circumstances and marry the men of their choice. The behavioural norms associated with male and female are reversed as these women author identities that see them securing their own destinies. Through displays of strength, bravery and rebellion the three women successfully challenge male authority and, consequently, not only absorb the focus of their internal readers, the men whom they pursue, but have also remained the central focus of critical scholarship. To date, criticism has been mostly limited to how Cervantes creates these *mujer varonil* types with an emphasis on the clever strategies that the women skilfully employ in order to navigate societal demands and ultimately escape the labyrinth. Taddeo, for instance, remarks that Cervantes 'is exceptional in making women [...] the protagonists rather than merely the muse or the temptress who leads men into a web of confusion'.[83] The women of *El laberinto* become protagonists by means of the powerful and dynamic ways in which they usurp parental authority in order to achieve a degree of autonomy. Studies have established that these women particularly manipulate speech and role-play/disguise in their bid to exercise a discriminating capacity to choose.[84] For Ellen Anderson, for instance, Rosamira, Julia and Porcia are skilful actors who 'display *ingenio* by artfully employing silence, language and disguise to work their will on the world',[85] while Taddeo remarks that the women practice 'artful dominion of the spoken word [...] Even when imprisoned, they create their own stories'.[86] Friedman comments that the women 'attempt to control the dramatic events by becoming actors themselves, creators of plays designed to bring amorous rewards'.[87] Within this context of linguistic analyses, criticism has identified the dialectic of truth and fiction in *El laberinto* and interrogated these polarities in light of the fundamental function which they perform in the drama.[88] The evidence for such an approach is incontrovertible considering that the labyrinth is founded on a lie, constituted by deceit and exited when the truth is proclaimed. In fact, Zimic sees truth as being a 'lucero redentor' which delivers the protagonists from ignorance and falsehood and saves them from loveless marriages:

> Como causa particular de todas las dificultades se destaca la falsificación de la verdad. El conflicto entre ésta y la mentira predomina en toda la obra, constituyéndose, de hecho, en su tema fundamental, por encima de todos los otros, según lo indica ya la gran frecuencia de los vocabulos *verdad*, *mentira* y sus sinónimos en el texto, además de muchísimas expresiones de perplejidad que los personajes enuncian frente a la realidad desconocida o falsificada.[89]

Existing scholarship has also explored the far-reaching implications of this artful use of language and the freedom that Cervantes grants his women characters to express themselves.[90] These lines of enquiry inevitably highlight the resourcefulness of *El laberinto*'s female characters beyond their linguistic facility and have consequently prompted critics to evaluate Cervantes's treatment of 'freer' female expression in light of the limiting realities of seventeenth-century Spanish life.[91]

Anderson's analysis of the play remains the only study which engages with the idea of labyrinth as metaphor: 'identity itself is the labyrinth constructed in the play, and by implication, in the larger society from which its audience is drawn'.[92] The seventeenth-century Spanish subject, of course, lived in a world not unlike a confused and contradictory labyrinth.[93] As Bruce Swansey has noted, 'the labyrinth motif was a pervasive presence in Hispanic Baroque writing. The tense relationship between monstrosity and sentimentality that drew writers to it seemed to encapsulate the contradictory dualities of the age'.[94] The structural and symbolic value of the labyrinth image readily lends itself as a useful symbol for literature and provides fertile ground to explore and interrogate the contradictory and confusing paradigms of contemporary life and the human condition. Moreover, as aesthetic symbol, the labyrinth draws its power from paradox. As Penelope Doob has noted, it is 'a great and complex work of art and a frightening and confusing place of interminable wandering — the labyrinth as order and as chaos, depending on the observer's knowledge and perspective'.[95] The motif is derived from the classical myth of the Cretan labyrinth which appears in Ovid's *Metamorphoses VIII* and Catullus 64 as well as other perhaps less influential texts.[96] As the unchallenged and significant source of mythological material for the seventeenth-century Spanish playwright, Ovid's version of the myth is of fundamental importance to this study.[97] As recounted by Ovid, King Minos orders Daedalus to build a labyrinth to house the Minotaur; the hybrid offspring of his wife, Pasiphae, and a bull sent by Neptune. Minos feeds the Minotaur with youths from Athens as a tribute which he demands in atonement for the death of his son, Androgeos. Theseus arrives in Crete as one of the Minotaur's intended victims but Minos's daughter, Ariadne, falls in love with him and secretly brings him thread which he uses to chart his path, re-trace his steps and exit the maze. In return, Theseus promises marriage to Ariadne and after killing the Minotaur, escapes to Naxos where he then abandons Ariadne and sails for home.

Golden-Age dramatists, as readers and re-writers of canonical classical texts, conflated aspects of the Cretan labyrinth myth in order to produce drama appropriate to the domestic realities of contemporary Spain.[98] During the Renaissance the labyrinth myth was particularly subject to allegorical interpretations and readings; as exemplified by the publication and popularity of Pérez de Moya's sixteenth-century mythographic manual *Philosofía secreta*.[99] However, as Michael Kidd notes: 'despite the claim of traditional criticism that classical mythology in early modern Spanish literature is always "intended" allegorically in the manner of Juan Pérez de Moya's *Philosofía secreta*, the basic concerns of the mythological plays coincide with those of the broader *comedia*'.[100] The majority of playwrights elected to manipulate the Ovidian source overtly inviting the spectator to engage in a process of retrospection which compelled the audience to look back to the past. This dialogical process requires that the spectator look simultaneously backward and forward as past and present fuse. The dramatist's revision of the classics functions as a constant reminder of the original text and both acknowledges and reminds the viewer of its canonical status. The 'new' text, then, uses a classical garb to lend authority to its re-creation of the ancients. Significantly, this re-writing obliges the spectator to engage intellectually with the intricacies of the mythological revision and identify how the playwright has exploited the myth and for what purposes. In this sense, the dramatist is a reconceived mythographer who utilises the interpretive potential of the myth and 'corrects' his classical predecessors so that his audience might 'estimate differently' the canon.[101] Such a strategy culminates in a re-reading and re-creation of the myth which ultimately addresses contemporary concerns on both socio-cultural and aesthetic levels. The pervasiveness of this strategy with respect to the labyrinth myth, in particular, is evidenced in the number and variety of textual reconstructions, post-Cervantes, undertaken by other Golden-Age dramatists. For instance, Lope's version of the myth is adapted in order to suit the demands of the contemporary honour code.[102] *El laberinto de Creta* (1612–15) not only raises pertinent issues concerning the inflexibility of the honour system, but also plays with *mise en abîme* and calls attention to the theatrical conventions which are employed within the drama. Calderón's *El laberinto del mundo* (1636) manipulates the motif within a theological framework exploring issues of free will, fate and destiny while Tirso de Molina's *El laberinto de Creta* (1638) is, perhaps unsurprisingly, a blatant example of the exploitation of the myth for religious purposes. Tirso's Theseus is 'an allegorical pre-figuration of Christ' who saves and redeems Ariadne, a symbol of humanity.[103] Each of these plays retains aspects of the original text producing Golden-Age versions of the Ovidian protagonists, Theseus, Ariadne and Minos.[104] Throughout the seventeenth-century, then, the main events of Ovid's narrative were exploited to produce plays in accordance with *comedia* conventions which engaged contemporary intellectual sensibilities.

Despite critical interest in the mythological *comedia* few critics have examined Cervantes's *El laberinto de amor* in relation to its mythological framework, much less interrogated the play in light of the Ovidian model which informs it, despite the drama's evocative title.[105] This is, perhaps, symptomatic of a general critical tendency within Cervantine studies which overlooks the writer's relationship with the classics. Frederick de Armas has recently commented that: 'Throughout his literary career Cervantes was engaged in a conversation and a context with the classical authors of Greece and Rome [...] his work constantly calls upon the textual remains of the ancients'.[106] Cervantes's 'conversation' with the classics, as Pedro Ruiz Pérez has recently shown, was not uncontentious. Ruiz Pérez's analysis of *Viaje del Parnaso* explores how Cervantes domesticates Parnassus and places poetry and poetic practise into the hands of the contemporary Spanish writer: 'Cervantes ofrece en su poema la presentación de un parnaso netamente español y estrictamente contemporáneo, sin lugar para los clásicos, sean los poetas grecolatinos o sean los escritores en lengua vulgar, si pertenecen a tiempos pasados'.[107] Ruiz Pérez's prioritisation of *inventio*, as the determining methodology of Cervantes's creative practice, locates it within an established doctrine of *imitatio* and its reverential attitude toward the classics, while also significantly recognising the writer's freedom to interpret and re-create classical texts.[108] Such an approach foregrounds original and creative individuality over slavish imitation. In *El laberinto de amor* Cervantes's exploitation of classical sources to create a maze through which his characters journey on their voyage of self-discovery and realisation could be said to emblematise *inventio* and the paradoxes which inform it. The re-configuration of mythical roles in *El laberinto* is complex. For instance, Ariadne as model, is dispersed across all three female protagonists; informing the characterisation of Rosamira, Porcia and Julia. As well as representing Ariadne, the women also resemble Daedalus and the Minotaur. Cervantes's use of Ovid, therefore, highlights the fluidity of *inventio* and de-centers the authority of the ancient model. It is evident, therefore, that Cervantes manifests a different attitude toward authorities and strategies of writing than that of many of his contemporaries. As we will see in our study of *El laberinto*, the dramatist understands the creative process as one in which the author is free to express him/her self and to remain unshackled concerning dominant authorial practices.

The dramatist's promotion of a very liberal concept of *inventio* is apparent from the outset. The myth of the Cretan labyrinth is not evoked explicitly in *El laberinto de amor*. Rather, the threads of the myth are woven together in subtle nuances and allusions. It is, however, suggested by one of the drama's female characters, Porcia, in Act I: 'Ya en el ciego laberinto / te metió el amor cruel; / ya no puedes salir dél / por industria ni distinto. / El *hilo* de la razón / no hace el caso que prevengas' (I. 282–87). Porcia's summation of her situation deliberately parallels the conduct of Ariadne, Ovid's heroine, who successfully leads

Theseus through the maze by means of a ball of thread. It is appropriate that it should be Porcia who alludes to the classical roots of the play, considering that the women in the drama display characteristics and behavioural patterns which are analogous to that of Ovid's female protagonist. Ariadne is purposeful, determined and courageous as she obtains Theseus's freedom at great personal cost. It requires that she not only wilfully disobey her father, but also that she aid Theseus in the execution of her half brother, the Minotaur. Regardless of familial and societal duty, Ariadne defies convention in order to secure Theseus's liberty and earn his hand in marriage. Her situation parallels that of the three female protagonists of *El laberinto de amor* who are all destined for loveless marriages. Their desperate circumstances compel the women to defy parental authority and to pursue actively the men whom they wish to marry. For Julia and Porcia, this entails escaping from prison-like homes where desires and ambitions are repressed by overbearing fathers. All three, like Ariadne, usurp male influence and command powerful spaces in which they demonstrate a potent sense of self-belief.

The women of *El laberinto de amor* are, then, authors and artists at work. They function on every plane of theatrical communication as actors, actresses, spectators and most significantly, as directors. It is the women's cunning that leads the men into and out of the maze. The heroines write their own script and their male counterparts, Dagoberto, Manfredo and Anastasio, unwittingly become their audience and co-actors. It is, therefore, the women who construct the labyrinth; mirroring the role of the original creator of the Cretan labyrinth, Daedalus. Ovid writes: 'Daedalus ingenio fabrae celeberrimus artis / ponit opus turbatque notas et lumina flexa / ducit in errorem uariarum ambage uiarum' (VIII. 159–161).[109] Just as Ovid's Daedalus is a talented craftsman who fashions the intricacies of the maze, Cervantes's female protagonists are artists who dictate the path which the men take. It is the female protagonists, then, who exercise authorial power and control the characterisation of the men. Although scholarship has identified the women as performers and directors, critics have neglected to interrogate how the female authorial role influences the way in which the reader/spectator might consequently interpret the actions of their male counterparts. In fact, studies of *El laberinto* tend to pay little critical attention to Dagoberto, Anastasio and Manfredo. Moreover, persistent evaluation of the strategies which the women employ has led to a one-dimensional argument which has failed to take into account the circumstances and conditions which drive the women to extreme and desperate measures. In other words, their struggle to assert themselves as individuals has been overlooked. This struggle is, in fact, reflected in the attitudes exhibited by the male protagonists as personifications of seventeenth-century Spanish patriarchy. *El laberinto de amor* appraises the condition of patriarchy from the margins inhabited by those who are subject to its authoritarian values. The women, then, occupy an interestingly 'central' position from which to survey social and aesthetic realities from a peripheral perspective.

The centrality of the female voice in Cervantes's drama is particularly significant considering Ovid's own exploitation of this theme in the *Heroides*. The twenty-one texts collectively represent letters written by legendary classical women to their lovers. Laurel Fulkerson challenges those critics who would view the *Heroides* as ineffectual letters written by abandoned women to men who abandon them. According to Fulkerson, Ovid's heroines are reading and writing women who tell their side of the story, their letters being 'men-centred' only on the surface.[110] The letters, therefore, grant these classical women a voice which they can employ to depict themselves and their lovers in whichever way they choose.[111] Fulkerson notes that it is Ariadne, in particular, who asserts a powerful and effective influence over the other members of the community of heroines and 'seeks to become the spokeswoman for deserted women [...] providing an *exemplum* for the other women of the *Heroides*'.[112] In Cervantes's play, Rosamira, Julia and Porcia could also be said to fulfil the role of 'spokesperson' who highlights the seventeenth-century Spanish woman as an individual in her own right. Moreover, their female-authored drama ventriloquises female desires and objectives through a subjective depiction of the men whom they cast as co-players.

This brief study of the play will examine how Cervantes carves out a metaphor for the condition of the seventeenth-century marginalised Spanish woman. Rather than focus on the linguistic strategies of the female heroines in *El laberinto*, which, as we have seen, has been extensively treated already, I will investigate how the women fulfil roles analogous to key characters in the Ovidian myth. This approach will consider scenes in which the characterisation of the men is not only influenced by the strategies which the craftswomen employ, but is entirely contingent upon the conduct of the female protagonists. My reading will develop the argument of Cervantes's heroines as creators/artists by extending the ramifications to consider their authorial role in the light of the playwright's own dramatic marginality and engagement with his craft.

The Women at Work

The opening scene of the play sees the Duke of Novara orchestrating plans for the marriage of his daughter, Rosamira, to the nobleman Manfredo. Rosamira, however, is absent from the stage and her life is, therefore, effectively decided for her. The Duke's plans are thwarted when the son of the Duke of Utrino, Dagoberto, levels an accusation at Rosamira's honour which threatens her family's name and reputation: 'Digo que en deshonrado ayuntamiento / se estrecha con un bajo caballero, / sin tener a tus canas miramiento, / ni a la ofensa de Dios, que es lo primero' (I. 62–65). Dagoberto accuses Rosamira of showing contempt and impudence toward the very structures that underpin society. However, Rosamira's submissive and virtuous character had only just been confirmed for the audience: '¿Y Rosamira, la duquesa vuestra, / pone de voluntad el yugo de cuello? / Nunca al querer del padre fue siniestra; / cuanto más que se vee que gana en ello, / siendo el duque quien es.' (I. 13–17). Dagoberto prepares the ground for his accusation by using his status and gender as leverage in manipulating the Duke's response: 'que sabes bien quién soy, y que me aplico / contino al proceder más virtüoso' (I. 40–41). The Duke considers Dagoberto's accusation in light of the fact that his daughter has an unblemished record of compliance to his will (I. 76–77). Nonetheless, he acknowledges and affirms Dagoberto's social standing: 'considero quién eres, e imagino / que sólo la verdad pudo traerte / a cerrar de mis glorias el camino' (I. 71–73). Rosamira is brought before her father but chooses to remain silent, making no attempt to dispute the accusation which could ruin her family in a world where the power of 'el que dirán' ruled. In the face of her silence, the Duke assumes his daughter's guilt: '¿Qué dices, hija? ¿Cómo no respondes? / ¿Empáchate el temor, o la vergüenza? [...] Culpada estáis; indico es manifiesto / tu lengua muda, tu inclinado gesto.' (I. 126–27; 132–33). Rosamira, in fact, remains wilfully quiet. She represents a stark contrast to Isabela in *El burlador de Sevilla* who attempts to defend her illicit relationship with Don Juan but is silenced by her father the King:

> Di mujer:
> ¿qué rigor, qué airada estrella
> te incitó, que en mi palacio,
> con hermosura y soberbia,
> profanases sus umbrales? [...]
> Calla, que la lengua
> no podrá dorar el yerro
> que has cometido en mi ofensa (I. 163–67; 168–70)[113]

Isabela's silence, unlike that of Rosamira, is imposed against her will. As Tirso's play progresses it becomes clear to the audience that Isabela's disdain for social standards requires a linguistic ability to out-manoeuvre the situation which she does not possess. Rosamira, however, exhibits a silence which is both astute and resourceful. Although she is characterised as a weak and acquiescent individual, it soon becomes apparent that she is, in fact, an arch-plotter who concocted the scheme with Dagoberto so that she might evade marriage to Manfredo.

In Act I Rosamira anticipates that Dagoberto's lie and her lack of self-defence will, taken together, result in condemnation and, therefore, manipulates the connection between silence and culpability. Agapita Jurado Santos comments that:

> El silencio suele interpretarse como ausencia de palabras, como una interrupción en la comunicación, sin embargo resulta evidente que el silencio es

un signo fundamental en la obra literaria, pues forma parte de las instancias narrativas con una intensidad no menor que la de las palabras.[114]

Rosamira's silence remains connected with her guilt via Dagoberto's accusation throughout the play (I. 526-29; II, 1973-76). Her mute voice, conveniently, is no match for Dagoberto's 'truth'. Rather than an objective presentation of reality, truth is revealed to be biased and subjective and to present a perspective which can be readily manipulated in order to serve one's own purposes. Rosamira, via Dagoberto, confronts her father with a situation which is paradoxically both real and not real. Moreover, Dagoberto's words are framed by aristocratic standing and status. The Duke is, therefore, unable to permeate the superficiality of the situation and accepts at face value the affront to his honour. Zimic contends that Rosamira displays 'absoluta pasividad en todas sus relaciones con los demás'.[115] He fails to recognise that her silence is an ironic illocutionary act which sets the wheels in motion for her marriage to Dagoberto. Rosamira and Dagoberto's success is wholly contingent on Rosamira's ability to enact the role of a guilty, tainted woman. Anderson remarks that: 'Her silence is the silence of any author of any drama, who is usually invisible on stage, but everywhere in the story'.[116] Her silence, then, cannot be mistaken for passivity. Furthermore, Rosamira's speechlessness reveals that the Duke is more willing to believe in status and rank than in the reputation of his daughter and, therefore, exposes how patriarchy is willing to trust readily in outward appearances. In her 'play', Rosamira casts Dagoberto as the voice of power and authority manipulating the fact that his word 'as bond' will inevitably function as a verbal sword to mutilate her character. Rosamira's silence is a paradoxical representation and deconstruction of the seventeenth-century Spanish woman. Dagoberto's ventriloquising of Rosamira reveals her silence to be eloquent and powerful. Furthermore, Dagoberto's role in Rosamira's play not only casts doubt upon his individual integrity, but raises questions concerning society's collective patriarchal structure. Zimic reflects:

> Al declarar que Rosamira está ilícita y secretamente relacionada con un 'vil y bajo caballero', dice dos verdades incuestionables, pues, aunque su fin sea bueno, los medios que ha escogido para conseguirlo son, en efecto, viles y bajos, por la infamia que cae sobre toda la familia de su amada, como consecuencia de ellos.[117]

Patriarchy, then, does not only exercise faith in external signs, but in signs which are less than virtuous and honourable. Interestingly, Dagoberto can also be said to be a script-writer. He sends a letter to the Duke which attempts to lay the blame at the feet of the latter: 'La presta resolución que tomaste de entregar a Manfredo por esposa a tu hija Rosamira me forzó a usar de la industria de acusalla, por evitar por entonces el peligro de perdella' (III. 2870). Unlike Rosamira who respects her father and only employs desperate measures to avoid a loveless marriage, Dagoberto is discourteous and dismissive of the older man's social position. Rosamira does not, in fact, lie and her silence is that of an artful author, rather than indicative of callous and egotistical manipulation.

Rosamira's performance culminates in her confinement to a tower.[118] However, it is her imprisonment which functions as the impetus for the action of the play. Fernández-Loza comments that: 'alrededor de ella girarán todos los demás personajes'.[119] Imprisoned in the centre of the labyrinth, Rosamira dictates how the drama unfolds as each player gravitates towards her in pursuit of a love match. Anderson states:

> The tower is meant to remind the spectator of the labyrinth of the play's title, for like Daedalus's creation, it is a prison in whose center resides an offspring who has brought dishonor to the man whose name as father it bears [...] Rosamira, then, for very beauty, enacts the role of a female Minotaur, in Cervantes's play the first inversion of the original myth's masculine and feminine roles.[120]

Rosamira is not the only character who suffers imprisonment in *El laberinto*. Both Julia and Porcia are incarcerated within the homes of their fathers. Julia explains how she has been contained and repressed: 'Teníame mi padre / encerrada do el sol entraba apenas; / era muerte mi madre, / y eran mi compañía las almenas / de torres levantadas, / sobre vanos terrores fabricadas' (II. 1625–30). Therefore, each of the women in the play can be viewed as female Minotaurs; prisoners of the patriarchal system which dictates their limited social space and role. However, such an association with the mythological figure would also suggest that the women typify monstrosity. The Minotaur is monstrous as a result of his hybrid constitution as half man and half bull.[121] Similar to the Minotaur, the women in *El laberinto* represent a hybridity of feminine and masculine behavioural norms. On the one hand, their desire to marry is entirely feminine. On the other, they fulfil their desire in a decidedly masculine fashion which sees them utilise their intellectual capacities as authors to adorn masculine dress and actively combat the restrictions imposed upon them.[122]

Rogelio Miñana's analysis of the monster motif in *El rufián dichoso* highlights that the word 'monster' derives from the Latin '*mostrare*'. Covarrubias's *Tesoro* offers a corresponding definition: 'Monstro: latine monstrum, a monstrando, quod aliquid significando demonstret'.[123] Miñana states that such a definition connotes 'lo que es digno de mostrarse [...] Un monstruo lo es sólo por cuanto se diferencia de lo que le rodea'.[124] The monster, then, merits contemplation for its rare and atypical constitution. The women in *El laberinto* embody unorthodox characteristics because they shun conventional behaviour. However, just as Minos conceals the Minotaur, Rosamira, Julia and Porcia are hidden away in an attempt to obscure the dishonour which they represent. Notably, it is the men in *El laberinto* who construct the women as minotaurs; that is, as potentially threatening and destructive creatures. In reality, the women represent little threat to established order as, like Marcela of *La entretenida*, they desire marriage to men of their own rank. In fact, what is 'monstrous' about the women, in all definitions of the term, is the way in which they are mistreated. Rosamira is imprisoned despite the fact she is known to be honourable and Julia is incarcerated as a result of 'vanos temores fabricadas' which have no substance or legitimacy. The treatment which they incur reflects the values of a society which posit women as economic commodities. This is ratified by Rosamira's father who remarks that she will be confined 'hasta que alguna espada o pluma borre / la mancha que en la honra lleva puesta' (I. 144–45).[125] Nonetheless, Rosamira infringes the male space and exploits the 'pluma' to her own advantage. Her ability to negotiate her situation is contingent on an innate sense of self and her own resourcefulness, rather than dependence on the male characters of the play. Cervantes, therefore, literally places in Rosamira's hand the power to re-write her future.

The heroines' skill in directing and performing their drama is particularly exemplified in Julia's pursuit of Manfredo. From the outset of the drama, Manfredo is portrayed in an unfavourable light and referred to as 'un Narciso' (I. 10). Such a description appropriately fits his self-centred behaviour and is, in fact, reflective of the attitude which characterises the male protagonists of the play as they seek to guard and preserve their social reputation at the cost of marginalising and imprisoning the women. Julia disguises herself as the student Camilo in order to narrate a story of how 'he' met Julia who proceeded to tell 'him' the story of her love for Manfredo. Camilo exercises a powerful authorial voice in order to detail Julia's confinement and subsequent decision to pursue her love in masculine disguise. Julia, as Camilo, is, therefore, able to relay her feelings truthfully for the man in front of her without paying heed to rank, role or appropriate modes of conduct. This scene is informed by the relationship between Camilo, the author, and Julia, the subject of 'his' narration. Camilo performs the role of director controlling 'his' character and presents Julia on stage in a fashion that captivates Manfredo's attention. The nobleman declares: 'que el *modo* de decirlo me enamora' (II. 1562). Camilo artfully presents the situation of Julia as one which demands Manfredo's attention, conjuring up the image of a woman who has surrendered everything for his love: 'Dejé mi padre, ¡ay Cielos / dejé mi libertad, dejé mi honra, / y, en su lugar, recelos / y sujeción tomé, muerte y deshonra' (II. 1771–74). Julia dramatises her situation in order to impress the realities of her cosseted existence upon the nobleman. Thacker states that: 'Patriarchal society can be characterized by its oppression of the individual in the interests of stability. Men may be almost entirely ignorant of this oppression because society apparently directly serves their interests'.[126] Moreover, Julia purposefully represents the feminine in a way that Manfredo will find pleasing. As narrator, author and lead player, Julia can wield the same linguistic sword Dagoberto used to slay Rosamira's character in order to fabricate a picture of herself that will pique Manfredo's curiosity: 'Volví, miréle, y vile / lloviendo perlas de sus bellos ojos' (II. 1571–72). In other words, Julia constructs herself as the object of masculine desire and performs a role in order to arouse Manfredo's interest and secure her goal. In this sense, Julia is a strong and aggressive heroine playing the part of a repressed and needy woman.

For Howard Jacobson, Ovid's Ariadne in *Heroides X* is above all a role-player who 'becomes' the epic poet taking on the role of abandoned heroine.[127] She manipulates narrative devices as a means to portray herself as the deserted woman, but has little interest in reviving Theseus's love for her. Instead, she wishes for her own survival: 'si non ego causa salutis, / non tamen est, cur sis tu mihi causa necis'.[128] Julia also manipulates authorial devices by depicting herself as an oppressed victim as she highlights the consequences of a life dominated by patriarchy: 'En fin, yo, de curiosa, / en agujero hice en una puerta, / que a la vista medrosa, / y aun al alma, mostró ventana abierta / para ver a Manfredo' (II. 1643–47). Nonetheless, Manfredo recoils in horror at the revelation that Julia has adopted masculine disguise in her attempt to pursue him: 'Envilla al padre suyo: / que con esto restituyo / mi inocencia y su querella' (II. 1850–52). Although Manfredo also adopts disguise as a student he finds fault only with Julia and is immediately concerned for his reputation. His narcissism is further confirmed when he resists all blame for Julia's behaviour: 'Si la recibo, me hago / en su huida culpado; / si la vuelo, habré mostrado / que a ser quien soy satisfago, / excusaré el desafío, / cobraré el perdido honor' (II. 1881–86). Julia, unswayed by Manfredo's response, continues to manipulate his reaction and in Act III Camilo tells the aristocrat that Julia has fled in desperation that Manfredo will not reciprocate her love. Rather than be jailed by Manfredo's conceited response, Julia draws out his true feelings toward her as well as determining his reaction to the situation: '¿Qué es lo que tengo de hacer?' (III. 2081) to which she answers: 'Ni reñilla, ni afrentalla, / ni al padre suyo envilla' (III. 2082–83). Julia engineers the situation until the moment when she reveals her true identity by presenting herself as the ideal female object. Stage directions denote: '*entra Julia muy bien adrezada de mujer, cubierta con su manto hasta los ojos, y pónese de rodillas ante Manfredo*' (III. 2700). Julia's submissive behaviour is undermined by her dynamic conduct and the spectator is aware that, once again, Julia is performing a role. Her protean ability to be brave, resourceful and yet 'conventionally' feminine eventually wins over Manfredo. She proves herself to be more than worthy of his love and he eventually exclaims 'eres mi igual, y aun mejor' (III. 2783). Julia has not only outwitted her future husband but has surpassed him in ingenuity, despite Manfredo's privileged social position. The episode clearly exemplifies the lengths to which the women have been driven in order to assume a level of control over their lives. As McKendrick observes, in *El laberinto* 'repression encourages not obedience but revolt'.[129] Moreover, it is evident that Julia's complex self 're'-fashioning challenges male/patriarchal definitions of female identity. Julia's control of her situation expresses a sense of self which is potentially threatening to an ideologically homogeneous society.

Julia and Rosamira demonstrate that society's attack on the female subject may affect the external, but its power over the internal is severely limited. The women's behaviour exposes patriarchy as a controlling device which compels and obliges the seventeenth-century woman to believe in the 'reality' of her repressed and subordinate position in patriarchal hierarchy. The women of *El laberinto* undermine and challenge this 'reality' and unmask it as a prejudiced representation of contemporary life which merely serves the interests of their male counterparts. The prevailing view of the female as incapable of forging her own path intelligently in life is shown to be fiction disguised as truth and paradoxically founded on the illusory nature of appearances. Society, therefore, misinterprets and misuses its authority in an attempt to thwart the natural abilities of *El laberinto*'s female protagonists. Unlike the men in the play, the women are unable to reconcile their desire for love and marriage with their natural capabilities, as though these were mutually exclusive.[130] The potential of the women to undermine imposed restrictions carries implications for all types of social conditioning as the ability of the collective order to impinge upon the individual is weakened. *El laberinto de amor* shows societal structures to be fallible and assailable when the individual utilises a strong sense of self and inner freedom in order to counter-act its enveloping control.

As a result of their female-authored drama, the women receive praise from the men when they realise that they have played second fiddle to the superior plotting and planning of the female protagonists: 'Tu industria y el Cielo han hecho / que les seamos esposos; / ellos son lances forzosos; / no hay sino hacerles buen pecho' (III. 3039–42). On a more significant note, the women are now able to express freely an authentic sense of self. Porcia joyfully asserts 'soy la que, en traje mudado, / trayendo amor en el pecho, / procurando tu provecho / he mi gusto procurado' (III. 2999–3002). She uses '*ser*' no less than seven times to make firm affirmations of selfhood. This can be viewed in the light of Dagoberto's 'sabes bien quién soy' (I. 40). As Dagoberto played on his gender and rank to see Rosamira imprisoned, so Rosamira is now free to define herself as she pleases. The women have procured their own pleasure, transcending restrictions, yet respecting social rules. The conflict inherent in this notion highlights what we have previously termed 'Baroque tension'. The women, torn between duty and desire and driven into dangerous behaviour, are ultimately presented as conflicted subjects. Cervantes leaves us in no doubt that society's tight rein on the freedom of the individual is the driving force behind the women's compulsion to create and perform. This creativity is born paradoxically from a peripheral perspective. In this respect, the women are not unlike Cervantes himself who shared no part in the dramatic monopoly of the contemporary stage and whose creativity flourished from a decidedly marginal position. Just as *El laberinto*'s female protagonists are 're-writers' who confront the limitations imposed upon them and create a drama which challenges established social principles, Cervantes mobilises his negligible status in order to call into question contemporary theatrical conventions. Such a strategy is indicative of Cervantes's self-conscious awareness of his role as a poetic practitioner. Theory and practice amalgamate as *inventio* becomes the context in which Cervantes establishes his own creative selfhood. It is clear, then, that Cervantes re-writes the classical tale in order that he might express himself more freely as artist.

Unlike *La entretenida*, the ending of *El laberinto* must conclude with marriage and, in the case of Porcia, with a promise of Papal dispensation. Friedman views the closing scene as an affirmation of skilful role-play: 'Those who clearly triumph do so not because the gods have favoured them but because they have played their self-imposed roles with the greatest vigor and ingenuity'.[131] Clearly, marriage functions as a reward for the heroines and an acknowledgement of their successful schemes. Zimic observes the following:

> los multiples casamientos con que se concluye esta comedia no pueden considerarse como un procedimiento artificial, calcado de la convención teatral lopesca. Con base en el contexto de la obra entera, como también del tema fundamental, ese remate nos resulta no sólo artística e ideológicamente lógico, sino obligatorio.[132]

The absence of marriage at the end of the play would entail that the dramatist usurp the authorial power accorded throughout to his female protagonists. Rather, Cervantes permits his heroines to write their own ending to their story as a natural extension of the goals which have motivated and driven their actions throughout the entire play. Notwithstanding the fact that the heroines choose men of equal status, the dénouement does not neutralise a conclusion which is fabricated as a result of disregard for social structures. The multiple marriages cannot eradicate the fact that the heroines have adopted social roles which are inappropriate to their social position and that these roles have undermined their fathers' rule. Here, as elsewhere, Cervantes 'challenges the assumptions of that paternal power which the dominant social order promulgates as a norm'.[133] The Cervantine representation of marriage and, thus, the very structures which uphold society, resists the dominant order. Cervantes frees woman of her traditional dependence upon and dominance by the male subject. The Cervantine heroines do not refuse to accept their place in society but they do insist on articulating *how* they will fulfil their social role. They refuse to be victims of arranged marriages and prejudiced attitudes which deny women the right to discriminate intelligently. In other words, the heroines demand recognition as individuals. In *El laberinto* the status quo may be restored with marriage, but it is not restored unchanged. The drama's conclusion, then, is only superficially conventional and, thus, can also be viewed as a Cervantine response to the *comedia nueva*. David Castillo views the ending of *El laberinto* as 'another form of parodic inversion of the Lopean model insofar as it endorses the transgressive behaviour of the protagonists'.[134] As authors, the women simultaneously embody new social possibilities and challenge conventional theatrical conclusions. In this sense, the heroines re-write Lope's *comedia nueva*. By means of a powerfully paradoxical 'authorial' voice, the women provide an orthodox ending in a wholly unconventional fashion. Moreover, like the monster, the women demonstrate that they merit an audience that recognises their remarkable and extraordinary characteristics. The heroines are, therefore, symbolic of Cervantine theatre which draws attention to itself by refusing to comply with the uncontested and homogenous voices that regulate and control contemporary theatre.

The drama ends on the realisation that the control of individual liberty will always represent a problem for society. Rosamira, Julia and Porcia expose conventional prejudiced attitudes toward women just as Ariadne captures Theseus's cruel abandonment on paper in the *Heroides*. The reality and, indeed, the redundancy of the limitations of the female world are made apparent: 'Di: ¿No puede acontecer, / sin admiración que asombre, / que una mujer busque a un hombre, / como un hombre a una mujer?' (II. 1146–49). Anastasio's question involves a transferral of subject and object positions. Significantly, the nobleman objectifies himself and, in so doing, acknowledges the capability of women to choose wisely. As a representative of Spain's ruling classes, his summation of the situation undermines well-established social parameters which designate women as subservient to an obdurate system.

The anachronisms of restrictions placed upon women are compounded by the play's meta-strategies. The women, like Daedalus, become authors who direct their performances to achieve the admiration of their audience and more significantly, to merit definition as autonomous individuals. Cervantes permits his heroines a voice through which they can artfully objectify the men. Art is utilised as a powerful instrument to overrule convention and ensures that Rosamira, Julia and Porcia become subjects rather than subject to unjust and inhibiting values. Cervantes demonstrates how the women exploit their authorial position to bring centre-stage a powerful self-portrait while simultaneously exposing the realities of life on the periphery of society. In this sense, *El laberinto* makes apparent the ease with which theatre, and namely Lope's *comedia*, can transmit social propaganda. The women are representative of the stage itself and act as a mirror which reflects the intolerant attitudes of the day as exemplified by the male protagonists. Nevertheless, this mirror is not conventionally mimetic but constitutes the women's deviant voices.[135] They can, therefore, be read as rebellious creators who work against the grain of dominant dramatic practise. My reading of the heroines of *El laberinto* as the protagonists of the Ovidian myth, therefore, offers a way of understanding Cervantes's relationship to his own craft and to his audience. The struggle of the women to obtain a measure of independence can be likened to the dramatist's effort to position his own marginal voice centre-stage. Like the heroines of *El laberinto de amor* Cervantes demonstrates that his voice merits attention and that his theatre merits an audience; if only for its blatant refusal to conform.

1.3 Manipulative Magic in *La casa de los celos y selvas de Ardenia*

Critical 'encounter' with Lope has taken much longer in the case of *La casa de los celos y selvas de Ardenia*; an observation which is not unsurprising given the play's challenging nature. However, Marcella Trambaioli has recently contended that *La casa de los celos* is 'una especie de protocomedia burlesca'; specifically a parody of Lope's *Las pobrezas de Reinaldos* (1588–9), *Los celos de Rodamonte* (1588), *El casamiento en la muerte* (1595), *Angélica en Catay* (1599–1603), and *Adonis y Venus* (1597–1603), all of which are heavily influenced by Ariosto and chivalric material.[136] Trambaioli's interpretation not only affirms Cervantes as an attentive reader and/or spectator of Lope, but highlights *La casa de los celos* as a highly self-conscious text which draws attention to itself and the Lopean texts with which it engages as works of fiction.[137] Following Trambaioli, my own reading will highlight that the play's dialogue with Lope is much more prevalent than has been realised.

Given the complex nature of the play, a brief synopsis of events is useful. *La casa* dramatises and parodies the love plots of chivalric and pastoral literature. The main plot chronicles Reinaldos and Roldán's (Charlemagne's paladins) romantic quest for Angélica. The play's bucolic sub-plot mirrors the frustrated amorous relationship. In addition to the convolutions of these love triangles, Marfisa and Bernardo del Carpio appear in Ardenia in search of adventure. The drama is also 'peopled' at times by allegorical figures such as Buena and Mala Fama. Given that so many diverse reactions and analyses of the drama have raised more questions than answers, a review of critical scholarship is also beneficial.[138]

Labelled 'la más anómala de todas las *Ocho comedias*', *La casa de los celos* is particularly complicated by its confusion of chivalresque, epic and pastoral genres which collide in a disorientating fashion to forge a highly inverisimilar plotline which often appears incongruent and chaotic.[139] The abrupt and uncomfortable shifts in time and space only serve to contribute to the difficulty the reader/spectator may have in discerning what is, in fact, the focus of this play. What has emerged from studies of Cervantes's 'anomaly' is a series of polemical issues around which there is little consensus. Virtually every reading of *La casa* stands in uncontested isolation. In fact, the meagre debate which the play has generated tends to centre on structural rather than aesthetic issues. For instance, the date of the drama's composition has incited some interest due to the fact that, like the *Quijote*, *La casa de los celos* draws heavily on chivalric material.[140] Most critics place the play as a product of Cervantes's first period of dramatic production.[141] More recently, however, Trambaioli has argued persuasively that *La casa de los celos* was composed in the first years of Cervantes's second writing period.[142]

Critical attention also tends to prioritise a focus on the play's unifying themes (or lack thereof) given the drama's depiction of seemingly incompatible environments. Lewis-Smith contends that '*La casa de los celos* is, as yet, far from revealing a definite thematic unity under rigorous critical inspection'.[143] Despite the fact that the play's title suggests that 'jealousy' will play a significant role in the drama, '*celos*' is generally not thought to be a fundamental theme.[144] Rather, attention has remained firmly fixed on the play's thematic disorganisation. Friedman, for instance, contends that the drama is not unified thematically, but notes that it has literature as a unifying 'point of reference'.[145] Ruiz Pérez's methodical reading of the play, however, sheds light on *La casa*'s structure and contends with critical judgements that condemn the play's lack of cohesion:

> La complejidad de la estructura de personajes y el desarrollo argumental de la pieza, con sus figuras secundarias, sus digresiones y su carácter abierto, no debe ocultar una unidad esencial y una coherencia interna, que responden a una unidad de concepción y a un planteamiento temático plenamente cervantinos. El mundo caballeresco y el mundo pastoril no son dos universos opuestos, sino dos caras de una misma realidad, perfectamente entrelazadas en el conjunto de la comedia.[146]

Ruiz Pérez's appraisal would appear to have functioned as a catalyst for critics keen to identify the factors which unite the superficially chaotic play.[147] Amanda Meixell, for instance, has recently argued that the role of the *Espíritu de Merlín* reveals 'thematic unity among the seemingly unrelated elements'.[148] Within the broader context of the play's theme there are some overlapping critical concerns regarding *La casa*'s portrayal of conflicted relationships. Lewis-Smith analyses the protagonist's irrational conduct and concludes that the play derives coherence from the theme of human absurdity.[149] This line of enquiry has also been explored by both Zimic and Illuminada Amat who pay attention to the play's intimate depiction of the individual's struggles.[150] Such an approach clearly highlights the Cervantine prioritisation of 'conflicto interior' rather than a plot which, like Lope's *comedia*, relies heavily on action.[151]

This critical preoccupation with structure and protagonist interaction has led to discussion of the function of the pastoral genre in the play. The rural environment of Act II is peopled by a shepherdess, Clori, whose decisions are financially motivated, while two shepherds viciously mock a 'pastor bobo' type character. This Cervantine inversion of bucolic literature has traditionally been interpreted as a rejection of its values.[152] For Morley Hawks Marks, Cervantes's treatment of the genre represents a degradation of the pastoral.[153] Nonetheless, Rosalie

Hernández-Pecoraro's analysis of Clori as a 'self-determining subject' leads her to conclude that the pastoral metaphor with its exploitive stance toward female agency and desire is radically assaulted in *La casa*.[154] The drama's bucolic space emerges as a site of liberation and Hernández-Pecoraro's reading, therefore, hints at the reinvigoration, rather than degradation of the pastoral. Cervantes's regeneration of the pastoral is reflective of the ways in which contemporary poetry, in particular, exploited the genre as a means to generate debate and to interrogate dominant ideologies. These positive connotations contribute to the perception of the pastoral as an active locus of investigation which encourages and opens up more constructive approaches to the play.

Undoubtedly, *La casa de los celos* has a decidedly mulitgeneric composition. As Childers comments: 'Debates over Cervantes's attitude towards pastoral, picaresque, and chivalric fiction have tended to settle into a general acknowledgment that he wrote in all of these modes, but never in a pure form'.[155] *La casa de los celos*, in fact, draws heavily on chivalric material and as such, has a closer connection to *Don Quijote* than the other *comedias*. The drama adapts episodes of both Matteo Boiardo's *Orlando innamorato* and Ludovico Ariosto's *Orlando furioso* to form a plot which invites the audience to laugh at the comic re-fashioning of Roldán and Reinaldos's pursuit of Angélica.[156] Analysis of *La casa* as a parody of chivalric literature and the play's complex intertextual relationship with its Italian predecessors, however, remain relatively unexplored as Cervantine critics have, not surprisingly, prioritised the parodic attitude that finds fuller and more artistic expression in the *Quijote*.[157]

Both Trambaioli and Friedman have underscored the drama's literary self-consciousness.[158] Friedman remarks that:

> *La casa de los celos* is Cervantes's literary macrocosm for the stage, designed to create a progressive distancing from the real [. . .] *La casa* puts reality in its place through the ironic force of negation. This is not a defeat for the real but an unmasking of fiction — a show of the tools of the trade — on stage and at the height of illusion.[159]

In *La casa de los celos* Cervantes elevates fiction as he creates a theatrical spectacle which is completely defined and informed by literature. Such a tactic serves to ensure that the absence of reality is patently conspicuous. This 'distancing' is in itself an illusion as the denial of reality functions on an entirely ironic plane. As with *La entretenida*, the theatre of *La casa de los celos* is not permitted to be a substitute for reality and reality 'is never absent from the message systems that play at denial'.[160] The result of this strategy, in both *La entretenida* and *La casa*, is that the mechanisms of the stage are 'unmasked' and made plainly visible to the *vulgo*. Despite the fact that Friedman and Trambaioli have both shown *La casa* to be a play which reveals itself to be fiction, no attention has been drawn to how this 'unmasking' might function on a dramatic level. The dismantling of illusion is particularly pertinent from the perspective of the spectator who is confronted throughout with a range of special effects. With reference to *Don Quijote*, Arboleda notes:

> A través de sus personajes, Cervantes vuelve al acto mismo de representar desenmascarando ese mismo acto, recurriendo *al mismo discurso dramático*. Hace que su público (externo e interno de la obra) o lector (externo e interno de la obra) 'despierte' y observe (vea, lea) que el acto de representar es producto de la manipulación de ciertas convenciones literarias (dramáticas) y que por lo tanto no es una 'historia verdadera' en el sentido literario del término.[161]

In *La casa de los celos* 'representar desenmascarando' is the key illusion-breaking strategy comprising various 'shock tactics' which arouse the *vulgo* out of passivity by means of a magician, Malgesí. Meixell has recently highlighted the function of Malgesí's dramatic productions as particularly interesting 'because it focuses on the question of the magician as creator of fiction'.[162] This analysis of the wizard underscores Malgesí as an ineffectual creator who is unable to control his social environment. Meixell's study, however, scrutinises Malgesí in isolation of the strategies which he employs to promote the breakdown of illusion and her conclusions can, therefore, only be partial. Meixell contends that Malgesí's shortcomings as a creator reflect personal inefficacy, but there is more to it than this.

I would argue that in *La casa de los celos* Malgesí is the primary vehicle through which the transient and illusory nature of the stage is revealed. Such a strategy is indicative of Cervantes's aversion for illusion-oriented theatre despite the fact that *La casa*, unlike *La entretenida*, seems not to engage with Lope's *comedia nueva*. Trambaioli comments that: 'no se puede pasar por alto que la praxis teatral que la informa no es la de la comedia nueva propiamente dicho'.[163] Certainly, *La casa*'s subject matter, the palpable absence of honour and *capa y espada* plots and archetypal *comedia* figures attest to a composition date prior to the establishment and maturity of the *comedia nueva*.[164] It advocates, nonetheless, a self-reflexive theatre that punctures the fiction which Lope's drama would both promote and promulgate. As Arboleda states:

> Es de admirar cómo para Cervantes esta polémica con Lope y contra algunas de sus ideas dramáticas, ahondó en un mayor desarrollo de su metaficción y su metadrama. La necesidad de producir obras autoreflexivas, en las cuales el lector/espectador pudiere tomarse el esfuerzo de descodificar las esencias, las significaciones, ayuda mucho a que Cervantes desarrolle sus ideas y sus obras.[165]

La casa de los celos is, however, much more than a platform for Cervantes's grievances with Spanish theatre and is not restricted to aesthetic concerns which show the 'tools of the trade'. My reading re-affirms the views of Trambaioli and Friedman, but also explores the implications of illusion-shattering techniques beyond the theatrical frame. 'Desenmascarando' has special effects for the seventeenth-century Spanish audience in light of the highly unstable contemporary context in which this play was produced. In fact, this early drama anticipates the anxieties of the Baroque and attempts to awaken the spectator to the realities of the environment in which he/she lives. It is not my intention to offer a full re-evaluation of the play, but rather to illustrate one very significant, but overlooked aspect of *La casa de los celos*. Analysis of Malgesí's role allows us to recuperate this much maligned play as a powerful dramatic statement of Cervantine theatre.

Malgesí the Magic Maker

Malgesí is Cervantes's adaptation of Ariosto's Malagigi; cousin to Rinaldo and one of Charlemagne's twelve paladins.[166] Stolen at birth by a slave but rescued by the fairy Oriande, Malagigi learns the magic arts and puts his powers into practice in order to help the paladins secure success. Although not a principal character, Ariosto's sorcerer is exploited to advance the plot, set up humorous situations and resolve complex circumstances via displays of supernatural powers.[167] Likewise, Cervantes's enchanter operates, ostensibly, on the edge of the paladins' pursuit of Angélica and exercises his magical powers in a bid to cure his brother, Reinaldos, of his debilitating passions. In the play's opening scene, which clearly signposts Ariosto, Reinaldos threatens violence against Roldán. Malgesí, very rationally, attempts to defuse his anger whilst Charlemagne and a knight, Galalón, appear on stage. Via Carlomagno, our attention is drawn to a book carried by Malgesí. Detailed stage directions state:

> Apártase Malgesí a un lado del teatro, saca un libro pequeño, pónese a leer en él, y luego sale una figura de demonio por lo hueco del teatro y pónese al lado de Malgesí; y han del haber comenzado a entrar por el patio Angélica, la bella, sobre un palafrén, embozada y la más ricamente vestida que ser pudiere; traen la rienda dos salvaje[s] vestidos de yedra o de cáñamo teñido de verde; detrás viene una dueña sobre una mula con gualdrapa; trae delante de sí un rico cofrecillo y a una perrilla de falda; en dando una vuelta al patio, la apean los salvajes, y va dónde está el Emperador (I. 184).

Malgesí's 'libro pequeño' is most likely a book of spells, just as Ariosto's Malagigi carries a book through which he is able to charm giants into sleep and fly through the air on magical creatures. Malgesí's actions here indicate the direction which the remainder of the play will take and it is clear that we have entered a magical realm where reality is subject to the manipulations of illusion and where anything is possible. In the instant that Malgesí opens his book of spells and Angélica arrives on stage, a chain of events is put in place which drives the rest of the plot. As Ruiz Pérez notes: 'el juego queda insinuado con la posibilidad de que todo el desarrollo de la trama constituya una ilusión surgida de la magia de Malgesí, cuyo conjuro aparece relacionado en expresa acotación con la aparición de Angélica y su cortejo'.[168] Malgesí is exposed as a 'magic maker' who skilfully fabricates illusions which assume the appearance of reality. From the outset of the play the spectator is made aware that he/she cannot accept unproblematically the machinations or 'cajas chinas' of the play whether the enchantor is Malgesí or Cervantes.[169] The action of the drama is shown to be motivated entirely by Malgesí's manipulation of illusion which in turn spawns the spectacle. *La casa de los celos*, therefore, affirms itself as a work of fiction from the outset, one which will depend upon audience expectations to create dramatic conflict. Spadaccini and Castillo have observed: 'el lector del teatro cervantino nunca pierde de vista los mecanismos de la teatralidad'.[170] What hasn't been addressed, to date, is the effect of this self-reflexive strategy, these 'mecanismos', on an audience.

Central to a discussion of Malgesí's role is the motivation which informs his authorial function. While the conduct of other characters in the play is driven entirely by self-interest, Malgesí is not only devoted to helping Reinaldos but, significantly, is always on hand to explain, reveal and clarify the events of the play for both the internal and external audience.[171] In this sense, the enchanter functions as a type of dramatic commentary which elucidates the action of the plot. As the dramatist, he is an 'outsider' with insight and the only character that is not manipulated by the play's course of events; fully aware of the 'reality' impinging on each person's situation. As such, Malgesí astutely observes people and situations. In the opening scene he reacts to his brother's violent rage and remarks on his lack of judgement. Malgesí asks '¿No ves que desatinas?' (I. 47) as he tries to convince his brother that Roldán is not mocking his poor attire. In fact, this is the first of many instances in which Malgesí exercises clear-sighted discernment. Such a strategy underscores the didactic function of drama and indicates that it serves an informative, as well as an ethical purpose. As Cervantes himself argues, it is this combination of 'delectare et docere' which underpins his exemplary *novelas*:

> Quiero decir que los requiebros amorosos que en algunas hallarás, son tan honestos y tan medidos con la razón y discurso cristiano, que no podrán mover a mal pensamiento al descuidado o cuidadoso que las leyere. Heles dado nombre de *ejemplares*, y si bien lo miras, no hay ninguna de quien no se pueda sacar algún ejemplo provechoso.[172]

Considered in the context of Cervantes's Horatian aesthetics, Malgesí's perspicacity endorses prudent use of illusion. Meixell observes that the magician 'is associated with the truth on every occasion'.[173] When Angélica appears to attain easily the affection of Charlemagne's paladins, Malgesí dissuades their ill-fated passion. The magician reveals that Angélica's pleas for help are manipulative and deceitful (I. 214–59): '¡Qué bien que lo relata la hechicera!' (I. 260); '¡El mismo engaño en esta falsa vive!' (I. 278) and '¡Oh ciego engaño, / oh fuerza poderosa / de la mujer que es, sobre falsa, hermosa!' (I. 336–38). Malgesí expone Angélica's ability to fabricate a credible story and demonstrates to Roldán and Reinaldos the Princess's awareness of the powerful effects of her discourse. If Malgesí *has* conjured up Angélica, then the magician has both constructed and deconstructed his own magic. He wants to share his 'inside' knowledge with the characters who are not privy to this irony. The off-stage audience, already aware of what's happening, is invited to 'see double' as they watch Malgesí perform the role of playwright and Angélica act out the script. Both internal and external audiences are entertained and instructed through this highly complex metatheatrical environment.

Malgesí soon lays bare Angélica's true motivation: 'mas su intento, / que el Cielo le corrija, / es diferente del fingido cuento, / porque su padre ordena / tener tus doce Pares en cadena [. . .] La lanza es encantada, / y tiene tal virtud, que, aquel que toca, / le atierra, y es dorada' (I. 298–302; 309–11). The magician endeavours to ensure that Angélica's attentive audience perceives her tale as fraudulent and he warns Carlomagno that her objective is to protect her father's imperialistic interests (I. 321–25). Moreover, Malgesí is the only character who deduces Galalón's untrustworthy qualities. The knight secretly hopes for the deaths of Roldán and Reinaldos in battle in order that he might win influence with Carlomagno. Roldán, however, believes Galalón to be a loyal friend: 'Reinaldos, no le tengas ojeriza / a Galalón, que a fe que es nuestro amigo' (I. 161–62). Malgesí expresses his suspicion and unease: '¡Así le viese yo hecho ceniza, / o de la suerte que en mi mente digo! / Éste es el soplo que aquel fuego atiza / y enciende, por quien siempre es enemigo / nuestro bien rey de nuestro buen linaje' (I. 163–67). Malgesí's suspicions are proved correct at the end of the play when the enchanter arrives on the scene just as Galalón is misrepresenting his heroic deeds to Carlomagno. When Malgesí reveals Galalón to be a liar, the knight rages: 'La ciencia deste enemigo / honra y vida y más me cuesta' (III. 2665–66).

Malgesí's persistent assertions that Angélica and Galalón are not who they appear to be break the suspension of disbelief and cause the spectator to take note of how dramatic action manoeuvres and controls audience response. The magician's comments concerning Angélica and her 'fingido cuento' particularly reveal how linguistic manipulation operates as a dramatic device which can create and sustain illusion. It is through Malgesí's interventions on stage that Cervantes encourages both the on-stage and off-stage audience to recognise the creative potential of language to conceal and mislead. The sorcerer's spectators, however, are not persuaded of his judgement; Reinaldos and Roldán remain in pursuit of Angélica, whilst Galalón is allowed to persist with his deceitful schemes. Thus Meixell views Malgesí as a type of defective storyteller who is unable 'to resolve issues through his own powers of persuasion' and 'does not know how to use his knowledge to direct a different course of action'.[174] She does, however, acknowledge that the blame cannot be placed on Malgesí alone:

The play illustrates that the people whom Malgesí is trying to assist do not make the magician's task any easier: Charlemagne, Roldán, and Reinaldos do not want to believe the truth if it contradicts what they want or hope to be the case. By underscoring the various characters' reluctance to give credence to Malgesí's claims, Cervantes is commenting upon people's general hesitation to embrace new ideas.[175]

I would argue that the drama's depiction of the paladins and the Emperor's resistance to Malgesí's proclamations of truth has much less to do with a wilful reluctance to be proved wrong, and more to do with the inability to perceive truth for what it is and, indeed, to recognise their own role as receivers of powerfully influential devices. Despite the fact that Malgesí persistently comments on and, therefore, shatters illusion, his audience is unable to see through the fictions which Angélica and Galalón create. It is not that Malgesí is an incompetent creator, rather that his audience is so susceptible to illusion that they are incapable of accepting his protestations for the truth that they reveal. Malgesí's strategy is designed to provoke the on-stage audience to assess critically the spectacle with which they are faced. It is a type of 'metacommunication' defined by Gregory Bateson as 'a device which informs the participants in an interaction about the nature of what is going on [...] Reflexive comments which cue and explain'.[176] Nonetheless, Malgesí's audience display indifference in the face of his interventions and comply with the deceiving fictions which the stage creates.[177]

In the final act of *La casa de los celos* Malgesí's role as a puppeteer in control of the stage is particularly prominent. Stage directions indicate that Malgesí is 'de dentro' (III. 2410) yet he voices Marfisa's thoughts before she has the opportunity to speak them aloud: '¿Quién sabe el intento mío? / Los versos dicen lo mismo / que imaginé en mi intención.' (III. 2416-18). Such a strategy prompts an audience to recognise their position as receivers of dramatic strategies. The magician reveals theatrical artifice precisely because he is aware that the spectacle derives its very power from the inability of the audience to reflect upon it. This is also evident in Act II when Malgesí vainly conjures up figures such as Temor, Sospecha, Desesperación, Curiosidad and Celos and questions why his magic has failed to rouse Reinaldos from his madness: '¿Cómo que con la invención / de quien yo tanto fié / no se cela el corazón / de mi primo?' (II. 1343-46). Anthony Close offers an interpretation of Malgesí's magic which contends with Meixell's view that the enchanter is questioning 'the ineffectualness of his intricate performance'.[178] Close argues that Malgesí's trickery is 'una especie de terapia de choque' which ends in failure precisely because the sorcerer 'no puede forzar el libre albedrío'.[179] I would note, however, that there is much more at stake in this scene than the fact that the paladins cannot be forced against their will to comply with the possibility that Angélica is not what she appears to be. Malgesí summons up five allegorical figures before Reinaldos and blatantly breaks suspension of disbelief as he explicates and defines the appearance of each figure and the function that it performs: 'Esta figura que ves / es el Temor sospechoso' (II. 1283–84); 'Ésta es la infame Sospecha, / de los celos muy parienta' (II. 1293–94) and 'La vana Curiosidad / es ésta que ves presente' (II. 1303–04). Malgesí both constructs and 'unmasks' these figures; imposing upon the scene a commentary which operates as a type of script (II. 1263–1337). The paladin, however, remains utterly unmoved by his brother's attempt to free him of his madness. This would suggest that Cervantes is not merely depicting a wilful compliance with fiction, but uncontrollable surrender to the mechanisms of the stage.

The final scenes of *La casa de los celos* see Malgesí explain to Reinaldos that the appearance of Angélica is merely a product of an enchantment: 'Aquesa enterrada y muerta / no es Angélica la bella, / sino sombra o imagen della, / que tu vista desconcierta' (III. 2135–38). Once again, the magician simultaneously constructs and sabotages his magic. Malgesí can, therefore, be said to embody a Cervantine appraisal of the role that a dramatist should perform. Rather than create a spectacle which oppresses the receiver, Cervantes's on-stage playwright provides the means through which the spectator can exercise discrimination and discernment. This confirms Arboleda's view that: 'El teatro de Cervantes es un teatro de ruptura, de distanciamiento, de choque y de confrontación con el ilusionismo en que la representación tiende a sumergir al público'.[180] Unlike the *comedia nueva*, Cervantine theatre seems less interested in sustaining illusion. Rather, as demonstrated in *La casa de los celos*, the priority is to bring sharply into focus the responsibilities of both the playwright and the audience. The stage must not exploit or control and the spectator must not receive the *comedia* passively nor unproblematically.

This unmasking of illusion is, therefore, much more than an observation about 'people's general hesitation to embrace new ideas'. In fact, Cervantes's dismantling of the stage not only challenges his audience to discern and resist the dramatic devices to which they are susceptible, but operates as a type of 'des-engaño' which obliges the spectator, as Arboleda would have it, to 'wake up' and perceive the realities of an increasingly unstable seventeenth-century Spain.[181] For it is likely the *corral* audience, conditioned by the illusion-making devices of the stage, would otherwise accept unproblematically dramatic representations of Spanish imperial grandeur. Cervantes's portrayal of inept squabbling knights and an epic hero, Bernardo del Carpio, who suffers a crisis of identity shatters the illusion of a unified Spanish empire.[182] This is compounded by Malgesí's persistent admonitions to perceive the transient and manipulative qualities of his magic. Via the strategy of unmasking 'engaño', Cervantes advocates a responsible engagement with the socio-cultural and political messages at play. If Cervantes read Lope as many in the twentieth-century did — as a playwright whose work endorsed the regime — then this play might be read as a reaction against the ideology advocated by Lope's highly influential *comedia nueva*.[183] Certainly the *Quijote* attests to Cervantes's unease with Lope's popular theatre as is seen both in chapter XLVIII of part I of the novel, but also in chapter XVI of part II when the novelist's anti-hero offers a definition of poetic art which reveals Cervantes's anxieties concerning theatre as a marketable commodity fashioned to suit the taste of an indiscriminate audience:

> La poesía [. . .] es como una doncella tierna y de poca edad, y en todo extremo hermosa, a quien tienen cuidado de enriquecer, pulir y adornar otras muchas doncellas, que son todas las otras ciencias, y ella se ha de servir de todas, y todas se han de autorizar con ella; pero esta tal doncella no quiere ser manoseada, ni traída por las calles, ni publicada por las esquinas de las plazas ni por los rincones de los palacios [. . .] no ha de ser vendible en ninguna manera [. . .] no se ha de dejar tratar de los truhanes, ni del ignorante vulgo, incapaz de conocer ni estimar los tesoros que en ella se encierran. Y no penséis, señor, que yo llamo aquí vulgo solamente a la gente plebeya y humilde, que todo aquel que no sabe, aunque sea señor y príncipe, puede y debe entrar en el número de vulgo (pp. 666–67).

Art, then, must not be exploited as a tool to serve the interests of a particular group or class of people. Once again we see the dramatist promoting theatre which has an ethical point of origin. As Arboleda states: 'Cervantes rechaza la manipulación y uso del teatro como objeto propagandístico de las ideas y mitos nobles como el *amor, honor y monarquía*. Como alternativa de estas desviaciones, Cervantes insiste en la imprescindible necesidad de la integridad artística'.[184] The dismantling of illusion in *La casa*, therefore, not only promotes dynamic audience participation, but debunks any sense of self-delusion or deception. It coaxes the spectator to be a responsible individual in collective society; sensitive to the powerful subtleties of the stage.

This is why the ending of the drama, like that of *La entretenida*, concludes in such an unconventional fashion. Close comments that: 'La acción de la comedia, atrapada en un círculo vicioso, acaba volviendo a su punto de partida'.[185] In fact, there is effectively no plot progression in *La casa de los celos* and any sense of a concrete ending is pointedly avoided. Interestingly, in the play's closing scene an *Ángel*, in epic mode, foretells the fate of *La casa*'s protagonists (III. 2691–2723). The messenger predicts the military campaigns in which Spain will be involved and concludes by warning Charlemagne that he will lose in battle (line 2715). This speech is couched in the future tense, but for Cervantes's audience it refers to events which are, in fact, part of their past, and compels them to confront the reality of failed and disastrous campaigns of yesteryear. This is further compounded by Roldán's dismissive and arrogant attitude toward the angel's proclamations. The paladin asserts: '¡Morirán luego a mis manos / andaluces y africanos!' (III. 2741–42). Malgesí vainly attempts to caution Roldán: '¡Vano saldrá vuestro intento!' (III. 2743) and 'No te alargues, arrogante, / que Dios dispone otra cosa, / como en efecto verás' (III. 2747–49). These predictions only serve to lend credibility to the magician's status as a 'truth-teller' given that

Roland died in the battle of Roncesvalles in 778. As the audience watches Roldán make his way determinedly to certain death dramatic irony gives way to disillusionment. Cervantes thus exploits the past as a lens through which the spectator is compelled to face the present. Roldán's situation mirrors that of the contemporary audience who are blind to the realities of an aggressive imperialistic policy and a Spain that is descending into decline. The stark reality of past defeat is juxtaposed against an equally precarious present in order that the seventeenth-century Spanish spectator might interrogate the climate in which he/she lives. *La casa de los celos*'s final scene is, therefore, a violent unmasking of *engaño* which utterly destroys the façade of the stage and forces an audience to realise its vulnerable position as consumers of powerful representations and to exercise responsibility accordingly. In this play it is Malgesí who fulfils the role of Cervantes himself as the magician coaxes his audience out of complacency. In *La casa*'s final scene on-stage fantasy cedes to an uncomfortable off-stage reality.

Cervantes's preoccupation with dramatic manipulation is affirmed in *Don Quijote II* (chapters XXX–LVII) in the episode which sees the *ingenioso hidalgo* stay with the Duke and Duchess. Cervantes's protagonist's inability to separate fiction from illusion is cruelly exploited for the purposes of entertainment. When Don Quijote leaves the castle he is immediately conscious and appreciative of his newly found freedom in the 'campaña rasa':

> La libertad, Sancho, es uno de los más preciosos dones que a los hombres dieron a los cielos; con ella no pueden igualarse los tesoros que encierra la tierra ni el mar encubre; por la libertad así como por la honra se puede y debe aventurar la vida, y, por el contrario, el cautiverio es el mayor mal que puede venir a los hombres (pp. 984–85).

Don Quijote is not only liberated from the confinement of the castle, but from the oppressive illusion-making tactics practiced by the Duke and Duchess. When the knight leaves: 'le pareció que estaba en su centro y que los espíritus se le renovaban' (p. 984). In *La casa de los celos* Don Quijote's physical separation is prefigured by a dramatic strategy in which Malgesí persuades both the on-stage and off-stage audience to perceive the mechanics of dramatic fashioning. From the opening scene of the drama Malgesí is aware of the lengths to which he will have to go to rescue his brother from his lovesick delusion: 'El laberinto he entrado / que apenas saldré dél' (I. 335–36). Fiction is a dangerous labyrinth in which one can lose him/herself when illusion and reality are blurred. Reinaldos is unable to exercise free will and mobilise any sense of perception as he is subject and subordinate to the manipulations of the stage. Fact and fiction have become so intricately linked that they are inseparable and indistinguishable. Just as Don Quijote is confined to the *duques*' castle and exploited for entertainment, the characters of *La casa* are imprisoned in a universe where illusion and reality mutually shape each other. Moreover, Malgesí's labyrinth metaphor not only reflects Reinaldos's inability to respond to and engage with dramatic illusion, but, as discussed above, is indicative of the confusions of the highly unstable and uncertain world in which the contemporary subject lived.[186]

La casa de los celos y selvas de Ardenia is a showcase for the potentially liberating nature of Cervantine theatre itself and offers a radical re-conception of the early seventeenth-century Spanish stage. The play's focus on the shattering and disintegration of illusion should not be perceived negatively as the promotion of a stage which is formless, incoherent or disinclined to entertain. Rather, *La casa de los celos* should be understood as freedom from a theatre in which the spectator experiences a conditioned horizon of expectations. As Alcalá Galán remarks, Cervantes's theatre offers an alternative 'renewing' vision: 'Pienso que con sus *Ocho comedias* [...] Cervantes trata, y consigue, un intento de renovación del teatro que no pase por los postulados de la comedia nueva y que constituya a la vez una alternativa a ésta'.[187] This alternative is a theatre that promotes reciprocal communication and which depends on the dynamic participation of an audience. This is the safety device which prevents the proliferation and passive reception of powerful propaganda. In other words, Cervantine theatre gives voice to the interests which he believes were silenced by the repressive nature of the Golden-Age stage.

This study of *La entretenida*, *El laberinto de amor* and *La casa de los celos y selvas de Ardenia* exposes the dualities and oppositions at the heart of an abstruse and conflicted seventeenth-century Spanish society. These notions are inherent in Cervantes's portrayal of the female protagonists of *El laberinto* and *La entretenida* who transgress boundaries in order that they might successfully perform their social role and through a magician in *La casa*, who acts as the lens through which the instabilities and manipulations of the age are seen. The manner in which freedom is presented affirms the forces, external and internal, which operate upon the individual. Exercise of individuality and free will, in this theatre, is revealed as the antidote for the repressed and oppressed subject. *La entretendia* and *El laberinto* particularly focus on the individual's reaction to the limits and margins imposed by society and allow the human subject to overcome these. There is a sense of both social and poetic justice in the victories of Marcela Osorio, Rosamira, Porcia and Julia. Liberty is not exploited for the good of self nor is it manipulated for the purposes of altering social structures. Fidelity to self is clearly offset against recognition of the value of societal configuration. Free will is mobilised for the greater good of society, and strategies employed by society in order to contain are portrayed as outmoded and redundant. As McKendrick has pointed out, Cervantes believed that confinement of the individual 'was not the soil in which moral responsibility flourished'.[188] Cervantes leaves us in little doubt that autonomy is synonymous with progress and that restriction is an unparalleled threat to humanity.

Cervantes's understanding of freedom in individualistic terms, as represented by the three plays under consideration in this chapter, is reflective of his theatre in general. Just as moral responsibility does not prosper under the shadow of societal confinement, nor, does the artist flourish within the parameters of highly restrictive formulas designed to pander to the *vulgo*. As Alcalá Galán notes:

> No es aceptado [el teatro de Cervantes] precisamente porque huye de los recursos fáciles y estereotipados demandados por los gustos tiránicos del público, en lo que no deja de tener parte la irresponsable complacencia de los dramaturgos adscritos a las modas y modos del momento.[189]

Cervantes's theatre is clearly not enslaved to the *comedia nueva*, demonstrated by its refusal to be a propagandistic vehicle to protect the 'values' of the ruling class, nor is it any sort of marketing machine for a monarcho-seigneurial system. *El laberinto de amor*, *La entretenida* and *La casa de los celos* manifest Cervantes's interpretation of the function of the theatre as an institution which should not submit to social dictates. Rather, Cervantes advocates the freedom of the artist to create. In *La entretenida* and *El laberinto* the women exploit their marginality to position their voices centre-stage and overturn their father's will. In *La casa de los celos* Malgesí fashions a theatre which exposes its own ability to exploit, thus awakening his passive audience to the potential of a stage which thrives on mutual communication. Cervantes, then, rejects Lope's formula in favour of an ethical *inventio*; a methodology which frees the author to be innovative and creative whilst promoting illusion responsibly. In sum, these plays constitute a collectively potent statement of a theatre designed to liberate both author and spectator and to promote a stage which requires active scrutiny and discrimination in order for its words to resonate meaningfully in the seventeenth-century world and beyond.

Notes to Chapter 1

1. Jean Canavaggio, 'De un Lope a otro Lope: Cervantes ante el teatro de su tiempo', *Anuario Lope de Vega*, 6 (2000), 51–59 (p. 51).
2. Friedman, *The Unifying Concept*, p. 108.
3. The play is generally considered to be Cervantes's 'dramatic anomaly'. Canavaggio states that: 'tanto por su estructura como por su versificación 'primitiva' se diferencia de las demás comedias de la edición de 1615'. 'Las figuras del donaire en las comedias de Cervantes', in *Risa y sociedad en el teatro español del Siglo de Oro. Actes du III Colloque du Groupe d'études sur le Théâtre Espagnol, Toulouse* (Paris: Éditions du Centre National de la Recherche Scientifique, 1981), pp. 51–67 (p. 52).
4. Marcella Trambaioli, 'Una protocomedia burlesca de Cervantes: *La casa de los celos*, parodia de algunas piezas del primer Lope de Vega', in *Cervantes y su mundo I*, ed. by Eva Reichenberger and Kurt Reichenberger (Kassel: Reichenberger, 2004), pp. 407–38 (p. 424).
5. See Friedman, *The Unifying Concept*; Carmen Cubero, 'En torno a *La entretenida* de Cervantes. El teatro dentro del teatro y el teatro sobre el teatro', in *El teatro dentro del*

teatro: Cervantes, Lope, Tirso y Calderón. Actas del 'Grand Séminaire' de la Universidad de Neuchâtel, 18–19 de Mayo de 1995, ed. by Irene Andrés-Suárez, José Manuel López de Abiada and Pedro Ramírez Molas (Madrid: Editorial Verbum, 1997), pp. 59–72; Jonathan Thacker, *Role-play and the World as Stage* and Eric J. Kartchner, 'Empty Words: Promises and Deception in *La entretenida*', *Bulletin of the Comediantes*, 56 (2004), 327–43.

6. Thomas Austin O'Connor, 'Is the Spanish Comedia a Metatheater?', *Hispanic Review*, 43 (1975), 275–89.
7. Thacker, *Role-play and the World as Stage*, p. 54.
8. Casalduero, *Sentido y forma*, p. 164.
9. Friedman, *The Unifying Concept*, p. 107.
10. Margaret A. Rose, *Parody: Ancient, Modern, and Post-modern* (Cambridge: Cambridge University Press, 1993), p. 52.
11. Friedman, 'The Comic Vision of Cervantes's *La entretenida*', *Theatralia: Revista de Teoría del Teatro*, 5 (2003), 351–59 (p. 356).
12. Stanislav Zimic, 'Cervantes frente a Lope y a la comedia nueva: Observaciones sobre *La entretenida*', *Anales Cervantinos*, 15 (1976), 19–119. Zimic perceives *La entretenida* 'como una representación de un drama íntimo de su autor', p. 21. Francisco José López Alfonso, '*La entretenida*, parodia y teatralidad', *Anales Cervantinos*, 24 (1986), 193–205. Juan Bautista Avalle-Arce offers a study of the sonnets in the drama which are, in his opinion, exploited for the purpose of parodying Lope's model. The critic notes that *La entretenida* is 'una voluntariosa imitación de las comedias de Lope; pero una imitación, sin embargo, que tiende hacia los efectos de la parodia'. 'On *La entretenida* of Cervantes', *Modern Language Notes*, 74 (1959), 418–21 (p. 419).
13. Melveena McKendrick remarks that in seventeenth-century drama 'marriage is used at the end of a play as a symbol of the restoration of the good order of society'. 'Women against Wedlock. The Reluctant Brides of Golden Age Drama', in *Women in Hispanic Literature: Icons and Fallen Idols*, ed. by Beth Miller (Berkeley: University of California Press, 1983), pp. 115–46 (p. 145).
14. George Mariscal, 'Woman and Other Metaphors in Cervantes's comedia famosa de *La entretenida*', *Theatre Journal*, 46 (1994), 213–30.
15. Linda Hutcheon notes that the use of parody implies 'an informed reader'. See *A Theory of Parody: The Teachings of Twentieth Century Art Forms* (New York; London: Methuen, 1985), p. 27.
16. Rose, *Parody*, p. 38.
17. Rose, *Parody*, p. 39.
18. Ironically, modern audiences have accessibility to *La entretenida* which was unavailable to seventeenth-century audiences. *La entretenida* was first performed in 1995 and was later adapted and performed in 2005 by *La Compañía Nacional de Teatro Clásico de España*.
19. Hans Robert Jauss, *Toward an Aesthetic of Reception* (Brighton: Harvester, 1982).
20. Jauss, *Toward an Aesthetic of Reception*, p. 15.
21. Iser, 'The Reading Process', p. 279.
22. Simerka, 'Early Modern Skepticism and Unbelief', p. 46.
23. Greenblatt, *Renaissance Self-Fashioning*, p. 2.
24. Catherine Connor (Swietlicki), 'Marriage and Subversion in Comedia Endings: Problems in Art and Society', in *Gender, Identity, and Representation in Spain's Golden Age*, ed. by Anita K. Stoll and Dawn L. Smith (Lewisburg, Pennsylvania: Bucknell University Press, 2000), pp. 23–46 (p. 28).
25. Friedman, 'The Comic Vision', p. 356.
26. Friedman, 'The Comic Vision', p. 352.

27. Melveena McKendrick, *Women and Society in the Spanish Drama of the Golden Age: A Study of the Mujer Varonil* (London: Cambridge University Press, 1974).
28. McKendrick, *Women and Society*, p. ix.
29. Mary Beth Rose, 'Gender, Genre, and History: Seventeenth-Century English Women and the Art of Autobiography', in *Women in the Middle Ages and the Renaissance: Literary and Historical Perspectives*, ed. by Mary Beth Rose (New York: Syracuse University Press, 1986), pp. 245–74 (p. 251).
30. McKendrick, *Women and Society*, p. 74.
31. Taddeo supports McKendrick's argument by asserting that Cervantes gives equal weight to the voices of his women characters. See 'De vox extremada: Cervantes's women characters speak for themselves', in *Women in the Discourse of Early Modern Spain*, ed. by Joan F. Cammarata (Gainesville, Florida: University Press of Florida, 2003), pp. 183–98 (p. 187).
32. Connor, 'Marriage and Subversion', p. 36.
33. Thacker, *Role-Play and the World as Stage*, p. 40.
34. Casalduero, *Sentido y forma*, p. 165.
35. James Casey, *Early Modern Spain: A Social History* (London; New York: Routledge, 1999), p. 202.
36. Elizabeth Closs Traugott and Mary Louise Pratt, *Linguistics for Students of Literature* (San Diego; London: Harcourt Brace Jovanovich, 1980), p. 227.
37. In Lope's *El perro del hortelano*, for example, Diana dictates a letter to her scribe which is in reality, intended for him. Although the countess exploits the opportunity to re-affirm her social status, it is clear that her servant, whose profession requires him to take dictation, would have no reason to believe that he is the recipient of her words. The plot is, in fact, often spurred on by comedic instances of miscommunication. For relevant studies on the play from a linguistic perspective see Edward Friedman, 'Sign Language: The Semiotics of Love in Lope's *El perro del hortelano*', *Hispanic Review*, 68 (2000), 1–20 and Isabel Torres, '"Pues no entiendo tus palabras / y tus bofetones siento". Linguistic subversion in Lope de Vega's *El perro del hortelano*', *Journal of Hispanic Research*, 5 (2004), 197–212.
38. See Duncan Moir, 'The Classical Tradition in Spanish Dramatic Theory and Practice in the Seventeenth Century', in *Classical Drama and Its Influence*, ed. by M. J. Anderson (London: Methuen, 1965), pp. 193–228 (p. 209).
39. Moir, 'The Classical Tradition', p. 208.
40. Iser, 'The Reading Process', p. 284.
41. Emilie L. Bergmann, 'Acts of Reading, Acts of Writing', in *Heavenly Bodies: The Realms of La estrella de Sevilla*, ed. by Frederick A. De Armas (Lewisburg, Pennsylvania: Bucknell University Press, 1996), pp. 221–34 (p. 225).
42. Mariscal, 'Woman and Other Metaphors', p. 214.
43. Marcela's choice of husband, therefore, neither compromises the double context of '*honor*' nor '*honra*'. Her suitable decision subverts the typical *comedia* honour plot in which a female character's honour may be in doubt or put at risk and thus, impinge on her family's public image and good reputation. See Gustavo Correa, 'El doble aspecto de la honra en el teatro del siglo XVII', *Hispanic Review*, 26 (1958), 99–107.
44. Iser, 'The Reading Process', pp. 284–85.
45. This is perhaps a result of the multifaceted and difficult relationship which exists between modern critical theory and the early modern. Despite the complexities of this relationship critics have employed and tested theoretical modes of thought against early modern material. Michael Moriarty notes: 'theory has proved fruitful in its application to any modernity, early or late, and served to legitimate their claim to our interest'. See 'Theory and the Early Modern: Some Notes on a Difficult Relationship', *Paragraph*, 29 (2006), 1–11 (p. 3).

46. Jürgen Habermas's highly influential study states that a new civic society began to emerge during the period of the Enlightenment when social sites came into being which produced rational critical debate. See *The Structural Transformation of the Public Sphere* (Cambridge: Polity, 1989).
47. William Childers, 'The Baroque Public Sphere', in *Reason and Its Others*, pp. 165–85 (p. 165).
48. Childers, 'The Baroque Public Sphere', p. 166.
49. Bergmann, 'Acts of Reading, Acts of Writing', p. 226.
50. An example of contrived matrimonial closure can be seen in the conclusion to Lope's *Los locos de Valencia*.
51. Robert Phiddian, *Swift's Parody* (Cambridge: Cambridge University Press, 1995), p. 13.
52. B. Ritchie, 'The Formal Structure of the Aesthetic Object', in *The Problems of Aesthetics*, ed. by Eliseo Vivas and Murray Kreiger (New York: Rineheart, 1965), pp. 225–33 (p. 230). See Iser, 'The Reading Process', p. 292.
53. McKendrick, *Women and Society*, p. 323.
54. McKendrick, *Women and Society*, p. 323.
55. Thacker, *Role-play and the World as Stage*, p. 12.
56. Erving Goffman, *The Presentation of Self in Everyday Life* (Harmondsworth: Penguin, 1969), p. 247.
57. Mariscal, 'Woman and Other Metaphors', p. 222.
58. Iser, 'The Reading Process', p. 293.
59. See Mariscal on this topic, *Contradictory Subjects*. The critic observes that 'the subject is constituted by multiple and often contradictory subject positions and thus is always only a provisionally fixed entity located at various sites (positionalities) within the general relations of production, systems of signification, and relations of power', p. 5.
60. A prime example would be *El perro del hortelano*'s Teodoro. Also see pp. 36 of this study.
61. Hornby, *Drama, Metadrama and Perception*, p. 71.
62. Butler, *Gender Trouble*, p. 188.
63. In *Pedro de Urdemalas* Pascual changes his name to Roque and in *El rufián dichoso* Lugo becomes Cruz.
64. Friedman, *The Unifying Concept*, pp. 110–11.
65. Donald R. Larson, '*La Dama Boba* and the comic sense of life', *Romanische Forschungen*, 85 (1973), 41–62 (p. 57).
66. Robbins, *The Challenges of Uncertainty*, p. 119.
67. Robbins, *The Challenges of Uncertainty*, p. 131.
68. For María Ángela Celis Sánchez, Cervantes's portrayal of the servant's individualism 'es uno de los más obvios reflejos del Cervantes-hombre renacentista que descubre la autonomía del ser y la miseria de la condición humana en la conciencia de serlo'. 'Planos de comunicación en las comedias cervantinas: el juego metateatral', in *El teatro en tiempos de Felipe II: Actas de las XXI Jornadas de Teatro Clásico* (Almagro, Julio de 1998), ed. by Felipe B. Pedraza Jiménez and Rafael González Cañal (Almagro: Universidad de Castillo-La Mancha, 1999), pp. 83–98 (p. 93). Zimic comments that the servants are depicted as people with 'una gama amplia y honda de preocupaciones, sentimientos y emociones, muy dignos de atención'. *El teatro de Cervantes*, pp. 239–40.
69. Larson states that characters find an 'authenticity' when they take up their social roles. '*La Dama Boba* and the comic sense of life', p. 57.
70. This is exemplified, for instance, when Torrente and Cardenio consistently reveal their true identity when playing the roles of Don Silvestre and servant in the closing scene of Act I.

71. See Northrop Frye on this topic: 'The Argument of Comedy', in *Comedy: Developments in Criticism*, ed. by D. J. Palmer (London: Macmillan, 1984), pp. 74–84.
72. Northrop Frye, *A Natural Perspective: The Development of Shakespearean Comedy and Romance* (New York: Harcourt, Brace and World, 1965).
73. Connor, 'Marriage and Subversion', p. 29.
74. Iser, 'The Reading Process', p. 282.
75. Connor, 'Marriage and Subversion', p. 28.
76. Lope's dramatic treatise *El arte nuevo de hacer comedias en este tiempo* prioritises plot and action: 'Ponga la conexión desde el principio / Hasta que vaya declinando el passo, / Pero la solución no le permita / Hasta que llegue a la postrera scena, / Porque en sabiendo el vulgo el fin que tiene / Buelue el rostro a la puerta, y las espaldas / Al que esperó tres horas cara a cara' (232–38). For this traditional view of Lope's theatre, see A. A. Parker, *The Approach to the Spanish Drama of the Golden Age* (London: Hispanic & Luso-Brazilian Councils, 1957). Ellen Anderson suggests that for Cervantes 'the decorum of character in drama is elastic, open, necessarily responsive to circumstance'. She sees this sense of flexibility as the dramatist's greatest challenge to the *comedia nueva*. See 'Mothers of Invention: Toward a Reevaluation of Cervantine Dramatic Heroines', *Bulletin of the Comediantes*, 62 (2010), 1–44 (p. 38).
77. See section 3.2 'Pedro: a contrapelo del siglo de oro' for a reading of Belica's legitimate anagnorisis in *Pedro de Urdemalas*.
78. The failure of *La entretenida*'s characters to attain their goals clearly undercuts Lope's formulaic 'mirror'. In his *Arte nuevo* Lope contends that the *comedia nueva* is like a mirror which depicts life: 'espejo / de las costumbres, y una viva imagen / de la verdad' (123–25).
79. Spadaccini, 'Cervantes and the Spanish comedia', p. 64.
80. For instance, see Schevill and Bonilla, *Comedias y Entremeses* and Luis Astrana Marín, *Vida ejemplar y heroica de Miguel de Cervantes Saavedra, con mil documentos hasta ahora inéditos y numerosas ilustraciones y grabados de época* (Madrid: Instituto Editorial Reus, 1948). Astrana Marín denounces the many 'enredos, disfraces y confusiones, que enmarañan la acción, hasta el punto de obligar al lector o espectador a una atención continua y a no perder el menor detalle', p. 220.
81. Ynduráin, ed., *Obras dramáticas de Miguel de Cervantes*, p. xli.
82. Zimic, 'Sobre la clasificación de las comedias de Cervantes', *Acta Neophilologica*, 14 (1981), 63–83 (p. 75).
83. Taddeo, 'De vox extremada', p. 185.
84. Pilar Alcalde Fernández-Loza notes that: 'Palabra y vestido son dos formas mediante las personas manifiestan su identidad social y ejercen su poder'. 'La verdad y la mentira en el teatro de Cervantes: El caso del *Laberinto de amor*', in *Memoria de la palabra: Actas del VI congreso de la asociación internacional Siglo de Oro*, ed. by María Luisa Lobato and Francisco Domínguez Matito (Madrid; Frankfurt: Iberoamericana-Vervuert, 2004), pp. 193–99 (p. 195). For Desirée Pérez Fernández, 'el tema de disfraz es el verdadero eje dramático de la obra'. '*El laberinto de amor* de Cervantes: análisis del texto y su puesta en escena', *Estudios humanísticos. Filología*, 28 (2006), 143–60 (p. 158).
85. Ellen M. Anderson, 'Refashioning the Maze: The Interplay of Gender and Rank in Cervantes's *El laberinto de amor*', *Bulletin of the Comediantes*, 46 (1994), 165–85 (p. 180). In a more recent study of *El laberinto de amor*, *La entretenida*, *La gran sultana* and *El gallardo español* Anderson examines ambiguous gender representation in key scenes in which the female protagonists 'play roles and manipulate language to work their will on the world'. See 'Mothers of Invention', p. 2.
86. Taddeo, 'De vox extremada', p. 189.

87. Friedman, 'Double Vision: Self and Society in *El Laberinto de amor* and *La entretenida*', in *Cervantes and the Renaissance*, ed. by Michael D. McGaha (Pennsylvania: Juan de la Cuesta, 1980), pp. 157–66 (p. 158). Taddeo concludes that: 'The long-suffering Cervantine heroines do not merely endure; their artful dominion of spoken and written language enables them to tell their own stories and thus triumph over their enemies'. 'De Vox Extremada', p. 187.
88. 'Truth' and 'fiction' are, of course, major themes in Cervantes's work. Spadaccini and Talens note that Cervantes's 'entire body of work revolves around the opposition between truth as such and truth as rhetorical construct'. 'Introduction: The Construction of the Self. Notes on Autobiography in Early Modern Spain', in *Autobiography in Early Modern Spain*, ed. by Nicholas Spadaccini and Jenaro Talens (Minneapolis: University of Minnesota Press, 1988), pp. 9–40 (p. 14).
89. Zimic, *El teatro de Cervantes*, pp. 206–07. Also see 'El laberinto y el lucero redentor: Estudio de *El laberinto de amor* de Cervantes', *Acta Neophilologica*, 13 (1980), 31–48 (p. 35).
90. See Agapita Jurado Santos, 'Silencio/Palabra: Estrategias de algunas mujeres cervantinas para realizar el deseo', *Cervantes*, 19 (1999), 140–53.
91. See McKendrick, *Women and Society*; María Soledad Carrasco Urgoti, 'Cervantes en su comedia *El laberinto de amor*', *Hispanic Review*, 48 (1980), 77–90 (p. 88) and Jurado Santos, 'Silencio/Palabra', p. 151.
92 Anderson, 'Refashioning the Maze', p. 167. Anderson also discusses how language and dress are the means by which identity is projected and understood in *El laberinto*. She particularly interrogates how the conduct of the drama's female protagonists challenges contemporary concepts of gender and rank in order to 'transform the calcified categories of conventional roles into the supple sinews of creatures who can move and be moved', p. 185.
93. Maravall notes that the Baroque world view 'which was tied to the consciousness of crisis, produced yet another image — or at least its diffusion and exacerbation — that was utilized by baroque writers: the world as a confused labyrinth'. See *Culture of the Baroque*, p. 153.
94. Bruce Swansey, 'From Allegory to Mockery: Baroque Representations of the Labyrinth', in *Rewriting Classical Mythology in the Hispanic Baroque*, ed. by Isabel Torres (Woodbridge: Tamesis, 2007), pp. 128–38 (p. 129).
95. Penelope Reed Doob, *The Idea of the Labyrinth from Classical Antiquity through the Middle Ages* (Ithaca: Cornell University Press, 1990), p. 18.
96. See, for example, Propertius, *Elegies* book II.
97. See Isabel Torres, 'Introduction: Con pretensión de Fénix', in *Rewriting Classical Mythology*, p. 7.
98. See Denise DiPuccio for a general discussion of how Golden-Age dramatists manipulated myth. *Communicating Myths of the Golden Age Comedia* (Lewisburg, Pennsylvania: Bucknell University Press, 1998).
99. Juan Pérez de Moya, *Philosofía secreta de la gentilidad*, ed. by Carlos Clavería (Madrid: Cátedra, 1995).
100. Michael Kidd, 'The Rise of the *Comedia Nueva*', in *Stages of Desire: The Mythological Tradition in Classical and Contemporary Spanish Theater* (Pennsylvania: The Pennsylvania State University Press, 1999), pp. 63–123 (p. 63). Kidd's reading of Golden-Age mythological dramas does not take into account Cervantes's *El laberinto*. It should also be noted that the use of the labyrinth myth experienced a transition from allegory to parody during the seventeenth century. See Swansey, 'From Allegory to Mockery'.
101. See Harold Bloom, *A Map of Misreading* (New York: Oxford University Press, 1975), p. 4.
102. Michael Kidd analyses the play in *Stages of Desire*, pp. 86–101.

103. See Swansey's study of the play: 'From Allegory to Mockery', pp. 129–31.
104. See, for example, Lope's *El laberinto de Creta*. The play includes characters such as Ariadna, Fedra, Teseo and Pasife.
105. Most commentators agree that the plot itself, especially that concerning Dagoberto and Rosamira, is taken from Ludovico Ariosto's *Orlando furioso* canto V. Moreover, among studies of the play, Anderson and Taddeo remain the few critics who mention the Cretan labyrinth. In her discussion of gender and rank, Anderson purports that: 'The story of the Daedalan labyrinth can be read as a myth of the different ways that men and women imagine and instruct'. Although this approach leads the critic to render some interesting observations on the fluidity of behavioural and social categories, the mythological context is explored as a means to a gender-centred end. 'Refashioning the Maze', p. 167.
106. Frederick A. de Armas, *Cervantes, Raphael and the Classics* (Cambridge: Cambridge Universty Press, 1998), p. 1. De Armas notes that 'there are very few studies that deal with Cervantes and the classics'. De Armas has also recently argued that *Don Quijote* is a 'deeply Ovidian text' which draws upon classical myths and themes. *Ovid in the Age of Cervantes* (Toronto: University of Toronto Press, 2010), p. xii.
107. Pedro Ruiz Pérez, *La distinción cervantina. Poética e historia* (Alcalá de Henares: Centro de Estudios Cervantinos, 2006), p. 84.
108. Ruiz Pérez, *La distinción cervantina*, pp. 128–32. Alban Forcione's article on 'Cervantes and the Freedom of the Artist' contends that Cervantes puts literary theories on trial in his prose fiction (he cites examples from the *Novelas* and *Quijote*). The critic concludes that Cervantes had a vested interest in the freedom of the creative imagination. See *The Romantic Review*, 61 (1970), 243–55.
109. 'Daedalus, most famous for his talent in the craftsman's art, set the building up, but confused its signs and led the eye into error with the twisted ramblings of its many ways'. See Publius Ovidius Naso, *Metamorphoses VIII*, with an English translation and notes by D. E. Hill (Warminster: Aris & Phillips, 1992).
110. Laurel Fulkerson, *The Ovidian Heroine as Author: Reading, Writing, and Community in the Heroides* (Cambridge: Cambridge University Press, 2005).
111. Sara H. Lindheim's analysis of some of the letters demonstrates how the Ovidian women manipulate two different tactics, either portraying themselves as strong and powerful or vulnerable and powerless. See *Mail and Female: Epistolary Narrative and Desire in Ovid's Heroides* (Madison: University of Wisconsin Press, 2003).
112. Fulkerson, *The Ovidian Heroine*, p. 142.
113. Tirso de Molina, *El burlador de Sevilla*, ed. by Antonio Prieto (Madrid: Editorial Biblioteca Nueva, 1997). All citations from the play are taken from this edition.
114. Jurado Santos, 'Silencio/Palabra', pp. 140–41.
115. Zimic, *El teatro de Cervantes*, p. 212.
116. Anderson, 'Refashioning the Maze', p. 173. This would appear to be a recurring attribute of Cervantine heroines. Marcela Osorio in *La entretenida*, of course, also fulfils the role of the unseen author.
117. Zimic, 'El laberinto y el lucero redentor', p. 39.
118. It is impossible not to anticipate here Segismundo's fate in Calderón's *La vida es sueño*. The Calderonian drama has been interrogated from the perspective of its engagement with Ovid's Cretan labyrinth myth. Shelley Chitwood explores how 'Calderón built *La vida es sueño* on the classical labyrinth myth in Ovid while making enough changes in it to allow the elaboration of key contrasts: illusion and reality and free will and fate'. Like Rosamira, Segismundo is imprisoned in a bid to maintain patriarchal control and authority. Moreover, Rosaura in *La vida* can be said to mirror the role of Rosamira, Julia and Porcia and, therefore, by implication the role of Ariadne, as she enables Segismundo to escape the labyrinth of his own confusion. See 'Calderón's Labyrinth: *La vida es sueño*',

in *Looking at the Comedia in the Year of the Quincentennial: Proceedings of the 1992 Symposium on Golden Age Drama at the University of Texas, El Paso, March 18-21*, ed. by Barbara Mujica and Sharon D. Voros (Lanham, Maryland: University Press of America, 1993), pp. 179-86 (p. 186). Isabela is also imprisoned in a tower in *El burlador de Sevilla* as a result of her inappropriate conduct with Don Juan (I. 177-79).
119. Fernández-Loza, 'La verdad y la mentira en el teatro de Cervantes', p. 196. This view is also held by Casalduero (1951), Zimic (1980) and María Soledad Carrasco Urgoti, 'Cervantes en su comedia *El laberinto de amor*', *Hispanic Review*, 48 (1980), 77-90.
120. Anderson, 'Refashioning the Maze', p. 168.
121. Calderón's Segismundo is also perceived as part animal: 'un monstruo en forma de humana' (I. 672) and 'una fiera humana' (III. 3175). *La vida es sueño*, ed. by Ciriaco Morón Arroyo (Madrid: Cátedra, 1989).
122. Again, the women are similar to Rosaura. Although Calderón's female protagonist is depicted as a strong and almost 'masculine' woman from the drama's opening scene, she is completely driven by a need to avenge her honour by ultimately becoming Astolfo's wife. *El laberinto*'s heroines can also be seen to be like Segismundo given that their imprisonment is physical rather than psychological.
123. Sebastián de Covarrubias, *Tesoro de la lengua castellana o española*, ed. by Martín de Riquer (Barcelona: Alta Fulla, 1998), p. 812.
124. Rogelio Miñana, '"Veréis el monstruo": La nueva "comedia" de Cervantes', *Bulletin of the Comediantes*, 56 (2004), 387-411 (p. 388).
125. Anderson observes that these are instruments wielded by men. 'Refashioning the Maze', p. 168.
126. Thacker, *Role-Play and the World as Stage*, p. 39.
127. Howard Jacobson, *Ovid's Heroides* (Princeton: Princeton University Press, 1974), p. 224.
128. 'If I am not the cause of your deliverance, yet neither is it right that you should cause my death'. Ovid, *Heroides and Amores*, with an English translation by Grant Showerman (Cambridge; London: Harvard University Press, 1921).
129. McKendrick, *Cervantes*, p. 244.
130. See McKendrick's argument concerning the early modern Spanish woman and the conflict between nature and society. *Women and Society*, p. 327.
131. Friedman, 'Double Vision: Self and Society', p. 158.
132. Zimic, 'El laberinto y el lucero redentor', p. 48.
133. Ruth El Saffar and Diana de Armas Wilson, eds., *Quixotic Desire: Psychoanalytic Perspectives on Cervantes* (Ithaca: Cornell University Press, 1993), p. 14.
134. David R. Castillo, *(A)Wry Views: Anamorphosis, Cervantes, and the Early Picaresque* (Indiana: Purdue University Press, 2001), p. 118. This judgement is expressed again by Castillo and Spadaccini: 'en *El laberinto de amor* las damas protagonistas rechazan identificarse con el código del honor y las exigencias de la razón cristiana prefiriendo seguir el rumbo de sus deseos. Lejos de ser castigados a cuenta de la justicia poética al uso en la Comedia, las damas lascivas del *Laberinto* son premiadas con la adquisición de los objetos de su deseo'. See 'Cervantes y la 'comedia nueva': lectura y espectáculo', *Theatralia: Revista de Teoría del Teatro*, 5 (2003), 153-63 (p. 161).
135. This is a mirror which does not reflect on stage the 'reality' of life. Rather, it reveals and exposes how the stage can mislead and distort. As in *La entretenida*, Cervantes undercuts Lope's 'espejo' analogy.
136. Trambaioli, 'Una protocomedia burlesca de Cervantes', p. 411.
137. See Trambaioli, 'Una protocomedia burlesca de Cervantes', p. 424.
138. Early twentieth-century criticism on *La casa* is particularly harsh. Cotarelo y Valledor comments: 'No hay que buscar aquí orden ni concierto, ni arte por algún lado'. *El teatro de Cervantes*, p. 494. Schevill and Bonilla state: 'el lector más benévolo reconocerá que

Cervantes erró fundamentalmente al escoger por argumento de una obra dramática una serie de incidentes que nada tienen de teatral'. *Comedias y Entremeses*, p. 107. In recent years the play has provoked hostile reactions from some quarters. For instance, Florencio Sevilla Arroyo and Antonio Rey Hazas label the play 'la pieza más floja del teatro cervantino', *Teatro completo*, p. 107.

139. Paul Lewis-Smith, '*La casa de los celos* y la Commedia dell'Arte', *Theatralia: Revista de Teoría del Teatro*, 5 (2003), 375–84 (p. 376).
140. Lewis-Smith remarks that: 'The drama's lack of single-mindedness is connected with its date of composition. This, on purely technical evidence, some of which critics have already uncovered, may be placed in a period preceding or overlapping with that of the writing of *Don Quixote, I*'. See 'Cervantes and Inversimilar Fiction: Reconsidering *La casa de los celos y selvas de Ardenia*', in *Golden-Age Spanish Literature: Studies in Honour of John Varey by his Colleagues and Pupils*, ed. by Charles Davis and Alan Deyermond (London: Westfield College, 1991), pp. 127–36 (pp. 134–35).
141. See Canavaggio, *Cervantès dramaturge*, p. 38. John J. Allen purports that *La casa* and *Don Quijote* were written in 1592. '*La casa de los celos* and the 1605 *Quijote*', in *Cervantes for the 21st Century: Studies in Honor of Edward Dudley*, ed. by Francisco Rubia Prado (Delaware: Juan de la Cuesta, 2000), pp. 1–9.
142. Trambaioli, 'Una protocomedia burlesca de Cervantes'.
143. Lewis-Smith, 'Cervantes on Human Absurdity: The Unifying Theme of *La casa de los celos y selvas de Ardenia*', *Cervantes*, 12 (1992), 93–103 (p. 95).
144. Lewis-Smith dismisses jealousy as a motif of the play. 'Cervantes on Human Absurdity', p. 95. Friedman judges that jealousy 'is not the motivating force of the play'. *The Unifying Concept*, p. 125. Morley Hawks Marks, however, contends that 'los celos y su persistencia e inmutabilidad son el tema unificador de la obra' although she does not expound on this conclusion. See 'Deformación de la tradición pastoril en *La casa de los celos* de Miguel de Cervantes', in *Cervantes and the Pastoral*, ed. by José J. Labrador Herraiz and Juan Fernández Jiménez (Cleveland: Cleveland State University, 1986), pp. 129–38 (p. 130).
145. Friedman, '*La casa de los celos*: Cervantes' Dramatic Anomaly', in *Cervantes: Su obra y su mundo. Actas del I Congreso Internacional sobre Cervantes*, ed. by Manuel Criado de Val (Madrid: EDI-6, 1981), pp. 281–89. Lewis-Smith criticises this approach and states that Friedman's stance arises from 'an excessively modern view of *Don Quijote*'. See 'Cervantes and Inversimilar Fiction', p. 128.
146. Pedro Ruiz Pérez, 'Dramaturgia, teatralidad y sentido en *La casa de los celos*', in *Actas del II Coloquio de la Asociación de Cervantistas* (Alcalá de Henares, 6–9 de noviembre de 1989) (Barcelona: Anthropos, 1991), pp. 657–72 (p. 666).
147. This would also indicate how approaches to the drama have changed over the course of the last century. Early twentieth-century criticism especially accuses *La casa de los celos* of lacking cohesion. Recent contributions by Friedman, Lewis-Smith and Ruiz Pérez have led to significant attempts to appreciate and recuperate the play.
148. Amanda S. Meixell, 'The Espíritu de Merlín, Renaissance Magic, and the Limitations of Being Human in *La casa de los celos*', *Cervantes*, 24 (2004), 93–118 (p. 94).
149. Lewis-Smith, 'Cervantes on Human Absurdity', pp. 95–96.
150. Zimic, 'Algunas observaciones sobre *La casa de los celos*', *Hispania*, 49 (1973), 51–58 and Illuminada Amat, '"And These Be the Fruits of Play": Sexuality in *La casa de los celos y selvas de Ardenia*', *Bulletin of the Comediantes*, 52 (2000), 31–51.
151. For Zimic, the play dramatises 'conflicto interior'. See also José Manuel Trabado Cabado, 'Lírica, mundo pastoril y discurso dramático en *La casa de los celos*', *Theatralia: Revista de Teoría del Teatro*, 5 (2003), 385–96 (p. 388). See also endnote no. 76 for a note on Lope's tendency to prioritise plot and action.
152. See, for instance, Cotarelo, *El teatro de Cervantes*, p. 501.

153. See Hawks Marks, 'Deformación de la tradición pastoril', pp. 129–38. Earl Thompson perceives the shepherdess's self-interest and corrupt values as symptomatic of the conflict between classical pastoral literature and the realities of sixteenth-century Spain. 'Shepherds as Spanish Society: Cervantes' View in One comedia', in *Varia hispánica: Homenaje a Alberto Porqueras Mayo*, ed. by Joseph L. Laurenti and Vern G. Williamsen (Kassel: Reichenberger, 1989), pp. 7–15.
154. Rosalie Hernández-Pecoraro, '*La casa de los celos y selvas de Ardenia*: The Pastoral Metaphor Disrupted', in *Bucolic Metaphors: History, Subjectivity, and Gender in the Early Modern Spanish Pastoral* (Chapel Hill: University of North Carolina Press, 2006), pp. 202–10 (p. 210).
155. William Childers, '*Correr la pluma*: Multigeneric composition in *Don Quijote* and *Persiles*', Mester, 25 (1996), 119–46 (p. 119).
156. See Canavaggio in particular for a detailed study of the play's literary sources. *Cervantès dramaturge*, pp. 103–10. Lewis-Smith thinks that the drama is heavily influenced by the 'commedia dell'arte'. See '*La casa de los celos* y la Commedia dell'Arte'.
157. For Lewis-Smith, the parodic treatment of *La casa de los celos* 'is a manifestation of Cervantes's rational sensibilities uncomplicated by an interest in illusion [. . .] As in *Don Quixote*, in *La casa de los celos* Cervantes parodies chivalresque literature as an incompetent imitation of epic, as bungling pseudo-history'. 'Cervantes and Inverisimilar fiction', p. 129.
158. See Friedman, *The Unifying Concept*, p. 127.
159. Friedman, 'Perspectivism on Stage: Don Quijote and the Mediated Vision of Cervantes' Comedia', in *Ideologies and Literature. Plays and Playhouses in Imperial Decadence*, p. 82.
160. Friedman, 'Perspectivism on Stage', p. 83.
161. Arboleda, *Teoría y Formas del Metateatro*, p. 46.
162. Meixell, 'The Espíritu de Merlín', p. 108.
163. Trambaioli, 'Una protocomedia burlesca de Cervantes', p. 426.
164. Trambaioli notes that *La casa* was most likely composed in Cervantes's second writing period 'tal vez en una fecha temprana del mismo, cuando las relaciones entre los dos ingenios [Cervantes and Lope] se enfriaron, es decir alrededor de 1603'. 'Una protocomedia burlesca de Cervantes', p. 426.
165. Arboleda, *Teoría y Formas del Metateatro*', p. 83.
166. Malagigi's literary roots are found in the character of Maugris from the Matter of France. In this account, Maugris was stolen at birth by a Moorish slave but eventually rescued by a benevolent fairy who taught him magical powers. See Philippe Vernay, *Maugis d'Aigremont: chanson de geste* (Berne: Francke, 1980).
167. See Julia M. Kisacky, *Magic in Boiardo and Ariosto* (New York: Peter Lang, 2000).
168. Ruiz Pérez, 'Dramaturgia, teatralidad y sentido', p. 662.
169. Ruiz Pérez remarks that 'el encantador, sea Malgesí o el propio Cervantes, abre un juego de cajas chinas, en el que la ficción se impone por completo sobre la realidad'. 'Dramaturgia, teatralidad y sentido', p. 662.
170. Castillo and Spadaccini, 'Cervantes y la "comedia nueva"', p. 159.
171. Most of the play's characters are motivated by less than honourable desires. Angélica desires to protect her father's imperial interests and Galalón strives to win influence with Carlomagno at the cost of the lives of others. In the pastoral scenes, Clori wants to marry Rústico as it will provide her with financial security. Lauso and Corinto's cruel conduct toward Rústico is motivated by jealousy as they endeavour to dissuade Clori.
172. Cervantes, *Novelas ejemplares*, ed. by Harry Sieber (Madrid: Cátedra, 1980), p. 52. All citations from the exemplary novels are taken from this edition.
173. Meixell, 'The Espíritu de Merlín', p. 103.
174. Meixell, 'The Espíritu de Merlín', pp. 103–04.

175. Meixell, 'The Espíritu de Merlín', p. 105.
176. Gregory Bateson, 'A Theory of Play and Fantasy', in *Steps to an Ecology of Mind* (New York: Ballentine, 1972), pp. 117–83 (p. 142).
177. The *furrier* in *El retablo de las maravillas* inadvertently performs the same role as Malgesí. He interrupts proceedings and attests to the empty illusion on-stage. Nonetheless, the *retablo*'s audience more actively engage with the spectacle as they vigorously challenge the *furrier*'s intervention.
178. Meixell, 'The Espíritu de Merlín', p. 102.
179. Anthony Close, 'La idea cervantina de la comedia', *Theatralia: Revista de Teoría del Teatro*, 5 (2003), 331–49 (p. 342).
180. Arboleda, *Teoría y Formas del Metateatro*, p. 57.
181. Robbins states that 'Deceit (*engaño*) was one of the obsessions of the period: how to detect it, how to avoid it, and even how to exploit it'. *The Challenges of Uncertainty*, p. 14.
182. Although Bernardo del Carpio is an epic hero and warrior, he is quick to state his distaste for war: 'Dura y detestable guerra' (I. 391). Moreover, he is constantly exhorted to return to his homeland and reminded that he has become too involved with inconsequential issues: 'Y tú, sin par, que aspiras a divina, / procura otras empresas, / que es poco lo que en éstas interesas' (III. 2502–04). Bernardo eventually returns to Spain by force when Castilla removes him from Ardenia.
183. See, for example, Karl Vossler, *Lope de Vega y su tiempo* (Madrid: Revista de Occidente, 1933) and José María Díez Borque, *Sociedad y Teatro en la España de Lope de Vega* (Barcelona: Antoni Bosch, 1978). Recent criticism, however, has shown that this view is not unproblematic. As McKendrick states: 'To claim that the theatre as a whole [. . .] was directly harnessed to the purposes of the government and class is seriously to underestimate the complexity of the relationship between the Spanish theatre of the day and the society that produced it'. See *Playing the King*, p. 5. See also Charlotte Stern, 'Lope de Vega, Propagandist?', *Bulletin of the Comediantes*, 34 (1982), 1–36 and Catherine Swietlicki, 'Lope's Dialogic Imagination: Writing Other Voices of "Monolithic Spain"', *Bulletin of the Comediantes*, 40 (1988), 205–26.
184. Arboleda, *Teoría y Formas del Metateatro*, p. 84.
185. Close, 'La idea cervantina de la comedia', p. 342.
186. See my introduction to *El laberinto de amor* where the exploitation of the labyrinth metaphor in this context is discussed.
187. Alcalá Galán, "Dios te dé salud y a mí paciencia", p. 269.
188. McKendrick, 'Writings for the stage', p. 154. McKendrick remarks that Cervantes believed in 'the absolute morality of freedom'.
189. Alcalá Galán, "Dios te dé salud y a mí paciencia", p. 260.

CHAPTER 2

∼

Staging *Libertad* in Cervantes's *Comedias de Cautivos*

'No hay en la tierra, conforme mi parecer, contento que se iguale a alcanzar la libertad perdida'
Don Quijote, I, XXXIX

Cervantes's *comedias de cautivos* have been considered by one critic as 'el resultado literario de una experiencia vital insoslayable, imposible de olvidar, que había marcado para siempre su biografía y su quehacer literario'.[1] Herein lie the two areas of investigation which have so concerned Cervantistas: the events of Cervantes's 1575–80 North African imprisonment and the impact that such a traumatic experience has exerted on his literary production. Critical interest has resulted in copious biographies and articles and the general consensus that Cervantes's experience as captive left an indelible mark on his work. Nonetheless, as George Camamis has noted, there is still work to be done:

> Si es verdad que hay muchos trabajos sobre ciertos aspectos del cautiverio de Cervantes y de sus obras que tratan de su cautividad argelina, no hay ninguno que estudie el desarrollo del tema desde sus comienzos hasta sus grandes éxitos en el teatro y la narrativa del Siglo de Oro, para destacar así la gran innovación de Cervantes en este campo.[2]

More than thirty years have passed since the publication of Camamis's study without any significant engagement with the theme in Cervantine theatre; despite the fact that three *comedias* — *El gallardo español*, *La gran sultana Doña Catalina de Oviedo* and *Los baños de Argel* — deal directly with the fraught situation of the *cautivo*. This section of the study will, therefore, seek to address this neglect and focus on the plays mentioned above not in terms of the fictionalising of biographical data, but rather in terms of how Cervantes's treatment of the captivity theme reveals a prevailing interest in how the seventeenth-century Spanish world is experienced by his conflicted and displaced spectator. While each of the plays under investigation can be termed *comedias de cautivos*, they depict *cautiverio* to varying degrees. For instance, *Los baños de Argel* offers a much darker portrayal of the horrors of physical incarceration than either

El gallardo español or *La gran sultana*. Nonetheless, each of these *comedias* dramatises the often complex struggle that wages between the captor and the captive. As such, they stress a heightened preoccupation with the individual who is both oppressor and oppressed. This captivity is illustrated in many forms; psychological, physical and ideological. As with the plays discussed in Chapter One above, Cervantes makes clear that the individual functions better and more productively outside confining conditions.

What emerges most significantly from a study of the *comedias de cautivos* is Cervantes's concern with the troubled realities of early modern Spain. The plays deal with multifaceted issues which interrogate notions of national identity, selfhood and nation formation; themes which have recently emerged in Cervantine criticism, as demonstrated by Fuchs's recent work which argues that Cervantes's texts 'consistently engage with the problems of the nascent Spanish nation'.[3] In fact, as I will argue in the analyses which follow, the dramatist is not as preoccupied with *cautiverio* as he is with the conflicted and precarious situation of the contemporary Spaniard. Analysis of how modes of subjectivity are constantly brought into question and contested reveals that early modern Spain is constructed upon transcendent but insecure and external signifiers, such as homogenous and exclusive nationhood. Ultimately, these analyses of the captivity plays consider the spectator's confrontation with political and socio-cultural illusions that disguise themselves as reality and expose how conventional value systems undergo interrogation as their inherent instabilities are revealed.

2.1 Playing the Past in *El gallardo español*

According to one commentator, *El gallardo español* 'is one of Cervantes's least known, little read, and most misunderstood plays'.[4] The tendency to 'misread' the drama undoubtedly lies at the root of *El gallardo*'s neglect. Like *La casa de los celos*, *El gallardo*'s ambiguous plot has resulted in a speculative search for meaning about which critical analyses are generally at odds. Even the drama's date of composition is disputed.[5] Interestingly, *El gallardo español* is Cervantes's only *comedia* which dramatises an historical event — the successful defence of the Spanish stronghold of Oran during the Ottoman-Habsburg struggle for control of the Mediterranean in 1563. Yet critics prefer to prioritise a focus on Cervantes's depiction of the better known siege of Numantia.[6] The fact that those commentaries which do exist can tend towards the idiosyncratic is further evidence of *El gallardo*'s obscurity. Among these are Zimic's focus on the drama's novelistic elements and De Armas's argument that the mythological relationship between Venus and Mars is a 'tema central' of the play.[7] Both readings remain isolated and uncontested. On the other hand, the drama's paradoxical portrayal of the protagonist, Don Fernando, as both deserter and hero who single-handedly secures victory at Oran, has incited more uniform interest.

For Casalduero, the character is an intrepid conqueror who upholds and embodies Spain's nationalistic spirit: 'El heroísmo se encarna en los hechos de un gallardo español — el gallardo español — don Fernando de Saavedra'.[8] Gethin Hughes's interpretation of Don Fernando is, however, not quite so forgiving. He perceives the protagonist to be narcissistic, self-obsessed and preoccupied by his own fame.[9] This notion of 'fama' is also the focus of William Stapp's analysis which explores the gulf between reality and the hype of Don Fernando's fame.[10] A more recent study by Minni Sawhney has sought to offer a more balanced reading of the protagonist on the basis of the drama's 'historical grounding'. She concludes that the soldier does not see himself as an 'epiphenomenon of his culture' but, rather, is a 'free floating cosmopolitan' individual.[11]

El gallardo español ends on a deliberately provocative note. Guzmán declares that it is time to draw an end to the *comedia* 'cuyo principal intento / ha sido mezclar verdades / con fabulosos intentos' (III. 3132–34). There has been considerable discussion surrounding the play's 'intent'. Commentators such as Casalduero and Friedman suggest that the 'truths' refer to those elements in the text which are based on history.[12] Canavaggio also assumes that 'verdades' equate to historical data in an analysis which deals specifically with historical verisimilitude and the extent to which it is faithful to historical events.[13] Friedman, on the other hand, views the 'fabulosos intentos' as a 'complex intrigue of love and honor [which] provides the predominant fictional interest' while Kartchner focuses on *El gallardo*'s intratextual mixture of truth and fabulous intentions.[14]

More pertinent to the present study, however, is Gerli's analysis which moves beyond conventional arguments which draw attention to the play's uses and misuses of historical data to focus on what Cervantes actually *does* with history.[15] Gerli interprets *El gallardo* as a highly self-conscious text which parodies Aristotle's claims of historical verisimilitude and exposes 'artificious uses of history' in the construction of verisimilar texts, thereby suggesting that writing is all fabrication. His insightful interpretation of a misunderstood text goes some way to illuminating the dramatist's preference for strategies of writing which draw on creative individuality or, as already established in this study, *inventio*.

Gerli's contention that history emerges as an unstable strategy in the context of artistic creation is, of course, confined to a literary context and his analysis takes no account of extra-textual concerns. The critic can be said to follow the Jaussian and Iser school of thought which limits the recovery of meaning to literary-based responses. As highlighted in my analysis of *La entretenida*, Simerka's adaptation of Iser advocates an interpretation of Golden-Age theatre that is inclusive of the historical, social and intellectual norms which informed early modern Spanish life and challenges those 'readings' which are wholly literary.[16] Gerli, like all those who have studied the play, has overlooked the fact that *El gallardo español*, as with all of the *Ocho comedias*, was intended for performance. The concluding lines, which have so interested and confounded critics, make explicit the work's generic status (*comedia*) and are addressed to the *corral* audience; a device which is not unlike that used by Tristán at the close of *El perro del hortelano* or Batín in the concluding lines of *El castigo sin venganza*. Nonetheless, Gerli's analysis of *El gallardo* leads him to question 'whether Cervantes ever meant *El gallardo* to be staged at all, and to consider the possibility that it was a drama destined solely to be read'.[17] In fact, Gerli's argument reduces the play's depiction of historical events to an 'experiment' which tests 'the abiding Aristotelian question of the legitimacy of texts which profess to stage empirical historical truths'.[18] By denying the play any status as a performance text, Gerli, and others, not only fail to consider audience reception, but crucially overlook the fact that the contemporary spectator received a play which not only re-presented their past but forced a confrontation with the realities of a fragile present.

The instability of history is, of course, brought to the fore by Cervantes elsewhere in his writings. The reader of the *Quijote*, for instance, must contend with the fact that the '*historia*' of Don Quijote is recorded by a Moorish historian, Cide Hamete Benengeli, whose credibility is perpetually brought into doubt. Wardropper explains this paradox as follows: that the reader is faced with 'a story masquerading as history, with a work claiming to be historically true within its external framework of fiction'.[19] Issues of authorial and historical reliability become of utmost importance in a work which exposes the fact that the 'historian can never operate on a purely factual or intellectual plane'.[20] This argument becomes even more pertinent in a performative context. In fact, Paul Hernadi conceptualises the issue in 'dramatic' terms; stating that the 'tales' of historiography are based on the 'plays' of history; that it is always the historian's ambition 'to do better than simply reproduce the past. He wants to re-present it with hindsight, disclosing patterns of cause and purpose of which the participants in the original events could not have been fully aware'.[21] We might even go so far as to say that history, in this context, therefore, *performs* history as it is tainted with subjectivities and biases that colour perceptions and understandings of the past.

This is precisely what we encounter in *El gallardo español*. By dramatising the events of 1563 Cervantes frames history with illusion and the spectator, therefore, is challenged with separating the 'verdades' from the 'fabulosos intentos'. Such a strategy is further compounded by the inclusion of the historical character, Don Martín de Córdoba who successfully led the military campaign to defend the Spanish hold of Oran. Separation of truth and fiction is made equally difficult by the fact that the drama's final statement shatters expectations made by the audience during the course of the play's action. The line between truth and illusion is blurred in *El gallardo* as the drama makes no attempt to disconnect truth and fiction, reality and illusion but, rather, focuses on the often indistinguishable line between these. Nothing is, in fact, stable in *El gallardo* as characters readily abandon lives and identities to pursue ideals and ambitions that they may or may not achieve or be expected to achieve. What, then, would the contemporary Spanish theatre-goer make of a play which re-presents their past, calls attention to the fact that the past is often not recuperated without prejudice and distortion and derives its dramatic action from this fluidity? These instabilities collectively place a burden on the spectator; not only to make sense of and derive meaning from the spectacle, but to deal with the past via its problematic and complicated representation on stage. The result is a confrontation with the past via the lens of a present mediated via performance and an inevitably heightened awareness of the realities of contemporary life and Spain's increasingly fragile condition. This is particularly pertinent in light of the fact that collective identities 'whether cultural/ethnic, national, or even transnational, grow from a sense of the past'.[22]

It is significant, but hardly surprising, that Cervantes should choose the theatre over narrative for the representation of significant historical events:

> the theatre very forcefully participates in the ongoing representations and debates about these pasts, sometimes contesting the hegemonic understanding of the historical heritage on the basis of which these identities have been constructed, sometimes reinforcing them. By performing history the theatre, at times even more forcefully than other discourses about the past like historiographic writing or novels about historical events, engages in such ideological debates, frequently intervening in them directly.[23]

I would argue that this is what *El gallardo español* both does and, indeed, thematises. Cervantes's drama directly 'intervenes' in the issue of national selfhood, representing it as unstable and problematic. Fuchs notes that various pressures of centralization, imperial ambition and religious dissidence contributed to the fact that 'the construction of national identity in early modern Spain was an enterprise fraught with difficulties'.[24] Weighed down by the past, *El gallardo* deals with Spain's struggle to affirm and project a collective identity as Spain's 'glorious' past cedes to a time of great difficulty replete with economic hardship, political instabilities and ineffective leadership under the Hapsburgs.[25] By dramatising the siege of Oran, Cervantes displays Spain's unquenchable thirst for imperial power and its ability to project this power in its successful defence of the North African coast.[26] For the seventeenth-century Spaniard, such a display of imperial politics juxtaposed against the background of Spain's present realities might have made for uncomfortable viewing. However, when Gerli's notion of the 'artificious uses of history', is applied to the extra-literary context, any sense of anxiety is forcefully counteracted. Drama's fluid representation of history is exposed, as is theatre's status as an unreliable device in providing a credible or wholly accurate picture of the past. Cervantes, it might be argued, effectively removes from the audience the burden of history. For what purpose, then, does Cervantes go to such lengths to enable the spectator to surmount the past? Rokem contends that:

> What may be seen as specific to the theatre in dealing directly with the historical past is its ability to create an awareness of the complex interaction between the destructiveness and the failures of history, on the one hand, and the efforts to create a viable and meaningful work of art, trying to confront these painful failures, on the other.[27]

The theatre, then, offers a space in which the spectator can paradoxically look back in order to look forward in an interaction which implies a recuperative process. Such an action emphasises, as Rokem would have it, 'the restorative potentials of the theatre in trying to counteract the destructive forces of history'.[28] For Spain, this is a matter of restoring a sense of identity which does not hinge on the weight of the past.

My reading of *El gallardo español* will argue that it is via the drama's protagonist, Don Fernando, the gallant Spaniard, that the 'destructive forces of history' are challenged. This analysis will demonstrate how Don Fernando is driven to find and project a strong sense of self; a development of Friedman's view that the Spaniard attempts to assert his authenticity as an individual.[29] The protagonist's self-fashioning is especially problematic given that other characters project upon him identities which have little bearing on reality. In fact, Don Fernando's identity stems from a reputation which precedes him; a notion which is inherently unstable. Significantly, Don Fernando can be viewed as emblematic of Spain itself as he attempts to escape a past which is constantly revealed as precarious and open to re-interpretation, in order to construct a future. Such an approach aims to consider the impact of Cervantes's negotiation of history on the early modern *corral* stage and, ultimately, examines how engagement with Don Fernando's struggle for individuality may free spectators from the burden of their own history.

Strategies of Self-Realisation

As established, critics have often debated Don Fernando's conduct in light of the fact that the gallant Spaniard deserts his duty and attends to the whims of a Mooress who desperately wishes to meet the man about whom she has heard so much. The difficulties experienced by commentators in reconciling the soldier's rebellious behaviour with the image of a brave hero whose fame is unparalleled is, in fact, a consequence of the critical tendency to neglect any study of *how* the spectator is invited to establish judgements and preconceptions of Don Fernando before the soldier has ever appeared on stage. In *El gallardo*'s opening scene we see Arlaxa demanding that her lover, Alimuzel, bring Don Fernando to her 'preso y rendido, / aunque sano y sin cautela' (I. 5–6). The wilful but beautiful Moorish woman promises her hand in marriage if Alimuzel fulfils her wishes. Notably, our first impressions of Don Fernando, who is absent from the stage, are heavily influenced by the perceptions of Arlaxa. She states:

> Quiero *ver* la bizarría
> deste que con miedo nombro,
> deste espanto, deste asombro
> de toda la Berbería;
> deste Fernando valiente
> ensalzador de su crisma
> y coco de la morisma
> que nombrar su nombre siente;
> deste Atlante de su España,
> su nuevo Cid, su Bernardo,
> su don Manuel el gallardo
> por una y otra hazaña (I. 33-44)

It soon transpires that Arlaxa's conception and ideas of Don Fernando's superhuman qualities stem from what she has *heard* about the great hero. Alimuzel tells the Spaniard: 'Tu fama, que no se encierra / en límites, *ha llegado / a los oídos de Arlaxa*' (I. 191-93). The many stories which she has heard about Don Fernando's heroic deeds stimulate a profound curiosity and desire to meet him (I. 700-09).

Interestingly, this compulsion to see the celebrated Don Fernando is mirrored by Margarita; a Spanish noblewoman who has left home to pursue marriage to Don Fernando. Margarita confesses that she is 'enamorada de oídas' (III. 2254) as a consequence of listening to tales about Don Fernando; a man 'tan gallardo en paz y en guerra, / que en relación vi a un Adonis, / y a otro Marte vi en la tierra' (III. 2220-22). The spectator is privy to the sort of stories to which Arlaxa and Margarita have been listening at the beginning of Act II when Oropesa, Arlaxa's 'cautivo español', relays how Don Fernando single-handedly captured a Turkish ship and extols him as unequalled among Christians or Muslims (II. 1146-1204). His eulogy prompts Arlaxa to proclaim: '¡Oh, qué famoso español!' (II. 1205). It is clear, then, that for Arlaxa and Margarita, Don Fernando is a character of legendary status who is worthy of their interest and devotion. Depicted as a 'Hércules, Héctor, Roldán' (II. 1206), the solider becomes 'a poetic creation larger than life'.[30] Moreover, as we can see from the accolades attributed to the gallant Spaniard, he is clearly elevated to mythological status; Alimuzel declares that he is an 'Ulises' (I. 211) and Arlaxa expresses that his '*nombre sobrehumano / me incita y mueve el deseo / de velle*' (II. 1135-37).

What is particularly important about these scenes is the analogical infrastructure constructed by the women as they refer to Don Fernando's reputation. Arlaxa and Margarita allude to mythological and epic literary figures to create and present a narrative based on the 'history' of the gallant Spaniard.

Significantly, these analogies are drawn from different times in literary history; for instance, the Greek warrior and hero, Hercules, is positioned alongside Charlemagne's paladin, Roldán. The women, then, dislocate these figures from their historical time and place; connecting them in a very fluid manner. Koselleck states that 'all historical knowledge is locationally determined and hence relative'.[31] As such, the disjointedness of the analogical structure employed by the interlocutors attests to a disregard for any sense of 'relativity'. Moreover, Margarita and Arlaxa's story-telling takes time for granted as they attempt to create a singular vision of the past and an impression of a continuous trajectory which charts the heroics of epic figures and ultimately culminates with Don Fernando. Following Ricoeur we might say that the women create an 'illusion of sequence' in their reconfiguration of time. Commenting upon the contribution of narrative to a phenomenology of time experience, Ricoeur argues:

> the temporal implications of the plot [. . .] are precisely those overlooked by anti-narrativist writers in the field of historiography and by structuralists in the field of literary criticism. In both fields, the emphasis on nomological models and paradigmatic codes results in a trend that reduces the narrative concept to the anecdotic surface of the story. Thus both the theory of history and the theory of fictional narratives seem to take it for granted that whenever there is time, it is always a time laid out chronologically, a linear time, defined by a succession of instants.[32]

The illusion of linear time, based on a 'succession of (analogical) instants' creates a narrative in *El gallardo* that appears continuous and invariant; a process which is lent considerable weight by the authority of the allusions exploited. This process, however, is ultimately exposed as misleading and deceptive given that it is stringent in structure and manipulative in purpose and, therefore, leaves little room for change, competing discourses or plurality of expression.

It is significant that Arlaxa and Margarita have both heard of Don Fernando's exploits via 'reliable' sources. In Arlaxa's case, Oropesa, her trusted servant has brought stories to Oran from Spain and Margarita has learnt of Don Fernando through the 'viejo', Vozmediano, given to her as a guardian and mentor by her father (II. 2207–08). Both Arlaxa and Margarita call attention to the fact that Oropesa and Vozmediano have *narrated* tales and painted verbal pictures of Don Fernando's deeds (I. 700–02; III. 2219). These men, then, can be said to function as historiographers as they 'recall' events from Spain's past which are subsequently received as statements of fact by Arlaxa and Margarita. John Loftis states that: 'history in any form in which we encounter it is culture bound, not objective, not immutable'.[33] The credibility of Oropesa and Vozmediano's accounts is, therefore, not without prejudice and distortion and is undermined by the fact that they are widely exaggerated and embellished. Moreover, Don Fernando's heroics take place outside of the theatrical frame and are narrated to the audience via other characters on stage. As Carlos Gutiérrez states: 'Cervantes tenía muy claro que Historia no equivalía a Verdad y, por ello, la narrativa histórica estaba sujeta, como cualquier otra, a los hábiles manejos del historiador-narrador'.[34] Don Fernando's reputation and 'fama', then, do not emerge from concrete evidence but, in fact, rest precariously on supposition and inflated oral accounts which are inherently unreliable.

Contrary to prevailing critical opinion, we should not, therefore, be surprised or challenged by the fact that Don Fernando is not, in reality, a 'Cid' or 'Bernardo'.[35] On hearing Alimuzel's challenge to a fight, Don Fernando is unconcerned about his allegiance to the defence of Oran and immediately begins to make underhand preparations to meet with Alimuzel, despite the advice and orders of his superiors. His character is far removed from the heroic and god-like stature attributed to him by Arlaxa in scene one. Our shifting impression of Don Fernando is not dissimilar to the aesthetic experience generated by Velázquez's painting of the god of war, Mars, which demands a negotiation of the gulf between preconceptions of a mighty warrior and the diminished, impotent figure on display.[36] Don Fernando's desertion, which has so occupied critics, is, among other things, a strategy employed by Cervantes to undermine our initial expectations and call attention to the fact that perspective is established and manipulated by the powerful and dynamic assertions of Arlaxa.[37] The gap which exists between audience expectation of Don Fernando and the reality of who he is, establishes a profound sense of ambiguity. This has further repercussions if we accept *El gallardo*'s protagonist as representative of Imperial Spain which is, therefore, as fictitious as the analogies evoked by Arlaxa and Margarita. His desire to forsake his duty and indulge his capricious nature destabilises the illusion of a glorious nation founded on absolutes. Maestro notes that the Baroque artist incorporated devices in their work which compelled the receiver to distrust appearances:

> Esta desconfianza en el mundo de los sentidos, unida a una experiencia inevitable de desengaños, induce al hombre del Barroco a discutir la percepción habitual de los hechos reales, a subvertir la interpretación de la experiencia cotidiana, a destacar [. . .] todo cuanto se sitúa más allá del mundo perceptible por los sentidos.[38]

The fact that both Arlaxa and the audience base their judgement of Don Fernando on mere stories infused with hyperbolic discourse demonstrates the fallibility of a 'mundo perceptible por los sentidos'. The idea of a Spain founded on 'one nation, one faith, one destiny' is, therefore, problematised by Don Fernando's arrival on stage.[39] The early-modern audience is confronted with the uncomfortable image of a Spain whose rhetoric and reality are violently at odds.

This instability is further heightened and made complicated by the details of the Spaniard's defection. When Alimuzel challenges him to a duel, Don Alonso, governor of Oran, attempts to dissuade Don Fernando by reminding him of his obligations as a solider: 'No quiero que allá salgáis, / porque hallaréis, si miráis / a la soldadesca ley, / que obligado a vuestro rey / mucho más que a vos estáis' (I. 242–46). He orders his subordinate not to squander his time on a 'simple niñería' and declares: 'En ningún modo sois vuestro, / sino del rey, y en su nombre / sois mío, según lo muestro' (I. 257–59). It is clear, then, that Don Fernando has no legitimacy as an individual. He is subjugated to prevailing hierarchy and his sense of identity is inextricably linked with ideals and values imposed upon him by the state. Not only does this profoundly undercut the portrayal of the soldier as a dynamic and heroic warrior, as established in the drama's first few scenes, but reduces him to a non-entity incapable of forging his own future. Don Fernando is stifled and unable to express an opinion. His immediate reaction toward Don Alonso's counsel is a concern with how Alimuzel will react: '¿Qué dirá el moro?' (I. 267). Ironically, for Don Fernando, the Moor's opinion is of particular value, given that the soldier's identity is entirely founded on what others say about him.[40] Deciding to disobey Don Alonso's warning, Don Fernando states his intent: 'Que me estará a mí muy mal / eso, es cosa manifiesta. / Sólo a mí me desafía, / y gran mengua me sería / que otro por mí pelease' (I. 290–94).[41] Hughes interprets this subject-centred speech as an indication of Don Fernando's reluctance to submit his self-interest to the common good.[42] I would agree that Don Fernando's motives are entirely self-motivated, but in the sense that they emerge from a desire to fashion an authentic selfhood. Hughes argues against such a reading, stating that Don Fernando's valour is already recognised and, thus, there is no reason to pursue Alimuzel's challenge. Nonetheless, as evidenced, the protagonist's deeds are based on 'oídas' and are, therefore, open to disrepute. Moreover, Don Fernando's response towards Don Alonso's counsel is especially telling: '¡De extraña seguridad / usa vuestra señoría / conmigo!' (I. 265–67). The solider is powerless to act in the face of the inflexible sense of honour imposed upon him by the stringent military code. This is further compounded by the fact that Don Fernando draws attention to the honour code once Alimuzel has issued his challenge: 'ya se sabe que suelo / a lo que es honra acudir' (I. 235–36). His personal sense of honour dictates that he should pursue Alimuzel, but his obligation to the 'soldadesca ley' states that his duty is solely to his superiors and the military campaign in Oran.[43] The honour code manifests itself in incongruous and irreconcilable forms, leaving Don Fernando incapacitated and unable to satisfy the requirements of military duty and chivalric codes of honour.[44] The seventeenth-century honour code can, therefore, be viewed as a mass of contradictions which serves to confuse and burden the individual with demands which are impossible to meet. It is little wonder, then, that Don Fernando's sense of self is fraught with difficulty and ambiguity. In this case, he chooses to place personal inclination before public duty and enlists the help of his general, Guzmán. Don Fernando is not unlike the women of *El laberinto* whose convoluted negotiation of self and duty emphasises the fact that oppression does not encourage obedience. Rather than remain shackled to uncompromising demands which dictate who he is, Don Fernando determines to forge his own future. This action sets the tone for the remainder of the play as the gallant Spaniard resists and subverts the expectations of both the on-stage and off-stage audience.

We next encounter Don Fernando toward the end of the opening act when we learn that he has allowed himself to be captured by Moorish soldiers and brought before Arlaxa. He declares that he has come 'a vuestra prisión de grado, / por no poder tolerar / ser valiente y mal pagado' (I. 822–24). As Kartchner acknowledges, Don Fernando's motives are often indecipherable.[45] However, his actions must be observed in the light of struggles of self-fashioning. Significantly, in the Moorish camp, he assumes an alternate identity as Juan Lozano and declares that he is one of Don Fernando's fellow soldiers. He identifies himself only as a 'soldado' and fields many questions about Don Fernando as though he were an entirely different person. This 'paradoxical nullification of the self' is a shrewd strategy which allows Don Fernando to distance himself from the burden of expectations which are inextricably linked to him.[46] Interestingly, he offers clues that he and the infamous soldier are one and the same person. He 'verifies' that Don Fernando is strong, brave and another 'Marte', yet asserts that the solider looks very like him and that they are equally valiant (I. 894–909). He pursues this strategy in the opening scene of the second act when he suggests that he is on a par with Don Fernando: 'He hecho las mismas [hazañas] que él, / con el mismo esfuerzo y pecho, / y ya me he visto con él' (II. 1110–12). When asked if he and the famous solider are friends, he replies enigmatically: 'Es otro yo' (II. 1114). Nonetheless, this 'engaño con la verdad' does not pique Arlaxa's interest and she does not recognise that he is, in fact, Don Fernando. In a twist of irony, he remains unidentified despite the fact that he is present when Oropesa relays his victorious capture of a Turkish ship and Arlaxa exclaims that she is desperate to see him. The on-stage audience's inability to realise that Don Fernando is standing in their midst again highlights the gulf which separates rhetoric and reality. The myths surrounding the soldier evidently surpass any sense of whom or what he really is. His name is, therefore, synonymous with fictions that have little bearing on reality. Although he declares that the name Juan Lozano is a 'nombre que es bien conocido' (II. 1101), Arlaxa retorts that she has never heard of him. She prefers, then, to place her faith in the arbitrary nature of Don Fernando's name rather than believe in the reality which confronts her.

It is this gap between signified and signifier which allows Don Fernando to forge an identity. Given that his audience have only *heard* of him, he can exploit the irreconcilable differences between reputation and reality to his advantage. In the enemy camp the Spaniard can safely construct any identity that he wishes;

he does not carry with him the burden of the past which dictates a code of expectations to which he must adhere. Paradoxically, as a prisoner of Moorish captors he is 'freer' than he is as a Spanish soldier defending his country. His venture into enemy territory and his conduct, then, are not as indecipherable as much as a clever strategy which permits the gallant Spaniard to defy the impositions which weigh him down. It is within this alien and contradictory space that Don Fernando can crucially restore some sense of selfhood. The manner of Don Fernando's interaction with the enemy of Spain undermines perceptions of univocal nation formation. For the early-modern audience, Spain, as represented by Don Fernando, cannot be received as an unchanging homogenous or 'ideal' nation state. As Etienne Balibar explains:

> The history of nations, beginning with our own, is always already presented to us in the form of a narrative which attributes to these entities the continuity of a subject. The formation of the nation thus appears as the fulfilment of a 'project' stretching over centuries [...] The illusion is twofold. It consists in believing that the generations which succeed one another over centuries on a reasonably stable territory, under a reasonably univocal designation, have handed down to each other an invariant substance. And it consists in believing that the process of development from which we select aspects retrospectively, so as to see ourselves as the culmination of that process, was the only one possible, that is, it represented a destiny.[47]

Don Fernando's conduct both challenges and undercuts the 'invariant' nature of history. The protagonist's self-fashioning highlights the fact that identity is not something fixed or static but, rather, that it is both constructed and contested.

How would the early-modern spectator react to a depiction of their nation as anything other than stable and uniform? I would suggest that audience response is mirrored by Guzmán and his inability to perceive Don Fernando as less than a faithful Christian and brave warrior. Guzmán fights with Robledo on the basis that the latter suggests that Don Fernando is possibly a renegade. Guzmán vehemently rejects Robledo's hypothesis and states: 'El renegar *no es posible*, / y si en ello os afirmáis / mentís' (I. 1070–72). Nonetheless, Don Fernando's motives are not transparent and his behaviour does not disprove Robledo's theory. Guzmán, however, manipulates Robledo's supposition to assert boldly that: 'ha afirmado que se es ido / a renegar don Fernando' (I. 1080–81). Each man, then, reaches a conflicting conclusion based on recent events and personal experience of Don Fernando; emphasising the subjectivities which are involved when recalling the past. Raymond Williams condemns conventional ideas of history for failing to take into account the plurality of discourses and their privileging of the dominant ideological viewpoint.[48] This is strongly countered in *El gallardo español* by Cervantes's use of multiperspectivity which allows the spectator to perceive a multiplicity of discourses at work from varying points of view. Cervantes's unease with a univocal view of history is evident also in the book-burning episode in *Don Quijote I* in which the priest and the barber elect to save a text which challenges Spain's imperial project: Cristóbal de Virués's epic poem *El Monserrato*.[49]

Throughout *El gallardo español*, debate concerning Don Fernando's behaviour is a constant theme. Margarita arrives in Oran to learn that people are proclaiming in the streets that the great Spaniard, Don Fernando, is a Moor (II. 1281-82). The noblewoman rejects the claims, declaring: 'Que *no es posible* sea moro / quien guardó tanto el decoro / de cristiano caballero' (II. 1553-55). Despite the fact that she has never seen nor met Don Fernando, Margarita founds her expectations on his heritage. Interestingly, both Guzmán and Margarita boldly assert the impossibility of Don Fernando betraying his country. However, this sense of 'impossibility' has much more to do with a refusal to call their own perspective into question than an objective assessment of Don Fernando's conduct. This is further compounded by the events which follow Don Fernando's promise to protect Arlaxa at the expense of Christian lives (II. 1623-40). This, of course, contradicts everything that Guzmán believes about Don Fernando, prompting him to ask: '¿Sois ya de Cristo enemigo? [. . .] ¿cómo sacas la espada / contra Él?' (II. 1750; 1752-53). When Don Fernando asserts that his allegiance is not in doubt, Guzmán is content to trust in this claim, despite the fact that his master's behaviour would suggest otherwise: 'A tu gusto me acomodo, / no quiero más preguntar' (II. 1765-66). He wilfully ignores the reality of the situation and chooses to rely on his conception of Don Fernando. This is again seen in the closing scenes of Act II when Guzmán defends Don Fernando in the face of Don Martín's angry denunciation of his errant subordinate (II. 1948-50). Guzmán and Margarita place their faith in the absolute truth that Don Fernando is the exemplary Christian Spaniard. They make assumptions, then, which leave little room for oppositional possibilities.

Regardless of the fact that Don Fernando ultimately proves himself to be a valiant solider, the dramatist compels his spectator to challenge his/her perspective of the past as something sure and established. This is especially significant in light of the fact that Robledo's counter-discourse is, quite literally, quashed as he is confined to a tower for daring to point out the fragility of Don Fernando's Spanish identity. In the final scene of the play, we are informed that he has died; thus suppressing his seditious opinions (III. 3089-90).[50] For the seventeenth-century Spanish spectator, it is a stark and unsettling reminder that their sense of national identity ominously operates on the basis of the exclusion of discourses which do not serve to consolidate national myths.

The idea of national identity as something much more volatile than that propagated in seventeenth-century Spain is particularly pertinent in *El gallardo español*'s final act. Don Juan, Margarita's brother, arrives in Oran and is taken prisoner by Moorish soldiers. He is eventually brought before Don Fernando/Juan Lozano who has made no attempt to distinguish himself from

Islam and is, in fact, wearing Moorish clothes. Although *El gallardo*'s protagonist protests that he is a Moor, Don Juan draws attention to the many similarities between the 'Moor' and Don Fernando: 'pienso que estoy mirando / el rostro de don Fernando / su habla, su talle y brío'; 'tanto te pareces / a un cristiano, que me admiro' (III. 2543–45; 2554–55). Don Juan is confused, but not deceived, as he declares: 'que es cosa desvariada / dar crédito a lo que veo' (III. 2586–87). The aristocrat evidently prefers to place greater stock on what he knows to be true than the 'reality' which faces him and is, therefore, the antithesis of Manfredo in *El laberinto de amor*. Claire Sponsler states that: 'Although clothing might seem to promise instant recognition of others, their social condition, and their relation to the viewer's self, it often leads to confusion, deception and misrecognition as well'.[51] As Don Fernando acknowledges, it is his Moorish dress which most confuses Margarita's brother and disallows 'instant recognition': 'le estorba este vestido / no dar crédito a sus ojos' (III. 2591–92). It is little wonder that Don Juan is so perplexed, given that he simultaneously encounters two contradictory images of Spain; the one that is symbolised by Don Fernando and a more fractured Spain whose identity is much less secure. Don Fernando's Moorish identity profoundly undermines the image of an exclusive unified nation. According to Fuchs: 'Spain attempted to construct a collective identity based on an ancestral devotion to Christianity [. . .] and a muscular defence of the faith'.[52] These are, however, conspicuous by their absence in *El gallardo* as Don Fernando's self-fashioning problematises what it is to be Spanish and to belong to Spain.

This is further compounded by Margarita's disguise as Fátima, the sister of Arlaxa. Although Arlaxa persistently states that Margarita is, in fact, Fátima, Don Juan refuses to believe her and declares to his sister: '¡Juro a Dios que eres mi hermana!' (III. 2721). Again, the nobleman reiterates that he will not trust in Arlaxa's claims or Margarita's Moorish identity: 'pues no me deja creer / lo que con los ojos veo' (III. 2738–39). Don Juan is subjected to the deception for a third time when Vozmediano, whom Don Juan also recognises, states that he is Pedro Álvarez. Exasperated at their scam, he decides to turn the tables on the tricksters by denying his own identity: 'Que si éste no es Vozmediano / y no es Margarita aquélla, / y el que causó mi querella / no es el otro mal cristiano, / tampoco soy yo don Juan, / sino algún hombre encantado' (III. 2912–17). As Kartchner observes: 'he creates a fictionalized double of himself to act in their fantasy world'.[53] In this sense, Don Juan does not allow the trickery to render him a passive participant in their scheme and he passionately contests the understanding on which Don Fernando and Margarita's Moorish identities are founded. These identities, which depend precariously on Don Juan's compliant acceptance, cannot be sustained and are ultimately exposed as fabrication. For Stapp, Don Juan's reaction signals 'el rechazo de la mundo visual y de la posibilidad de llegar a conclusiones basadas en él'.[54] In fact, Don Juan quite literally looks beyond the fragility of disguise to arrive at the truth. He is, therefore, a discerning and critical citizen unprepared to merely accept the rhetoric and appearances with which he is confronted.[55] The ease with which Don Fernando employs disguise coupled with sustained attempts to fool Don Juan is a model of Imperial Spain's attempts to project a certain 'story' and to ensure that this 'story' is corroborated. In *El gallardo* we encounter wily dramatists (Don Fernando, Margarita and Vozmediano) who attempt to pull Don Juan's strings but are counteracted by his incredulity. Such a strategy inevitably compels an audience to reflect on their own response to the irrefutable image projected by Spain and highlights the spectator's implicit and fundamentally complicit role in the formation of nationhood. Moreover, 'stable' signifiers of national identity are challenged and undermined by Don Juan's ability to see through the façade. Formation of national/collective identity is, therefore, revealed as strategic performance designed to disseminate and consolidate the myth of a fully realised and homogenous Spain. As such, this instability performs a perversely positive function and alleviates the audience from the burden of an 'incontrovertible' past and an immutable identity.

The protagonist of *El gallardo* assumes centre-stage at two vital moments of the drama's action; the beginning and the end. As this analysis demonstrates, the plot derives its action from a series of role-plays; Don Fernando negates himself to perform Juan Lozano, a renegade and a Moor. At the close of the play we no longer see the Spaniard as an insecure and subjugated solider. As war wages between the Spanish and the Moors for control of Oran, Don Fernando joins the battle at its most critical point. Fighting on behalf of the Christians, he clashes with Alimuzel much to the Moor's astonishment: 'Poco puedo y poco valgo / con este amigo enemigo. / ¿Por qué contra mí, Lozano, / esgrimes el fuerte acero?' (III. 2778–81). As the fight intensifies, Don Fernando's reaction is especially telling: 'Porque soy cristiano, y quiero / *mostrarte* que soy cristiano' (III. 2782–83). The protagonist can finally express 'authentic' selfhood and for the first time in the play, action and rhetoric, word and deed, are reconciled. Don Fernando, then, has 'become' the gallant Spaniard. However, the *corral* spectator is well aware that this victory and restoration of identity are the result of the hero's interrogation of dominant ideology via his participation in subversive activity. National identity, then, is not anchored on a solid foundation, but is an ever-changing process of making and unmaking. The 'fabulosos intentos' to which Guzmán draws attention in the closing line can, therefore, be viewed as fictitious identities which are represented as though they are something palpably real. The final scenes of *El gallardo español* forcefully counteract the failures of the past. Don Fernando makes a perfunctory apology for his behaviour, but ultimately declares: 'Pero no es éste lugar / para alargarme en el cuento / de mi extraña y rara historia, / que dejo para otro tiempo' (III. 3023–26). Don Fernando's decision to relate his story/history at 'otro tiempo', outside of the theatrical frame, alleviates the audience of the burden of history. Moreover, his marriage to Margarita in the play's final scene is not a union which is staged to hastily tie up loose ends but, rather, symbolises a new beginning for the soldier. Just as Don Fernando moves forward to a new future which is not contingent on the weight of the past, so must Cervantes's audience.

In *El gallardo español* Cervantes dialogues with the discourses which both form and inform the world of the seventeenth-century spectator in order to protest against the absolutes and assurances of Counter-Reformation Spain and the devices which the state utilises to ensure compliance and conformity. The drama, therefore, profoundly challenges the 'realities' of its moment of origin. As Mary Malcolm Gaylord notes with reference to *Don Quijote*:

> Cervantes takes on a very real, and often very serious national and cultural historiographic project that had been carried forward with special intensity since the end of the fifteenth century and continued to occupy the Spanish historical imagination into the seventeenth [. . .] the broad aims of the project are clear: to historify the new nation, giving it deep roots in Judeo-Christian time, to rewrite the past in terms of contemporary projects; to justify Spain's imperial status and messianic mission in the Peninsula, in Europe and the Mediterranean, on the American continents.[56]

The play strongly counters such a project by its blatant refusal to 'historify' Spain as it undermines the 'immovable' foundations on which it is constructed. As we have seen, this destabilisation operates on two levels; challenging the notion of history as undisputed and national/collective identity as immutable or invariable. Cervantes's portrayal of an historical event within the framework of theatre, as well as frequent instances when the past is subject to misrepresentation, calls into question the infallibility of history and its use as a stable basis for the formation of national identity.

The result is a profound sense of displacement and uncertainty; as exemplified by Don Fernando's anxious desire for authentic individualism. The idea of national identity as something cohesive is as mythical as the protagonist's god-like reputation. Nonetheless, Cervantes's purpose is not to further burden the audience with the reality of Spain's failures and tumultuous struggle for self-definition. Rather, an emphasis on the frailty of Spain's 'glorious' past, as propagated by the state, allows for an awareness that the future does not necessarily have to be shaped by the past; particularly a past that is open to wilful and strategic distortion. With *El gallardo español* Cervantes exploits drama as a 'form of liberation rather than a tool of repression' unshackling his spectator from the weight of history.[57] It is with this sense of hope and optimism that *El gallardo* concludes; so that the audience might leave the *corral* entertained, but also imbued with an understanding of the illusory and deceptive nature of history and instilled with a powerful knowledge capable of counteracting dominant and highly influential propaganda. It is little wonder, then, that *El gallardo español* is the first of the *Ocho comedias*. Just as *La gitanilla* begins with 'parece' and encourages careful consideration of the exemplary novels, so *El gallardo español* sets the tone for the way in which we might receive the *comedias*. As a theatre which heightens audience sensitivity toward the signifying systems at play, it is an error to take Cervantes's stage for granted.

2.2 All that Glitters is not Gold: *La gran sultana Doña Catalina de Oviedo* Re-considered

A Turkish audience would appear to have recently taken *La gran sultana Doña Catalina de Oviedo* for granted; a response ironically anticipated by early twentieth-century critical studies which suggest that the drama's misappropriation of historical fact deems it unworthy of serious scholarly attention.[58] Staged in Istanbul in July 2010 and directed by José María Pou, *Büyük Sultan Katalina* met with both controversy and acclaim. Various sectors of the audience objected to the adaptation on the grounds that Cervantes's text does not portray historical events of the Ottoman Empire with precision. Pou refuted the criticism by stating that the play was never intended as a 'texto histórico':

> La lectura que hacemos del texto de Cervantes ha sido revisada palabra a palabra, hemos estudiado frase a frase, sobre todo aquellas que podían molestar al pueblo turco, porque tenían que entender que Cervantes escribió un texto de libertad literaria, no un texto histórico, por lo que inventó e imaginó para escribir una obra de fantasía, un delirio turco y a ellos les cuesta entender que Cervantes no se ajustara a la realidad histórica.[59]

Pou's counter-argument which highlights *La gran sultana* as a work of fiction is indicative of more recent critical attention which points out that 'questions of historical authenticity and literary merit are often confused'.[60] Lewis-Smith notes that the play's debt to history is 'extremely rudimentary. If fact was Cervantes' inspiration, the product is nonetheless fiction'.[61] In other words, Cervantes was not interested in writing an accurate history, but nor did he reject history as a basis for *La gran sultana*'s plot.[62]

On occasions this critical focus on the use of history opens up to broach other concerns. Prominent among these, and linked to the ambiguity of the historical material, is the dialectic of truth and fiction. Cervantes's portrayal of an extravagant environment is framed by instances in which the on-stage audience question whether what they are seeing is, in fact, 'real'. For example, much attention is drawn to the disbelief experienced by the play's characters upon discovering that the Sultana is living openly as a Christian (II. 1320–21; II. 1660–74).[63] Lewis-Smith argues that Cervantes encourages the view that his principal action celebrates fact, while also promoting the view that the plotline is highly improbable. *La gran sultana* is, for Lewis-Smith, a type of *engaño* in which the dramatist pokes fun at an audience who are unable to discern between fact and fiction.[64]

It is a partial and problematic reading which Lewis-Smith himself acknowledges in a later article. Cervantes did not merely create his Sultana 'sólo para engañar y mofarse de los mosqueteros'. Rather, he fashions an excessively elaborate environment which is dispelled in the final scene when the *gracioso*, Madrigal, mocks the fantastical elements of the play.[65]

This *volte face* is symptomatic of a play which appears uncomplicated on the surface, but functions as a kind of kaleidoscope of multifaceted, shifting perspectives. This fluidity is particularly evident in its portrayal of ambiguous and unstable categories of gender and behaviour. The fact that Cervantes foregrounds a dynamic woman who forcefully asserts her Spanish identity at the very heart of the powerful Ottoman Empire has incited many varied gender-oriented responses. For instance, in an analysis of conventional role-reversal, Friedman views the Sultana as 'realistic, analytical, and clear-sighted', while her Muslim husband is 'idealistic, obsessive, and ingenuous', but ultimately concludes that Catalina is upstaged by the *Gran Turco*'s power and, thus, 'the result is a modified vision of sacrifice'.[66] The decidedly carnal atmosphere of the Turkish harem has led some commentators to read the play in terms of its more explicit 'sexualidad', with particular attention placed on the sub-plot which sees the Sultan choose a man (Lamberto/Zelinda), disguised as a woman, to sire his heir. Both Weimar and Connor explore the role played by the sexual in the play, with the latter noting that it is the *comedia*'s orientalism which 'facilita un tratamiento más explícito de la sexualidad del que se encuentra en las comedias situadas en Occidente'.[67] Undoubtedly the exotic setting provided Cervantes with the opportunity to depict the sexual, perhaps in a way that might have flouted conventional 'decorous' values of the time.[68]

What has clearly emerged from gender-based studies is a more significant recognition of how the 'other' functions in the play. In an alien and hostile environment which sees the Spaniard displaced and where there exists a fragile border between male and female, Cervantes provides ample room for an exploration of 'otherness' and its manifestations. Fuchs's study of the play advocates the idea that difference is incorporated and positively transformed in *La gran sultana*; that Cervantes depicts a tolerant and 'aggressively inclusive Ottoman world' which is underpinned by the accommodation of 'otherness'.[69] Such a view is upheld by Mariscal who argues that we should take Cervantes's heterogeneity seriously and consider the possibility that the potential for hybridization may not be monstrous but desirable.[70] In fact, Cervantine scholars generally agree that *La gran sultana* is a benign portrayal of an inclusive Ottoman Empire; an opinion encapsulated by Zimic's view that the play is 'una noble aspiración a la paz y a la armonía en el mundo por el cultivo de la tolerancia, de un deseo de comprensión y de amor genuino entre la gente'.[71]

This view of the drama as a defence of tolerance is, however, refuted by Díez Fernández:

Una lectura apresurada de la comedia daría la razón a los defensores de la admirada e inusual tolerancia, pues la obra dramatiza, con final feliz, los amores entre una Cristiana [. . .] y el sultán otomano, de manera que los dos amantes vencen los obstáculos de muy diverso tipo.[72]

He references and analyses scenes in the play, such as Madrigal's persecution of Jewish people (I. 421–75), in order to argue that Cervantes's drama is not, in fact, a ringing endorsement for mutual understanding. Nonetheless, Díez Fernández does not see intolerance as central to an interpretation of the play, focusing rather on how the drama exemplifies love's ability to overcome obstacles. In this sense, the critic appears to lack the courage of Cervantes's convictions.

Significantly, it is the idea of a 'liberal' message which has secured the play's popularity with theatre companies in more recent times. For instance *La gran sultana* was staged by the *Compañía Nacional de Teatro Clásico* in 1992, because its 'open-mindedness' ('"a la turca", de ambiente lejanamente exótico que constituye un mundo políglota, multicultural, de inquietantes ambigüedades posmodernas') was deemed appropriate in Spain's unsettled socio-cultural climate.[73] Adolfo Marsillach, the adaptation's director, labelled the drama 'un canto arrebatado a la tolerancia'.[74] Pedraza Jiménez, however, was to take exception to the way in which the production was marketed, in particular the cynicism behind the idea that tolerance 'es una idea que vende'.[75] Reading against the grain of prevailing criticism, Pedraza argues that interpretations such as that offered by Jurado Santos could be just as likely applied to Lope: 'Estoy convencido [. . .] de que, si aplicara el mismo método, la misma atención, el mismo rasero, en suma, a infinidad de comedias de Lope, podría llegar a conclusiones similares'.[76] Pedraza Jiménez, then, finds no basis in *La gran sultana* to suggest that the play is radical in this respect and cites examples from *La gitanilla* and *El coloquio de los perros* to remind his reader that Cervantes did not hesitate to poke fun at marginal groups. Pedraza's argument urges caution against potentially anachronistic interpretations which portray Cervantes as the spokesperson for a set of values which are decidedly 'modern' and have little bearing on the context in which the play was constructed: 'Cervantes tenía el sentido de tolerancia que era habitual en sus días, no en los nuestros. Es tan tolerante o intolerante como Lope, Tirso o Calderón [. . .] El dramaturgo Cervantes era hombre de su tiempo'.[77]

There is, as we shall see, sound evidence in the play for reading *La gran sultana* as a work which does not propagate values of tolerance. Notions of harmony and lenience function as an elaborate illusion disguising tensions, conflicts and sinister motives which inform the conduct of the drama's characters. It is, therefore, a much more unsettling and problematic drama than has traditionally been realised; and certainly not the 'comic' play that most critics have mistaken it for.[78] Indeed, the ludic element of the play functions as another layer of disguise which veils the more serious issues which impinge on the plot. This strategy operates on the premise of *ser/parecer* and as such, is inextricably connected to the multiperspectivity which defined Baroque reality. In *La gran sultana* the individual, for the most part, must contend with the disjunction between appearance and reality and as a result, experiences issues of conflicted selfhood. This is not true, however, of Doña Catalina who is constructed in terms of ideal Christian selfhood, emblematic (for Cervantes's audience) of an idealised homogenous Christian Spain, and in whom *ser* and *parecer* are entirely aligned. Problems of contradictory selfhood are, in fact, projected onto the Moor and it is the *Gran Turco* whose representation is at odds with contemporary reality. Cervantes, I will argue, uses the Turks and their empire as a metaphor for disrupted Spanish selfhood in a collective sense and, thus, situates the action of the play at an ironic distance in order to compel a more dynamic level of audience participation. This is, of course, a strategy which is not uncommon in Cervantes's writings (for instance in *La española inglesa* and *El amante liberal*).[79] By opposing two distinct ideologies of selfhood in *La gran sultana* in the relationship between Doña Catalina and the Sultan, the play connects signification to self identity and attaches 'value' to antagonistic subjective experiences. My reading of the play will investigate how subjectivity impinges particularly on the Sultan's responses to Catalina and on Catalina's insistence that all the signs of her identity are kept intact. This analysis will also take into account wider concerns, exploring how and why *La gran sultana* challenges its spectator to call into question, and even re-think their perception of, the values and ideals which inform their own world view.

Constantinople

La gran sultana opens in a world of opulence and excess. However, against a backdrop of images and symbolism which attest to the power, wealth and majesty of the Ottoman Empire, the spectator is faced with subtle signs which suggest that all does not glitter in this extravagant environment. The *Gran Turco*, Amurates, parades though the city with a large entourage while crowds gather to witness the spectacle. As the Sultan goes to worship at a mosque which is greater than any other (I. 37–39) six thousand soldiers on foot and horseback pass by. However, this display of splendour and authority is tainted by instances of disquiet which cast a prolonged shadow over the text. In the play's opening line the Sultan is described as a 'tirano'. His subjects are fearful of him and Salec, a renegade and servant, is unable even to stand in his presence. Instead he must keep his body bowed and his head inclined while the Sultan passes (I. 46). Moreover, the poor flock to see the Turk to present him with written petitions for help which are then given to two *garzones*, put into 'dos bolsas de terciopelo verde' and promptly discarded (I. 7–24 and description after line 33). The fact that these petitions are placed in *velvet* bags emphasises the distance between the petitioner and their patron, as well as the Turk's lack of empathy and understanding. Amidst the pomp and circumstance of the scene Salec asks Roberto, another renegade who has recently arrived in Constantinople: '¿Qué te parece, Roberto, / de la pompa y majestad / que aquí se te ha descubierto?' (I. 50–52). Like Roberto, the audience is a newcomer to this environment and Salec's question is just as relevant to the off-stage spectator who has been bombarded from the opening line with special effects. Tellingly, Roberto responds: 'Que no creo a la verdad, / y pongo duda en lo cierto' (I. 53–54). For Lewis-Smith, the 'pompa' and 'majestad' of the tyrant are 'so extraordinary that they defy spontaneous credence'.[80] The scene exposes the contrived aspects of this world, revealing it as spectacle and performance and Roberto's statement encourages a discriminating reaction toward the superficial elements which pervade *La gran sultana*. In fact, the renegade's comments frame the play to highlight the distorted and blurred line between illusion and reality. Interestingly, in the closing lines of this scene Salec states: 'aquí todo es confusión' (I. 178). This confused world defies categorisation. This is compounded by Roberto's observation that Salec has forgotten who he is: '¿cómo te has olvidado / de quién eres?' (I.186–87). In the ambiguous world of the Ottoman Empire, Salec has lost sight of his own identity. The renegade comments that, in fact, he doesn't believe in anything (I. 190–91). As we will see, Salec's feeling of displacement is the consequence of life in an environment without ideological certainty and, therefore, where the individual has little opportunity to forge a stable selfhood.

Intolerance is particularly exposed as the hallmark of the *Gran Turco*'s rule in Act II when the ambassador of Persia visits Turkey to plead for peace. He is grudgingly granted an audience with the Sultan, but is treated with contempt and eventually expelled from the court. This very short but significant scene reveals how the Turk deals with those to whom he is opposed. Interestingly, one of the Pashas advises him to make peace: 'que a nosotros la Persia así nos daña, / que es lo mismo que Flandes para España' (II. 1080–81). This reference to Spain's military campaign in Flanders brings Spain's political turmoil sharply into focus, a strategy which serves to dissipate the distance between the 'foreignness' presented on stage and the contemporary Spanish audience's personal experience of Imperial Spain as the Ottoman Empire and Spain are made interchangeable. López Estrada states: 'De esta forma inesperada, Cervantes entremete la mención de la paz en un asunto tan espinoso como era de las guerras de Flandes'.[81] The allusion to Flanders is framed within the context of the Pashas arguing whether they should pursue peace or war with Persia. Their decision-making is fraught with a volatility which serves to emphasise Spain's own political insecurities. This is further intensified by the fact that the *Gran Turco* is inept and effectively removes himself from the decision-making process, imposing accountability upon his servants: 'Mirad bien si la paz es conveniente / y honrosa' (II. 1074–75). Friedman remarks that the sultan 'actively pursues

Doña Catalina, but is passive as the agent of his people's fate'.[82] He is, in fact, an incompetent leader who threatens execution at the drop of a hat and is ruled by the desires of the flesh. His government is run by those who are just as ineffectual and the Cadí, the judge of the Turks, accepts as true Madrigal's assertions that he can teach an elephant to talk. Moreover, the *Gran Turco* is shown to be capricious in nature; a characteristic which is displayed when Catalina petitions the Virgin Mary and the Sultan encourages her to pray: 'Reza, reza, Catalina, [. . .] que no me espanta, / antes me parece bien, / a tu Lela Marién, / que entre nosotros es santa' (II. 1738; 1741–44). In light of Catalina's fervent religious devotion, the Turk is found hopelessly lacking. For the most part, his religion amounts to lip-service and a worship of Catalina as though she were a deity (II. 1749–52). Significantly, the Turk uses religious law to condemn Madrigal to death for an improper relationship with an Arab woman, even though he is blatantly flouting religious convention in his relationship with Catalina. Such hypocrisy is also evident when the Persian ambassador is accused of having consorted with the Spanish and is, therefore, considered a traitor to the faith. This 'betrayal' is used as leverage to insult and eject him from the court. These men face punishment because they are helpless in the face of the Ottoman Empire's supremacy.

The *Gran Turco* is such an inept ruler precisely because he relies on the abuse of power to rule. The depiction of a weak and pathetic leader is not uncommon in Cervantes's work. In *Pedro de Urdemalas* we encounter a king who, like the Sultan, cannot conquer his passions and exhibits an authority which is entirely self-serving.[83] As El Saffar notes: 'En su [Cervantes] obra los 'padres' u otras figuras de poder son típicamente ineficaces u objetos de mofa'.[84] In *La gran sultana* Cervantes paints a bleak and troubled picture of a society with little hope of escaping the turmoil insofar as it hinges on ineffective leadership. The reference to Flanders suggests that Spain suffers from similar problems under the reign of the Hapsburgs, and this is reinforced when the Persian ambassador's gushing praise of Philips II and III (II. 1042–57) is denounced as empty. In this way, Cervantes compels the Spanish spectator to see through Ottoman problems to their own. Edwin Williamson has read the play as a type of 'political fantasy' which expresses Spain's aspirations to one day overcome Islam.[85] I would suggest just the opposite — that rather than being a fantasy, the play exposes the fault lines in Spain's own imperial policies and revels in the unmasking of this illusion.

For a majority of commentators, the Turk is a tyrant who nonetheless displays tolerance and open-mindedness toward his Christian bride because he openly surrenders his will to hers. However, this 'tolerance' serves to mask a deep undercurrent of intolerance and prejudice which characterises his reign.[86] This is particularly demonstrated in his conduct toward Catalina. Against Díez Fernández's view that the Sultan's tolerance 'sólo se extiende a la sultana y es consecuencia inevitable del poder y del amor', I would argue that he is motivated by lust rather than love, and that his relationship with Catalina is further evidence of an insatiable imperial urge to conquer and take the spoils of war.[87]

At the beginning of the drama, the Turkish leader is informed that a beautiful Spanish captive has been hidden by Rustán, a servant, for many years. From the outset, Catalina is objectified and described as a 'gran tesoro' (I. 347) and as a rose in a walled garden (I. 353–55). Mamí, who has discovered Rustán's secret, uses decidedly hyperbolic language to paint a picture of Catalina's beauty: 'Quitó al cielo dos estrellas, / que puso en las luces bellas / de sus bellísimos ojos' (I. 366–68). Such language appeals to the sensory lusts and passions of the Sultan and he demands that his eyes see 'tan divinos despojos' (I. 604–06). Catalina is, thus, presented in a materialised manner and treated as though she were the *Turco*'s property.[88] When the Sultan finally sees her, he is overwhelmed by Catalina's beauty and on the basis of her appearance, re-defines her role in life: 'esta belleza es mi esposa' (I. 730). In spite of the fact that Catalina swears that she will not become his wife and, in so doing, commit a terrible sin, the Sultan declares that he is unconcerned which religion she follows and states that they are equals (I. 728–31; 768). However, the reason for this leniency and his willingness to let Catalina live as she pleases becomes apparent in Act II, when it transpires that he is only concerned with her external appearance:

> que a tu cuerpo, por agora,
> es el que mi alma adora
> como si fuese su cielo.
> ¿Tengo yo a carga tu alma,
> o soy Dios para inclinalla,
> o ya de hecho llevalla
> donde alcance eterna palma?
> Vive tú a tu parecer,
> como no vivas sin mí (II. 1239–47)

The Sultan is unconcerned about the inclinations of her soul as long as he can possess her body. Moreover, he suggests that he does not wish to take her by force, as it will benefit him sexually to allow her to live as she wants (II. 1278–85). Any concessions that the Turk makes regarding Catalina's Christian faith are not only the result of all-consuming passion rather than genuine love, but are precariously founded on what he stands to gain. Difference, then, is disguised as accommodation which is in actual fact exploitation. Catalina is merely an object to be owned and enjoyed. When the Turk proclaims: 'no eres mía, tuya eres' (II. 1324), he refers to the fact that she can live as she sees fit, but this does not alter the reality that she is unable to leave Constantinople and that she is under pressure to marry an infidel.

Mariscal interprets the *Gran Turco*'s comments as an 'invocation of basic human respect and self-determination for women'.[89] Nonetheless, Catalina's forceful declarations concerning her identity are eclipsed by the Turk's lack of interest in her person or individuality and are, therefore, rendered redundant. Despite her emphatic warnings: 'Advierte que soy Cristiana, / y que lo he de ser contino' (II. 1318–19), Catalina has no more rights than if she were a material possession. Fuchs states that the Sultana's ability to live as a Christian at the heart of the Ottoman Empire is 'due not so much to her own intransigence as to the Turks' ability to incorporate difference and transform it into a source of strength'.[90] The *Gran Turco*, however, does not so much incorporate difference as manipulate it in order that he might secure a favourable outcome for himself. This is especially evident when Catalina defends her reasons for marrying the Sultan: 'por quedarme / con el nombre de cristiana, / antes que por ser sultana, / medrosa vine a entregarme' (III. 2005–08). She keeps her name which, for her, signifies her selfhood, but for her husband means very little, given that she is under the control of the Turkish Empire. The Sultan, then, does not value nor attach any significance to Christianity, but he does contain it.

The *Gran Turco*'s attitude is indicative of that generally displayed toward women throughout the play. In Act II we learn that Madrigal, another Spanish captive, is involved in an illicit relationship with an Arab woman. While Madrigal is granted the opportunity to defend himself, the Arab woman, who remains both faceless and nameless, is incarcerated. Moreover, the final scenes of the closing act see the Sultan promote Lamberto to governor of Rhodes whilst Clara has little choice but to follow him. This is, therefore, not an environment which accommodates, but one in which exploitation is common currency. The marginal individual, whether female and/or Christian, is persistently objectified and manipulated to the advantage of others.

The *Gran Turco*'s penchant to engage readily with external appearance is especially evident in Act III when the Turk orders Lamberto's death on discovering that he is a man, after having chosen him to provide an heir for the empire. To save his skin, Lamberto fabricates a story in which he states that he was born Zelinda but petitioned Mohamed to become a man (III. 2721–48). This farfetched tale is, however, believed by the Sultan and Lamberto is awarded the title of Pasha. The Sultan's trust in the tale is based on the fact that he can *see* that Lamberto is now male: 'los cielos [. . .] / a Zelinda han convertido, / como hemos visto, en varón' (III. 2809; 2812–13). Ignoring the fact that Lamberto had previously expressed his desire to die as a Christian (II. 1458–59), the Turk is willing to believe that what he has heard is true. Fuchs interprets this as indication of an empire which 'refuses to ask too many questions of those it employs, benefitting instead even from the most improbable acts of allegiance'.[91] Once again, the Sultan and his empire gain from a very superficial engagement with the individual. This is compounded by the entry of the Sultana angrily proclaiming her jealousy and rebuking her husband for infidelity. The Turk responds positively to her reproach, believing that she is finally softening toward him. The Sultana's jealousy, however, has no substance.⁹² It is merely utilised as a tool to create a diversion in order to rescue Clara and Lamberto. Catalina has not previously demonstrated any amorous feelings toward the *Gran Turco*. Moreover, when Clara, disguised as Zaida, tells Catalina that Zelinda has been taken to the Turk, Catalina suggests that this is a positive occurrence: '¿Pues eso te da cuidado? / ¿No va a mejorar ventura?' (III. 2657-58). The Turk is not prepared to question the improbability of his wife's jealousy or of Lamberto's transformation for it is in his best interests to believe in the reality of what he has seen and heard.

The *Turco*'s belief in Lamberto's hasty conversion mirrors his insistence that Catalina can be who she wants to be. Significantly, not only does Catalina persistently draw attention to the fact that she is a Christian and intends to remain as such, but she protests that she must also dress as a Christian (II. 1757). For Catalina, her clothes are a sign of her faith and identity. In this sense, Christianity is presented as a reconciliation of *ser* and *parecer* and is, therefore, vastly different from the Moor's dominant gaze which relies on external authority to endorse perception. The Sultan is prepared to let Catalina dress as she wishes, stressing the fact that she is his and that he is especially interested in her beauty: 'Véase *mi* Catalina [...] Es *ídolo* de *mis ojos*, / y, en el propio o extranjero / adorno, *adorarla* quiero' (II. 1797; 1801-03). Catalina's Christian attire has no signifying value for the *Gran Turco* and it is again evident that he sees only what he wants. Cervantes's spectator is, thus, led to question the nature of his/her own subjective perspective. Moreover, by exposing the dominant gaze as unstable, as a force which makes only superficial gains; by extension Spanish imperial values are weakened and rendered potentially prejudiced.

In any other environment, Catalina's insistence on retaining her identity would present a radical challenge to prevailing authority. This is the experience of the heroines of *El laberinto de amor*. In the Ottoman Empire, however, Catalina's self-determination is redundant, given that this world functions on the basis of the external, attaching utmost importance to the illusory nature of appearance. In an environment which promotes façade and performance, the individual is a profoundly displaced entity. Individualism simply has no resonance. This is a stark, albeit hyperbolic, wake-up call for Cervantes's spectator, not unfamiliar with a world where personal inclination and societal standards often came into conflict.

Illusory appearances are of particular relevance to the scene in which the Turk states that he wishes to mix his blood with that of Catalina:

> que con la sangre otomana
> mezcle la tuya cristiana
> para darle mayor ser.
> Si *el fruto que de ti espero*
> llega a colmo, verá el mundo
> que no ha de tener segundo

el que me dieres primero.
No habrá descubierto el sol,
en cuanto ciñe y rodea,
no quien pase, que igual sea
a un otomano español (II. 1207-17)

Although this passage has often been cited as incontrovertible evidence of the *Gran Turco*'s tolerance and permissiveness, it is apparent that the Sultan wishes to use Catalina for the purposes of building an empire which will surpass any other. Mariscal comments that the *Turco*'s references to his future child 'strikes at the very heart of ideologies of purity'.[93] For a seventeenth-century Spanish audience, such a speech blatantly challenges socio-cultural values such as 'limpieza de sangre' which vigorously rejects hybridity — the antithesis of an 'otomano español'.[94] For the Sultan, however, 'limpieza de sangre' has no cultural value, which is entirely at odds with the dominant Spanish 'discourse of blood'.[95] Although the *Turco* and the off-stage audience perceive the issue from widely conflicting perspectives, both the Ottoman and Spanish empires deploy ideologies of blood for the purposes of fashioning a sense of exclusivity in the creation of superior and elitist states. As we have already seen, difference is, therefore, not incorporated but rather manipulated. In each case, emphasis is placed on the projection of an image of power and stability. Such an image operates on the premise of what is visible. This bears implications for the socio-cultural context in which a Spanish audience would have received this play, had it been performed. Written between 1606-10, *La gran sultana* enters public consciousness at a time when *moriscos* were being deported from Spain.[96] Cervantes's play gives voice, therefore, to the darker impulses which inform the idea that the state is founded on ideologies of blood. *La gran sultana* challenges the notion of 'clean blood' and exposes the fact that it rests precariously on exploitation.

The closing scene of *La gran sultana* is one of the most unsettling endings in the *Ocho comedias* and does little to soothe the anxieties experienced by the spectator throughout the drama. Its full significance is realised when considered in light of the scene which precedes it. In this penultimate scene, Madrigal is preparing to leave Constantinople and, prior to his departure, declares that he will put on a play in Madrid which will tell the story of Doña Catalina 'sin descrepar de la verdad un punto' (III. 2917). Madrigal anticipates that the audience will ask him such questions as: '¿es verdad que se llama la sultana / que hoy reina en la Turquía Catalina, / y que es cristiana, y tiene don y todo, / y que es de Oviedo el sobrenombre suyo?' (III. 2909-12). This metatheatrical strategy shatters the barrier between stage and spectator with the *gracioso* echoing, or indeed prompting, the thoughts of *La gran sultana*'s audience. If the play to which Madrigal refers, is the very play which the audience have just watched, then Cervantes has effectively dispelled the distance between Spain and Turkey, and has, quite literally, brought the play home. This scene, which makes clear that despite its setting is 'centred' on Spain, lays the foundation for the play's 'conclusion' in which Cervantes violently dismantles illusions of Spanish centrality.

The 'deceptively "open" dénouement' to the play is the key contributing factor to the sense of disquiet experienced by the audience.[97] As both Friedman and Díez Fernández note, Cervantes leaves his audience with more questions than answers.[98] These questions primarily revolve around the birth of Catalina and the Sultan's child. In the final lines, the *Gran Turco*'s *garzones* hurry through the streets of Constantinople proclaiming: '¡Viva la gran sultana doña Catalina de Oviedo! Felice parto tenga!' (III. 2952). The audience is not privy to any additional information regarding this child. The spectator is, therefore, inevitably left questioning the faith and allegiance of the sultan's heir. Moreover, Catalina's fate is unknown and we can only wonder whether she will remain in the favour of her husband. The closing line elusively promises a 'nueva y verdadera historia' of Catalina and her fame (III. 2961). We are keenly aware that this 'historia' and the birth of the child will occur outside the theatrical frame. This ambiguous ending opens a very ambivalent space for the audience and serves to reinforce the instabilities and uncertainties that drive the drama. This is complicated by the fact that relatively little has happened; Catalina is, after all, still captive. In fact, *La gran sultana* ends exactly as it begins — with a dialogue by Salec and Roberto. As if to reiterate the point that the play has come full circle, Cervantes writes: '*Salen Salec, el renegado, y Roberto, los dos primeros que comenzaron la comedia*' (III. 2940). The audience, brought back to the beginning, are aware that the uncertainties with which the play began have accumulated rather than dissipated.

Cervantes provides his spectator with the fundamental elements of the proverbial happy ending — marriage and an impending birth. This is undoubtedly one of the most contradictory elements of the play. In a different context, these would promote the family unit and safeguard the patriarchal structure. However, displaced against the backdrop of an alien, unorthodox environment, these conventional devices, so often used by Lope, become perversely disconcerting for the audience. Rather than resolving the confusion via the institution of marriage and family life (according to Frye's model), the ending of *La gran sultana* restates Salec's earlier claim that: 'aquí todo es confusión'. This refusal to propagate social models is similar to Cervantes's parodic portrayal of Lope's formulaic *comedia nueva* in *La entretenida*. However, *La gran sultana* goes further than this. By introducing the possibility of a 'hybrid' heir, Cervantes unsettles a Spanish audience obsessed with the idea of *limpieza de sangre*. In a contradictory fashion, the 'promotion' of the family unit perturbs rather than affirms or promulgates homogeneity. As Castillo remarks, Cervantes demonstrates that: 'Las nociones de esencialismo cultural están basadas en rígidos mitos como el código del honor, o la pureza de sangre, que no se pueden mantener en la práctica'.[99] In this sense, the profoundly unsatisfactory 'resolution' not only calls into question the conditioned aesthetic expectations of the *corral* audience, but very forcibly underscores the prejudice and intolerance projected by the Spanish subject toward those not aligned with seventeenth-century Spain's 'impermeable' cultural models. This disjunction is further compounded by the fact that in contrast to the Spaniard, for whom hybridity signifies an attack on Spanish supremacy, the servants of the *Gran Turco* react with obvious delight to the news, as evidenced in the play's final lines. Again, signification is connected to subjective experience and highly partisan perspective. The close of *La gran sultana*, therefore, advocates more mutable socio-cultural 'norms'. In fact, the 'otomano español' can be said to be emblematic of a rupture with conventional modes of classification. In its closing moments the play seems to propagate a discourse of blood that is far removed from established ideologies. Situated within its pertinent socio-historical context (racial tensions in Spain, expulsion of *moriscos* etcetera), *La gran sultana*'s audience is asked to question prejudices and biases that demarcate difference as something objectionable. This is not to say, however, that *La gran sultana* ultimately advocates inclusiveness and tolerance. Rather, the ending of the play thrusts Spain's 'ideals' into the spotlight as the drama exposes the counterfeit 'truths' on which Counter-Reformation Spain is precariously founded. In light of this, *La gran sultana*'s non-resolution represents a serious challenge to those readings which advocate that Cervantes's drama is an unproblematic portrayal of lenience and harmony.

Beneath the farcical and ludic elements which veil the play, lie complex issues which reflect the contradictory realities of seventeenth-century Spain. As we have seen, the play dismantles its own absurdities to reveal the dramatist's engagement with concerns that operate on individual and collective levels. The play explores the consequences of authority's ability to contain and curb individualism, while also challenging the cultural signifiers and models which underpin Spanish national selfhood. Within a conventional *ser/parecer* dialectic, it is *parecer* which is most compellingly disassembled in *La gran sultana*. Cervantes's Constantinople is one which actively endorses pretence, façade and subjective perception. Its ruler, the *Gran Turco*, is tyrannical, incompetent and manipulative. Spain, by implication, is criticised for its insistence on playing on an image of imperial might and political power which has very little bearing on contemporary realities.

The ambivalent space opened up by *La gran sultana* impacts reception of the text. As has already been established in this study, Cervantes makes plain that his theatre refuses to be an instrument of propaganda. As such, this play naturally resists those arguments which insist that the drama promotes a harmonious inclusiveness. Moreover, Cervantes does not make it easy for his spectator to read and interpret the signifying systems at play. The difficulty in peeling back the drama's layers of farce and rigorously determining the motivations which drive the play encourages both discrimination and active participation. In this sense, the uncertainties which characterise the drama can only serve to better equip the spectator to see 'beyond the veil' and deal with the paradoxes of early modern Spanish life. Ultimately, then, Cervantes does not abandon his spectator to find his/her way through the labyrinthine uncertainties and confusions which pervade *La gran sultana*. Rather, Cervantes complicates his audience's perception of their world so that they might question, confront and counter-act its dualities and failures.

2.3 Staging Spain in *Los baños de Argel*

Like much of Cervantes's writings for the stage, *Los baños de Argel* has been overshadowed by the infinitely more successful *Don Quijote*. Critical attention has, therefore, prioritised the better known and hugely popular interpolated short story, *La historia del cautivo*, from part I of the novel, with which *Los baños* shares a plotline. The tendency to overlook Cervantes's *comedia* is further compounded by the fact that its secondary plot is borrowed from the earlier four-act *El trato de Argel*, which is thought to have inaugurated Cervantes's career as dramatist.[100] *El trato*, labelled 'el drama de cautivos más poderoso de Cervantes', has attracted ample interest and most studies of *Los baños* are contained within articles which prioritise a reading of *El trato*.[101]

Scholars who have discussed *Los baños de Argel* generally follow two strands of argument: Cervantes's concern with 'otherness' and the staging/structure of the play. The question of the dramatist's anti-Semitism has specifically incited attention.[102] Scenes in *Los baños* in which the Sacristán, Tristán, relentlessly harass a Jewish man, recall Madrigal tossing bacon into the stew pot in *La gran sultana*. In *Los baños*, however, Tristán's actions are all the more contemptuous. Cervantes's portrayal of prejudice provoked Américo Castro to claim: 'No veo, pues, base sino para afirmar que por unas u otras razones — antijudaísmo de español, opinión formada en Argel [...] Cervantes aparece como lo que hoy llamaríamos un antisemita'.[103] Zimic, however, sees the Sacristán as a grotesque buffoon who represents 'un aspecto deplorable de la realidad española'.[104] Others, such as Canavaggio, tend to shy away from making dogmatic statements, preferring to focus on 'la expresión multidimensional de una difícil convivencia, contemplada por el espectador desde distintos puntos de vista'.[105] In other words, Cervantine multiperspectivism rescues the contemporary critic from the pitfalls of eliciting the author's personal ideology from a dramatic text.[106] Recent postmodern approaches take as their point of departure the view that Cervantes dismantles the 'noción de centralidad cultural'.[107] This is a line of enquiry which informs Irigoyen-García's recent study which argues that the play contests the process of cultural homogenization taking place in the Iberian Peninsula.[108]

Structural issues are central to articles by John J. Allen and López-Vázquez, with both critics suggesting that the drama was originally composed in four acts.[109] Issues of staging and performance concern Stackhouse, who argues that Cervantes did not expect his plays to be performed and, therefore, took liberties by utilising dramatic techniques which would not have functioned within the parameters of theatrical conventions. Interestingly, Stackhouse's reading contends that *El trato* and *Los baños* call into question contemporary ideologies and criticise the Spanish Crown for its inadequate response to captives languishing in jails in Algiers.[110]

These two opposing lines of argument which encompass ontological and aesthetic issues need not be seen as mutually exclusive. Some reconciliation of Cervantes's innovative dramatic tactics with the playwright's desire to destabilise central, absolute 'truths' would offer a more fruitful insight into the concerns which inform *Los baños*. This study will, in fact, explore how Cervantes employs such a strategy to confront and challenge the seventeenth-century Spanish spectator. As we will see, it is this sense of confrontation which underpins and drives the play. My own reading will draw on two very different interpretations which would appear to sit outside criticism offered to date: Maryrica Lottman's analysis which explores Cervantes's promotion of rural life, or the natural world, as a metaphorical representation; and Jorge Kühni's metatheatrical perspective.[111] What emerges from Lottman's study is the idea that the audience is compelled to engage with the symbolism at play. This notion is particularly relevant to the metaphorical space carved out by the play within the play performed by the captives in the concluding act; scenes to which Lottman makes scant reference. Kühni's interrogation of these scenes, however, offers a reading which draws attention to the powerful way in which the Cervantine 'word' fabricates both illusion and reality. Kühni concludes that the drama performed by the Spanish captives functions as 'la reflexión sobre un mundo exterior [. . .] y la autorreflexión sobre un mundo del teatro encarnado por el entreacto'.[112] The implications of this 'reflexión sobre un mundo exterior' have yet to be fully realised. My study, then, will explore how the spectator's perception of his/her world might be influenced by the symbolic dramatic space forged within the play's final scenes.

Any investigation of *Los baños de Argel* must be informed by an awareness that the work is potentially pseudo-autobiographical. As noted above, the *comedias de cautivos* are generally located within the context of testimonial and trauma literature: 'One wonders whether Cervantes could have become the great creative writer that he was had he not suffered the traumatic experience of his Algerian captivity'.[113] In fact, critics frequently turn to *El trato de Argel* in order to reconstruct the years that the writer spent as a prisoner in North Africa.[114] Written a short time after his liberation, the drama is laden with references which attest to the hardship suffered by the *cautivo*, as well as information which points to the physical, economic and political landscape of Algiers. Nevertheless, we must be cautious of overplaying Cervantes's captivity plays as a valid source of historical accuracy. As Enrique Fernández remarks: 'separar lo histórico de su elaboración literaria es difícil'.[115] In fact, *Los baños de Argel* is one of the playwright's most self-conscious *comedias*.

The drama begins with the abduction of Spanish Christians by Turkish corsairs as they are forced on board the enemy vessel and brought to Algiers as prisoners. The plot follows two couples whose relationships are fraught with difficulties. Costanza and Fernando are separated in Algiers and their love is complicated by the fact that Costanza's mistress, Alima, wife of Caurali, falls in love with Fernando, whilst Caurali desires Costanza. Meanwhile, Zara, a Moorish girl, falls in love with Lope, a Christian captive, and cleverly engineers circumstances so that she may leave with him and convert to Christianity. The play's conclusion sees these captives, and others, orchestrate a successful escape attempt. *Los baños* offers a vivid portrayal of the horrors of the bagnios and the impoverished state of the incarcerated *cautivo*.[116] In its depiction of captives who are cruelly subject to beatings, mockery, torture and children who are mercilessly snatched from their family and threatened with death unless they compromise their Christian faith, *Los baños* is an often disturbing picture of the fate which awaited those unfortunate enough to fall into the hands of ruthless captors in North Africa.[117] Rey Hazas comments that *El trato de Argel* and *Los baños*:

> son las más duras, las más tristes, las más sangrientas, las más próximas a la concepción trágica; porque, aunque a la postre los personajes principales se salven de la esclavitud y regresen, libres a España, otros muchos se quedan cautivos o se han quedado ya sin vida.[118]

In fact, *Los baños* closes with the haunting lines: 'Y aquí da este trato fin, / que no le tiene el de Argel' (III. 3092–93), allowing Cervantes to imprint on the mind of his audience the enduring horrors of life as a captive in Algiers. As Stackhouse notes: 'Cervantes had the opportunity to challenge in the play his audience's uncritically held assumptions about themselves and about their countrymen who were living as slaves in Algiers'.[119]

Captivity and its consequences are usually examined in Cervantes's drama in the context of the 'other'. *La gran sultana* is, of course, an obvious point in case. As Garcés remarks: 'Cervantes's interest in the marginal, his openness toward other cultures, and his respect for difference' are issues which emerge from critical interrogation of the captivity plays.[120] These are entirely legitimate approaches in light of the playwright's preference for shifting perspectives and his tendency to re-align the peripheral as something much more central: 'Maestro en el arte de insinuación, ambigüedad e ironía, Cervantes se complace en erosionar sutilmente sus convicciones más asentadas, orientándolo hacia un terreno sembrado de incertidumbres y enigmas'.[121] Cervantes's portrayal of a hostile and antagonistic North African environment in which he deals intimately with other *cautivos*, Muslims, Jews and renegades undoubtedly offers the possibility of viewing the 'outside', and especially Islam, from a paradoxically internal perspective.

The circumstances of Cervantes's own captivity are relevant here. Cervantes was in fact returning to Spain following a period of convalescence in Italy, where he had been recovering from serious wounds sustained during the battle of Lepanto in 1571 when he was captured. There has been a tendency to overlook the fact that the Miguel de Cervantes who was enslaved in captivity was a Spanish soldier who courageously fought for his country in the battle of Lepanto, 'a curiously deceptive triumph', whose success was more psychological than real.[122] It is, therefore, not inconceivable that *Los baños* is as much a statement about Spain as it is about the 'otherness' which impacted upon Cervantes while held captive.[123] Juan Goytisolo partially broaches this issue when he asserts: 'Cervantes elaboró su compleja y admirable visión de España durante su prisión en tierras africanas, en contraposición al modelo rival con el que contendía'.[124] Goytisolo makes the valid point that the Spain of Cervantes's work is forged from within the captive space but does not elaborate on how this 'vision' finds literary expression outside of the playwright's interest in 'otherness'.[125] I would argue that the bagnios of Algiers become in this play a microcosm of Spain itself; its paradoxes, difficulties and conflicts played out on the stage of North Africa. If the 'Spain' of Algiers is a portrayal of peninsular Spain, then the state of the captive has much to say about the fractured position of the seventeenth-century Spaniard. As we will see, the Spanish Baroque subject is no freer than the Spanish *cautivo* suffering the plight of Algerian incarceration. The seventeenth-century Spanish subject, then, is just as displaced as the captive shackled in a North African bagnio. This goes some way to explaining why Cervantes's depiction of the captive's suffering and distress is all the more acute in *Los baños de Argel*.

The pastoral interlude, a play contained within another play, is in itself a type of 'captive space', where theatre is reduced to 'aquel microcosmos de las mazmorras argelinas'.[126] Significantly, Osorio, a Spanish captive and the play's director, observes that: 'Argel es, según barrunto, / arca de Noé abreviada: / aquí están de todas suertes, / oficios y habilidades, / disfrazadas calidades' (III. 2064–68). His words establish that the spectator (both on and off-stage) should perceive Algiers as a microcosm of life itself. As such, analysis of the play within the play is of fundamental importance to this study. Given that metatheatrical devices permit a perceptive double vision: a theatre that 'se desdobla desde el punto de vista estructural', the Spanish spectator should see him/herself reflected in the captive.[127] In line with previous readings of *El gallardo español* and *La gran sultana*, this brief discussion of Cervantes's *Los baños de Argel* will situate these issues within the broader context of national selfhood, interrogating the dramatist's 'compleja visión de España' and exploring the implications of Spain's splintered depiction for the seventeenth-century spectator.

Play within the Play

The opening events of Act III function as a type of 'scene setter' which frames the impending play. Gathered to celebrate the Easter festival, the Spanish captives assemble in the king's prison to watch a pastoral colloquy directed and performed by other *cautivos*. Prior to the captives' performance, Cervantes meticulously depicts a 'pre-play' environment in which the mechanisms of theatre are re-represented on stage. As the crowd gathers in to the bagnio, Don Lope and Vivanco assume the roles of stage-managers and directors as they discuss the play's dialogue (III. 2097-107), the costumes which the actors will wear (III. 2108-09) and the absence of a *loa* (III. 2111-12). On seeing Tristán and Osorio dressed for the roles which they will assume in the production, Vivanco comments: '¡Oh, que mendigos están! / En fin: comedia cautiva, / pobre, hambrienta y desdichada, / desnuda y atarantada' (III. 2113-16). As well as calling attention to the play's generic status, Cervantes plays on the very genre which he created. Sevilla Arroyo and Rey Hazas have recently argued that Cervantes 'inauguró, así una suerte de minigénero teatral, las comedias de cautiverio, berberiscas o turquesas, que él mismo perfeccionó y enriqueció'.[128] Vivanco's comment serves to emphasise the plight of the captive and to focus the audience's attention on the *cautivo*'s conduct and speech throughout the play within the play. Therefore, before the pastoral interlude begins the spectator's perspective is aligned with that of the *cautivo*. As though to reaffirm and compound Vivanco's observation, Don Lope immediately comments: 'La voluntad se reciba' (III. 2117). Through this indirect address to the off-stage audience, Lope encourages careful and critical reception. In these first instances of doubling and identification, the seventeenth-century spectator is encouraged to see that the events of the play have less to do with Algiers and more to do with Spain.

What is particularly noteworthy about these scenes is the significant role that the Spaniard plays. Throughout *Los baños de Argel* the Spaniard, incarcerated in North Africa, shares the stage with his enemy, the Muslim captor. He is subordinate to those in a position of authority. For instance, during the course of the play we see many nameless *cautivos* suffering from beatings and verbal abuse. The *viejo* is cruelly taken from his homeland and can do little to oppose the Cadí from sequestering his children and from using every means possible, including brutal force, to convert Francisquito and Juanico to Islam. In short, the Spaniard is denigrated, treated with violent hostility and made to suffer on account that he has become, in this play, the marginal 'other'. However, in the play within the play, a *comedia cautiva*, it is the Spaniard who assumes centre stage. In fact, the interlude is an exclusively Spanish space in which the Spaniard is free to act, perform and engage with the spectacle. Ironically, it is the Muslim warden, now relegated to the audience, who creates this space: 'Los españoles, por su parte, hacen / una brava comedia' (III. 2027–28), 'Poneos tras el postigo, y veréis todo / cuanto hacen los cristianos en el patio, / porque es cosa de ver' (III. 2054–56). Osorio calls attention to the Spanish-dominated space when he states that their masters have allowed the captives opportunity to celebrate Easter mass and as such, 'De nuestras Pascuas tenemos / los primeros días por nuestros' (III. 2090–91). As the *cautivo* celebrates Christianity and performs a pastoral interlude by one of Cervantes's own precursors, Lope de Rueda, he claims ownership of the drama, but also of the events which follow. This is not dissimilar, of course, to the role reversal and challenging of social order which occurs within the *entremés* in the final act of *La entretenida* where the aristocracy assume the role of audience as they watch their servants perform.

The captor's subjection to the captive is most clearly demonstrated by the instances which see Tristán, the sexton, linguistically sparring with Cauralí, the captain of Algiers. Cauralí enters the bagnio and sits in symbolic submission to watch the play. Throughout the dialogue Tristán interrupts no fewer than six times and provokes frustration and tensions among both actors and audience. Significantly, the sexton manipulates many of these opportunities as occasion to address Cauralí. In fact, before he first interrupts proceedings, Cervantes's directions note: '*En acabando la múscia, dice el Sacristán (Todo cuanto dice agora el Sacristán, lo diga mirando al soslayo a Cauralí)*' (III. 2133). The sexton's deliberate eye contact with Cauralí, coupled with the provocative speech which follows, would suggest that Tristán's interventions are not those of the uninitiated spectator who interrupts because he is unable to discern fact from fiction. Rather, Tristán cleverly exploits his interruptions as a platform from which he can express the hardships of life as a captive. As Celis Sánchez observes, Tristán is 'bien consciente de su condición de actor [. . .] Cervantes confíe en su papel (en el metadrama) la posibilidad de hablar con absoluta libertad al turco y exponer dramáticamente la angustia que le produce su condición de cautivo'.[129] The opening lines of his first speech attest to the sense of displacement and alienation suffered by the *cautivo* upon arrival in a foreign and hostile environment: '¿Qué es esto? ¿Qué tierra es ésta? / ¿Qué siento? ¿Qué es lo que veo? / De réquiem es esta fiesta / para mí, pues un deseo / más que mortal me molesta' (III. 2134–38). He uses the performance, then, as a covert strategy which permits free expression of his anguish toward his captor. Moreover, he also exploits this particular instance to mock Cauralí for his love of Costanza, a Christian (III. 2142–53; 2156–65). The play within the play, therefore, provides a space whereby Tristán can temporarily leave his role as captive and openly and freely challenge his enemy's control: 'se sirve de su condición de actor para evidenciar su desdén hacia la humillación a que se ve sometido como prisionero y cautivo'.[130] When chastised by Fernando for his interruption and asked to pay attention, Tristán retorts: 'Sí haré; / pero no sé si podré, / según el diablo me tienta' (III. 2171–73). Yet we know that Tristán, as actor, is fully in control and that he uses this retort to insult the Moor further. He is not unlike Lugo from Cervantes's *El rufián dichoso* who, as we shall see in the following chapter, is also an astute actor; they are equally adept at controlling and manipulating the responses of others. In fact, Tristán (and Lugo) operate like puppeteers, pulling on Caurálí's strings. Unlike the sexton, the Moor is unable to discern whether Tristán's interjections are part of the scheduled performance: '¿Es esto de la comedia, / o es bufón este Cristiano?' (III. 2154–55).[131] Tristán capitalises on his enemy's inability to perceive the situation clearly and is, therefore, able to articulate his thoughts on captivity without fear of punishment. Kühni observes that Caurálí represents 'el prototipo del personaje encantado por la ilusión, desorientado en el laberinto que encierra lo real y lo irreal'.[132] However, it is not just the visual that is at stake here. Caurálí is not only captivated by the illusion, but is unable to perceive the linguistic games at play. As we will see, it is this inability which ensures that he remains subject to Tristán's manipulations.

When Tristán intervenes during the captives' performance in Act III, the audience understand that his interjections are the result of much anguish. The sexton's behaviour cannot be considered apart from the broader action of the play which depicts the ill-treatment suffered by the *cautivo* in Algiers. Caurálí, in particular, is a cruel and oppressive master. Even his wife, Alima, attests to the repression that she suffers: 'Sólo por estar sujeta / a mi esposo estoy de suerte / que el corazón se me aprieta' (II. 892–94). It is Caurálí who invades Spain in the opening scene of the play and takes Tristán and other Spaniards captive, treating them as little more than plunder. The devastation caused by the Algerians is so acute that an onlooker comments: 'Sólo habremos llegado a ser testigos / de que Troya fue aquí' (I. 115–16).[133] This scene switches to a prison in Algiers where we are privy to the stark realities of life as a captive. The Guardián Bají quickly affirms his role as a difficult task-master as he shouts abuse at an ill *cautivo* and beats him with a stick: 'Que os criasteis en regalo, / inútil perro barrunto [. . .] Pues yo os curaré en un punto / con el sudor deste palo' (I. 282–83; 85–86). In the following scenes we see a *cautivo* who has had his ears cut off as punishment for his attempt to escape. His desperate attempts to challenge his captors and attain liberty meet with disaster. At no other point in *Los baños* is the captive able to confront the enemy and evade the consequences. Even Francisquito, who resolutely pledges that he will not convert to Islam, suffers death as a result of his resistance. Tristán, then, takes advantage of the freedom which this dramatic space allows in order to defy his master and escape unharmed.

The sexton has, in fact, played the *gracioso*-type role throughout *Los baños*. The other *cautivos* rebuke Tristán's 'bufonería' in the scene for fear that he will antagonise Caurálí (III. 2238–39). As the captain becomes increasingly frustrated with Tristán's interjections and threatens to attack him, Don Fernando interrupts: 'que cuanto dice es donaire / y es bufón el pecador' (III. 2234–35). However, Tristán's transgression of conventional dramatic parameters and captive/captor boundaries to launch the drama's only uncontested challenge to Muslim autocracy, suggests that he represents much more than a *comedia* stereotype. Tristán gives voice to those who are marginalised, but forbidden to articulate their suffering. For the off-stage audience, aligned with the *cautivo*, Tristán's final interjection is especially resonant. The colloquy poses the rhetorical question: '¿Quién es este cuitado / que asoma acá entellerido, / cabizbajo, atordecido, / barba y cabello erizado, / desairado y mal erguido?' (III. 2219- 23). The sexton responds: 'Yo soy, cierto, / el triste y desventurado, / vivo en un instante y muerto' (III. 2224–26). Tristán, then, exploits the dialogue's portrayal of a dejected 'cuitado' to reflect the purgatorial position of the *cautivo* enslaved in Algiers.

Tristán is a device employed by Cervantes through which he endeavours to create what might be termed an 'ideal audience'; that is, an audience who comprehends and appreciates the playwright's agenda. Iser conceptualises the 'ideal reader' as a consumer who shares 'an identical code to that of the author'.[134] This notion, transferred to a dramatic context, suggests a spectator who responds to the messages played out on stage within their own frame of reference. Cervantes and the conventional *comedia* audience may not, of course, share an 'identical code' given that the dramatist's seditious theatre operates on the fringes of established theatrical codes and practices. We might view these scenes, therefore, as Cervantes's attempt to 'educate' his spectator by communicating what it is that his alternative drama does. For Iser, an ideal reader is a 'structural impossibility as far as literary communication is concerned' because authors:

> generally recodify prevailing codes in their texts, and so the ideal reader would also have to share the intentions underlying this process. And if this were possible, communication would then be quite superfluous, for one only communicates that which is not already shared by sender and receiver.[135]

Recodification of prevailing *comedia* codes is at the heart of Cervantes's theatre, as we have seen throughout this study. Cervantes's ultimate aim would appear to be the creation of an audience which shares his vision. His project is ambitious, and perhaps given the conditioning of the *comedia nueva*, unrealisable. Nonetheless, he clearly perceived it to be worth the effort, and potentially realisable, when he decided to communicate via publication; a gesture which we should not consider 'superfluous'. This might also explain why Cervantes chooses a Lope de Rueda play to be performed as the *entremés*. Cervantes displaces Lope de Vega with another Lope who is praised profusely in the prologue to the *Ocho comedias*. Cervantes credits the 'gran' Lope de Rueda as 'varón insigne en la representación y en el entendimiento' and extols the simplicity of Rueda's makeshift stage.[136] By positioning Lope de Rueda's interlude centre-stage, Cervantes transports his spectator to a time in which theatre was less commercial.[137] As such, Cervantes emphasises the type of spectator for which his own stage is best suited; an audience not dependent on special effects and able to engage discerningly with the signs at play.

In the context of *Los baños de Argel* Cervantes promotes a stage that requires active critical scrutiny via Tristán's interruption of the theatrical space. As the sexton depicts the anguish experienced by the *cautivo*, there exists the possibility that the off-stage Spaniard will associate his/her own situation with this suffering. For instance, just as the sexton does not recognise the alien land which he inhabits and becomes increasingly disconsolate, the fractured Baroque individual must deal with a Spain which is in the midst of imperial retreat and has radically altered. Like the captive, the Spaniard, then, is in no way free or liberated. Within this context the desperate attempts by *cautivos* to escape the hellish landscape of Algiers become even more pertinent. The captive who suffers from having his ears chopped off proclaims to his captor:

> aunque me desmoches todo
> y me pongas de otro modo
> peor que este en que me veo,
> tanto el ser libre deseo,
> que a la fuga me acomodo
> por la tierra o por el viento,
> por el agua y por el fuego (I. 532–38)

When Tristán expresses the miseries of life under tyrannical rule he may also communicate what it is to be subservient to any dictates and demands and to desire liberation. Although the spectator may not be physically incarcerated, he/she could empathise with what it is to be bound by diktats such as an intransigent honour code which permits the individual very little freedom of choice.

In the Algerian context of uncompromising authority freedom of speech is severely curtailed, as demonstrated by Hazén's ill-fated declaration of faith in Act I. When asked by the Cadí if he is a Christian, the renegade asserts: 'Sí soy; / y en serlo tan firme estoy, / que deseo, como has visto, / deshacerme y ser con Cristo, / si fuese posible, hoy' (I. 827–31). This passionate articulation of his belief results in impalement. There is little room in Algiers for counter-discourse. The depiction of dogmatic authority may produce anxieties concerning the realities of life under Hapsburg leadership and provoke identification with the subject's inability to question or interrogate the rhetoric propagated by his/her government. The Spanish subject exists within a system which advocates conformity to social models which insist on rigid hierarchical order, promotes collusion with Imperial Spain's aggressive policies and acceptance of the 'fact' that Spanish 'grandeza' is founded on a discourse of unpolluted blood. Throughout the play Cervantes conveys to his audience that restriction and confinement is not merely physical. In the play within the play Tristán is persistently petitioned to refrain from interrupting: 'Escuchad, [...] y callad, / que ésa es grande impertinencia' (III. 2184–86). He is eventually pressured to leave the theatre space so that the other actors/spectators can perform the colloquy undisturbed. Tristán does manage to enrage and challenge his captor. However, his dissident voice is ultimately quashed. Caurali labels the sexton a madman: '¡Echadle fuera a este loco!' (III. 2228). Dismissed as a 'bufón' who is less than lucid, Tristán leaves the *baño* with the true motives for his interjections concealed.

Tristán is not unlike Don Quijote who frequently challenges authority and counters the contemporary Spanish world view, but is not regarded seriously given that he is 'mad'. In one of the most subversive instances in part one of the novel, the would-be knight is horrified to encounter twelve men 'ensartados como cuentas en una gran cadena de hierro por los cuellos, y todos con esposas a las manos'. When Sancho explains that the men are galley slaves and 'gente forzada del rey' to go the galleys, Don Quijote responds: '¿Es posible que el rey haga fuerza a ninguna gente?' (p. 199). As he frees the slaves in an act which is undoubtedly heroic in intent but wholly unnecessary, Don Quijote pits himself against the authority of the king. His disproportionate sense of responsibility toward those whose liberty is curtailed, results in action which defiantly flouts authority. Like Tristán, the knight is a kind of spokesperson for the marginalised individual. Both of these instances in *Don Quijote* and *Los baños de Argel* demonstrate, in distinct ways, that the king (or authority) can and does force others to acquiesce. Tristán and Don Quijote, however, find covert means to bypass this power and oppose the status quo. The sacristán's ability to circumvent his circumstances identifies Cervantes's theatre as one of liberation. It opens up alternative perspectives and provides space for voices and discourse which otherwise might not be heard. In this context, Cervantes's 'ideal' spectator is one who can critically see through and beyond signifying systems both on stage and off. In the play within the play, then, Cervantes exploits Tristán's ability to make himself heard in order to carve out a space which potentially counter-acts the repression of the day.

Cervantes, however, complicates audience response to the suffering and repression experienced by the *cautivo*. The spectator is keenly aware that the sexton actively contributes to the subjugation suffered by others incarcerated in Algiers. Tristán, in fact, is responsible for mercilessly taunting a Jew throughout the course of the play. In this sense, the oppressed is also the oppressor. The sexton mocks the Jew's appearance and demands that he lift a barrel, despite the fact that it is the Sabbath and the Jewish man is forbidden to perform labour. He repeatedly calls the Jew a dog and viciously threatens: '¡Vive Dios, perro, que os arranque el hígado!' (II. 1285).[138] In a later scene, Tristán steals the Jew's stew on the Sabbath and demands that he pay a sum of money in order to 'ransom' the *cazuela* (II. 1682). Like many of *Los baños's cautivos*, the Jewish man is identified with his faith system throughout the play and remains nameless. Denied an individual identity, he is treated by prevailing authority as a nonentity. Tristán's persecution of someone from an opposing religious background renders the sexton no different from Caurali. Cervantes, therefore, exposes the other side of the coin as he highlights the contradictions of a fractured Spain. The Spaniard, who esteems himself on the basis of a 'pure' heritage and clean blood, is complicit in the racial prejudice and bigotry that define seventeenth-century Spanish life.

Of particular note is the wider context of the scenes in which the sexton terrorises the Jewish man. Prior to the drama's first anti-Semitic instance, Tristán is harassed by three young Moorish boys. They taunt the sexton and mock the fact that he is imprisoned in Algiers indefinitely: '¡Rapaz cristiano, / non rescatar, non fugir; / don Juan no venir; / acá morir, / perro acá morir!' (II. 1217–21).[139] The latter part of this insult is repeated four more times until the sexton exclaims: 'Sin duda que en el cielo / debía de haber gran guerra, / do el general faltaba, / y a don Juan se llevaron para serlo' (II. 1250–53). Despite the fact that Tristán heaps praise on Don Juan de Austria, who had commanded the triumphant forces at Lepanto in 1571 but died prematurely seven years later, the boys' taunting affirms that the sexton, like all captives, has been defeated by the Moor insofar as there is no hope of rescue. The Moorish boys draw attention to the bleak reality of the futile and miserable existence of the captive who is destined to languish in North African captivity. This episode suggests that the Spanish captives have been abandoned by their fellow countrymen and accentuates how Spain is perceived from the perspective of the other. For the Moor, Spain is an impotent power with few resources left to quash the enemy. There will be no grand rescue orchestrated by the Spanish, nor any display of imperial rigour and grandeur. If Don Juan represents an epoch in which Spain celebrated her supremacy, then this scene makes brutally clear that those days have vanished. The despondent state of the *cautivo* plays out on stage the harsh reality of Spain's declining influence. Moreover, Tristán's conduct toward the Jewish man depicts, again, as in others plays, a bleak (and, in fact, bleaker) picture of a society trapped in a vicious circle. Having been goaded by the Moorish boys, the sexton unleashes his frustration and anger on the Jew. In a desperate attempt to regain a sense of control, Tristán bullies the Jew and demands that he perform certain duties in order to exercise a measure of dominance. In fact, he echoes the insult ('perro') which has been thrown at him by the Moorish boys. Repression, therefore, breeds repression. Just as the Spaniard is oppressed by uncompromising authority, he/she disseminates this oppression by demonstrating intolerance and prejudice toward those marginal and minority groups which the state labels as inferior.

As in *La entretenida*, the play within the play device concretises this symbolic circularity. The spectators perceive Tristán, and by implication themselves, as they see the Moor's behaviour and attitude reflected in Tristán's abuse of the Jewish man — arrogant, hypocritical and aggressive. Tristán's second instance of anti-semitism calls into question the eulogistic depiction of Spain which precedes it. Zara, a Mooress, pretends to have been stung by a wasp or bitten by a spider in order that she can remove her veil and reveal her identity to Don Lope, a Christian captive whom she has paid to ransom. Lope understands that her behaviour is an elaborate ruse: '¿Hay tan discreta maraña?' (II. 1601). On revealing his own identity to the women on stage, he states that he is 'de una tierra / donde no se cría araña / ponzoñosa, si se encierra / fraude, embuste ni maraña, / sino un limpio proceder, / y el cumplir y el prometer / es todo una misma cosa' (II. 1623–29). He thus sets up Spain in opposition to Algiers as a pure and golden land, free from duplicitousness and deceit. As a titled and ransomed *cautivo* plotting his return to Spain, Lope, of course, can afford to have a romanticised vision of his homeland. The following scene reveals Don Lope's vision to be highly ironic and misleading. When Tristán harasses the Jewish man and callously steals the stew which he has cooked for the Sabbath, it is Spain which emerges as a land of 'fraude, embuste' and 'maraña'. *Los baños* does not offer an 'apasionada defensa de lo español', as Rey Hazas would have it, nor are the Spaniards in the captivity plays 'los más firmes, los más honestos, los más leales en el amor. Tanto en el sentimiento como en la fe, al igual en la religión que el nacionalismo'.[140] Rather, in those scenes in *Los baños* in which the Spaniard responds perversely to the oppression which he experiences, Cervantes confronts the spectator with a dark and unsettling depiction of 'lo español'. Spain, as emblematised in *Los baños*, sequesters power through exploitation and manipulation and provokes others to do likewise. Cervantes uses the illusion of the stage (the Moors as symbolic Spaniards exemplify *parecer*) in order to challenge realities and unsettle the idea of what it is 'to be' (*ser*) *español*.

The dialogue employed by the actors of the pastoral interlude contributes to this sense of deconstruction. Against the backdrop of the harsh realities of the *baños*, Guillermo, dressed as shepherd, recites a pastoral colloquy.[141] Canavaggio remarks that 'a discontinuity is immediately established [...] between the pastoral convention and the reality of the prison, a discontinuity which accentuates the reality of the play and underscores its value as witness to a historical reality which precedes all dramatic stylization'.[142] Certainly the presence of this *locus amoenus* represents a stark contrast which only serves to heighten the spectator's awareness of the misery suffered by the *cautivo*. For Irigoyen-García, the staging of a pastoral drama is particularly significant in that it is 'ideologically motivated'. That is, 'the convention of the dramatic shepherd in early modern Spain lies precisely in constructing a sharp opposition of unmistakable Old Christian shepherds against equally stereotyped Moors and Jews'. The Christian *cautivos*, then, choose a genre that 'celebrates Christian identity as opposed to its Other' within an exclusively Spanish space which symbolically challenges the Moorish captor.[143] This is further evidenced by the Christian tropes which Guillermo's colloquy employs; for instance, 'corderas' roaming freely. Thus Cervantes would appear to forge a bucolic, 'fictitious Arcadian place [...] in which Christians enjoy freedom'.[144] Nonetheless, it is precisely the enhanced artificiality of the pastoral scene which is disconcerting. Cervantes's interest in and engagement with the pastoral genre is, of course, well documented.[145] Barbara Mujica notes that 'the inevitable failure of the utopian vision was precisely what fascinated Cervantes'.[146] Significantly, in *Los baños de Argel*, the playwright evokes a perturbing scene which is only superficially utopian:

> Esparcíos, las mis corderas,
> por las dehesas y prados,
> mordey sabrosos bocados,
> no temáis las venideras
> noches de nubros airados,
> antes os andáy exentas,
> brincando de recontentas.
> No os aflija el ser mordidas
> de las lobas desambridas,
> tragantonas, malcontentas,
> y, al dar de los vellocinos,
> venid simpres, no ronceras,
> rumiando por las laderas,
> a jornaleros vecinos,
> o al corte de sus tijeras;
> que él sin medida contento,
> cual no abarca el pensamiento,
> os librará de lesión,
> si al dar del branco vellón,
> barruntáis el bien que siento (III. 2199–2218)

This speech, directed at the Spanish audience (both on and off-stage), conjures up a vision of an idealised environment which offers the spectator security and liberty; where the Spaniard can roam free unperturbed by lurking dangers. Underneath the surface of the dialogue's idyllic depiction of paradise there is, however, clear evidence of repressive propaganda. In fact, I would argue that this colloquy perilously lulls the Spaniard into a false sense of security. The rhetoric employed by Guillermo is, therefore, not so much about pitting the Christian captive ('corderas') against their Algerian captors ('lobas desambridas'), as Irigoyen-García would see it, but, rather, enforces the triumph of illusion over reality, and the suppression of reason. The dialogue, then, is emblematic of Spanish authority which would actively deceive its subjects and brutally gloss over the country's painful problems and failures. The audience is urged to disregard Spain's impending doom as symbolised by the starving wolf imagery and 'andar exentas, / brincando de recontentas'. Guillermo's *locus amoenus* has no bearing on reality on-stage or off. Rather, it is a scene of horror which ominously employs repressive mechanisms under the guise of optimism. The *cautivo* and the audience are effectively excluded from the pastoral dream or, in other words, a golden Spain. The meta-dramatic devices utilised in the play within the play, therefore, expose Spain's capacity for distorted self-representation. As such, the seventeenth-century Spaniard is encouraged to interrogate the repressive rhetoric to which they are subject and 'des-engañar' him/herself from its pervasive influence.[147]

Spain's substitution of reality for illusion is accentuated by the events which bring the captives' play to a premature end. The *cautivos* are abruptly interrupted by a Moor who brings news that a Spanish *armada* has been sighted off the coast of Algiers and as a result, janissaries are indiscriminately killing captives. As Guillermo expresses his disbelief, having heard nothing of such an *armada*, the Moor responds: 'Pues esta prueba / os desmiente y desengaña; / que a fe que dicen que asoman / más de trecientas galeras, / con flámulas y banderas, / y que el rumbo de Argel toman' (III. 2283–88). There is, however, no proof of an *armada* and the existence of the three hundred galleys uncomfortably rests on supposition. This is, in fact, shown to be the case when the warden hurries on-stage to say that the sun and clouds formed shapes over the sea which made him believe an *armada* was approaching. The Moor lays much emphasis on what he thought that he had seen:

> Tan claramente descubren
> *los ojos que la están viendo*
> de las fingidas galeras
> las proas, popas y remos,
> que hay quien afirme y quien jure
> que del cómitre y remero
> vio el mandar y obedecer
> hacerse todo en un tiempo (III. 2305–12)

Interestingly, he also draws attention to the instability of the vision: 'Salió el sol esta mañana, / y sus rayos imprimieron / en las nubes tales formas, / que, aunque han mentido, las creo' (III. 2297–300). Despite the fact that the imagery projected by the 'rayos' tends to 'mentir', the warden chooses to place his trust in a signifying system that is ultimately illusive. Especially pertinent in this scene are the elements of his vision which, for those who 'witness' the event, indicate a Spanish *armada*. He claims that someone saw an image of 'vuestro profeta' depicted on a flag; thereby marking the ship out as Christian. The warden conjures up a picture of military might as he notes: 'tan de cerca perciben / los oídos fuego y truenos, / que, por temor de las balas, / más de cuatro se pusieron / a abrazar la madre tierra: / tal fue el miedo que tuvieron' (III. 2319–24). Moreover, those who observe the approaching *armada* conclude that Don Juan 'venía a dar fin honroso / el desdichado comienzo / que su valeroso padre / comenzó en hado siniestro' (III. 2333-36). Significantly, the warden makes reference to Charles V's attack on Algiers in 1541, in which thousands of men and 150 ships were lost in a storm. Such a statement brings sharply into focus Spain's disastrous military campaigns and recalls the more recent fate of the Armada *'invincible'* in 1588. The 'fingida' *armada*, therefore, makes manifest metaphorically the mirage that is Spain's imperial power and splendour. Spain, in fact, is as impotent as the apparition which the sun creates in this scene. Interestingly, the Spanish empire was known as 'un Imperio dónde nunca se ponía el sol'; a statement which especially gained resonance in the time of Felipe II.[148] In this scene, however, the signs of Spanish glory are dismantled and the discourse of empire thereby exposed as empty and fraudulent. As news of the needless killing of thirty *cautivos* reaches the captives in the bagnio, reality invades the 'locus amoenus' and accentuates the costly mistake of having believed in the deception. In an episode which mirrors this disjunction of perspective and misconception of reality, Don Quijote battles with windmills in the opening chapters of Cervantes's novel. The knight sees giants where there are none, just as the warden sees an *armada* which does not exist. Don Quijote justifies his error of judgement: 'que las cosas de la guerra más que otras están sujetas a continua mudanza' (p. 76). Cervantes dramatises this sense of flux and instability in *Los baños* where it becomes increasingly clear that Spain's national identity is precariously founded on the fictions of the country's status as an invincible dominant power.

As my reading of *Los baños de Argel* suggests, Cervantes appears to engage more fully in this play with the fractured and disillusioned state of his early modern Spanish countrymen than in his other *comedias*. Self-conscious metatheatrical strategies permit the playwright to allegorise individual repression in the conditions of captivity. The play within the play, in particular, opens a space for interrogation which promotes sceptical evaluation of the wider issues at stake. Tristán's disruption of the pastoral drama, Guillermo's dialogue and the scene of the feigned *armada* together operate as a means to create and educate an audience capable of seeing through illusion. Cervantes's spectator is not permitted to tilt at windmills. The drama's closing lines reiterate that *Los baños* functions within the parameters of a broader ongoing project which explicitly involves the spectator: 'No de la imaginación / este trato se sacó, / que la verdad lo fraguó / bien lejos de la ficción [. . .] Y aquí da este trato fin, / que no le tiene el de Argel' (III. 3082-85; 3092-93). It is a play, then, which is fundamentally about freedom — thematised and symbolised. *Los baños* frees the spectator to recognise the extent to which their own conduct may be determined by the repression to which he/she is subordinated. Just as the captives orchestrate their escape at the end of the drama, a more critical awareness of society's capacity to contain and confine should enable the early modern Spanish subject to slip the shackles which determine his/her place in the world.

El gallardo español, *La gran sultana* and *Los baños de Argel* portray Cervantes's theatre as a stage that both reacts and counter-acts. Cervantes writes within an atmosphere of national disillusionment, and in these plays, in particular, responds to the decline of early modern Spain and the acute sense of displacement troubling the Spanish subject. There are undoubtedly darker voices at play in the *comedias de cautivos* than have previously been acknowledged. The playwright consistently disassembles the smokescreen in an attempt to create an audience that might think, question and engage more perceptively with the broader issues at hand. Hermenegildo reminds us that: 'Cervantes es maestro en el arte de abrir interrogantes'.[149] As such, Cervantes strikes the balance between optimism and pessimism even while he portrays the gaping chasm between illusion and reality.

In the captivity plays Cervantes grants a voice to the marginal and the oppressed. The peripheral individual is re-positioned centre-stage and presents a significant challenge to the early modern Spanish world view. In *El gallardo* it is the subjugated soldier who debunks over-inflated expectations to recuperate a sense of identity. Similarly, the imprisoned Spanish captive in *La gran sultana* functions as the catalyst which discloses the intolerance lurking under the guise of permissiveness, and the *cautivo* in *Los baños* boldly speaks out against the injustice of captivity. The problem of appearances and the reality they purport to represent is defied by those situated on the fringes. Cervantes's approach can be located within the context of what Egginton has called 'the minor strategy'. That is, in opposition to the major strategy which 'assumes the existence of a veil of appearances and then suggests the possibility of a space opening just beyond those appearances where truth resides', the minor strategy shows that the 'supposed purity behind the wall of appearances is already corrupted by the distinction that created it'.[150]

Cervantes's participation in the minor strategy has two pertinent functions. In the first instant, it draws attention to the playwright's own marginality and sheds some light on his 'failure' as a dramatist. As Egginton remarks, 'those who promoted the minor strategy in the seventeenth-century were in a tiny minority. The promise of a truth just beyond the veil of appearances proffered by the major strategy was powerful'.[151] From the outset, then, Cervantes had little hope of seeing his *comedias* performed considering that the balance of power rested with Lope and his followers. Nonetheless, as a minority dramatist working within the parameters of a seditious theatre, Cervantes subtly dismantled what was on offer in the seventeenth-century *corral*. Secondly, his drama offers an alternative to the messages perpetuated by those who would seek to manipulate appearances as part of an exploitative agenda. Cervantes demonstrates that any sense of stability will not be found in the representations of 'one nation, faith and destiny' projected by Spain. His theatre does not allow identification with or investment in a system which endorses appearance. This would explain why the spectator is consistently aligned with the *cautivo* and/or those who find themselves in opposition to the status quo. Thus, Cervantes's theatre takes on the very serious project of destabilising those mediums (Lope de Vega's stage, for instance) which attract and shape acquiescent followers. As such, Cervantes's non-conformist theatre actively sought to 'des-engañar' the early modern spectator.

Notes to Chapter 2

1. Antonio Rey Hazas, 'Las comedias de cautivos de Cervantes', in *Los imperios orientales en el teatro del Siglo de Oro, Actas de XVI Jornadas de Teatro Clásico, Almagro Julio de 1993*, ed. by Felipe B. Pedraza Jiménez and Rafael González Cañal (Almagro: Universidad Castilla-La Mancha y Festival de Almagro, 1994), pp. 29–56 (p. 34).
2. Camamis, *Estudios sobre el cautiverio*, p. 13.
3. Barbara Fuchs, *Passing for Spain: Cervantes and the Fictions of Identity* (Chicago: University of Illinois Press, 2003), p. 4. Anne Cruz's review of Fuchs's study surmises that it 'is a healthy sign that Renaissance scholars are finally looking to early modern Spain as a likely locus for the study of self-fashioning and the formation of the nation-state'. See <http://www.press.uillinois.edu/books/catalog/48ncy4pt9780252027819.html>.
4. E. Michael Gerli, 'Aristotle in Africa: History, Fiction, and Truth in *El gallardo español*', *Cervantes*, 15 (1995), 43–57 (p. 43).
5. Like all of Cervantes's *comedias*, it is difficult to pin down a date for the composition of *El gallardo*. The critics who have studied the play generally cannot agree on whether it was composed during Cervantes's first or second dramatic writing period. Moreover, it is surprising that the play's portrayal of Spanish confrontation with the 'other' in North Africa has not attracted the attention of postmodern critics interested in concepts of 'difference' and 'essentialism'. For instance, Fuchs examines how Cervantes's characters perform another gender or religion in order to 'challenge the attempt to identify and categorize "proper" subjects'. She does not make mention of *El gallardo* despite the fact there are frequent scenes when men and women cross-dress and also assume alternative religious identities. See *Passing for Spain*, p. 3. Vis-à-vis this line of enquiry, Anne Fastrup has recently explored cross-cultural identity in *El gallardo español*. Fastrup states that Cervantes often stages these identities 'in a space of limited State access' and analyses Don Fernando in relation to the *limited* reach of the State's power to control its subject. See 'Cross-cultural Movement in the Name of Honour: Renegades, Honour and State in Miguel de Cervantes' Barbary Plays', *Bulletin of Spanish Studies*, 89 (2012), 347–67 (p. 349).
6. See *La Numancia* in *Teatro completo*, pp. 918–91.
7. Zimic, 'Sobre la técnica dramática de Cervantes en *El gallardo español*', *Boletín de la Real Academia Española*, 54 (1974), 505–18. Zimic states that 'gran parte de la acción se nos ofrece por medio de narraciones y descripciones' (p. 506). Frederick A. De Armas, 'Los excesos de Venus y Marte en *El gallardo español*', in *Cervantes: Su obra y su mundo. Actas del I Congreso Internacional sobre Cervantes*, ed. by Manuel Criado de Val (Madrid: Edi-6, 1981), pp. 249–60.
8. Casalduero, *Sentido y forma*, p. 55.
9. Gethin Hughes, '*El gallardo español*: A Case of Misplaced Honour', *Cervantes*, 13 (1993), 65–75.
10. William A. Stapp, '*El gallardo español*: La fama como arbitrio de la realidad', in *Cervantes:*

Su obra y su mundo. Actas del I Congreso Internacional sobre Cervantes, ed. by Manuel Criado de Val (Madrid: Edi-6, 1981), pp. 261–72.
11. Minni Sawhney, 'Cervantes' Cosmopolitan *El gallardo español* during an Earlier Clash of Civilizations', *Theatralia: Revista de Teoría del Teatro*, 5 (2003), 167–75 (pp. 174–75).
12. Casalduero, *Sentido y forma* and Friedman, *The Unifying Concept*.
13. Canavaggio, *Cervantès dramaturge*, pp. 53–56.
14. Friedman, *The Unifying Concept*, p. 29 and Eric J. Kartchner, 'Dramatic Diegesis: Truth and Fiction in Cervantes's *El gallardo español*', *Yearbook of Comparative and General Literature*, 47 (1999), 25–35.
15. Cotarelo y Valledor argues that a persistent critical focus on Cervantes's work and its reproduction of historical and biographical information reduces the dramatist to a 'copiador de realidad'. See *El teatro de Cervantes*, p. 273.
16. Simerka, 'Early Modern Skepticism'. See section 1.1.
17. Gerli, 'Aristotle in Africa', pp. 46–47.
18. Gerli, 'Aristotle in Africa', p. 47.
19. Bruce Wardropper, 'Don Quixote: Story or History?', in *Critical Essays on Cervantes*, ed. by Ruth El Saffar (Boston: G. K. Hall, 1986), pp. 80–94 (p. 80).
20. Wardropper, 'Don Quixote: Story or History?', p. 82.
21. Paul Hernadi, 'Re-presenting the Past: A note on narrative historiography and historical drama', *History and Theory*, 15 (1976), 45–51 (p. 45).
22. Rokem, *Performing History*, p. 3.
23. Rokem, *Performing History*, p. 3. We should bear in mind that some of the playwright's short stories do, also, engage with history. For instance, *La española inglesa*.
24. Fuchs, *Passing for Spain*, p. 1.
25. Fuchs labels early modern Spain 'a nation in the making — by no means a fully achieved nation-state, but instead a polity in the throes of centralization and modernization, struggling to base a strong state on an older state of an ethnic or genealogical *natio*', *Passing for Spain*, p. 2.
26. Aaron Kahn's study of *La Numancia* argues that at the heart of the drama lies a message 'about the consequences of unjust imperial expansion'. *The Ambivalence of Imperial Discourse. Cervantes's La Numancia within the 'Lost Generation' of Spanish Drama (1570–90)* (Bern: Peter Lang, 2008), p. 75. Cervantes, then, was evidently preoccupied with such concerns as is also revealed in the *comedias de cautivos*.
27. Rokem, *Performing History*, p. 3.
28. Rokem, *Performing History*, p. 3.
29. Friedman, *The Unifying Concept*, p. 30.
30. Hughes, '*El gallardo español*: A Case of Misplaced Honour', p. 67.
31. Reinhart Koselleck, *Futures Past: On the Semantics of Historical Time* (Massachusetts: Massachusetts Institute of Technology, 1985), p. 132.
32. Paul Ricoeur, 'Narrative Time', *Critical Enquiry*, 7 (1980), 169–90 (p. 171).
33. John Loftis, *Renaissance Drama in England and Spain* (New Jersey: Princeton University Press, 1987), p. 6.
34. Carlos M. Gutiérrez, 'Cervantes o la relocalización del sujeto teatral', *Bulletin of the Comediantes*, 56 (2004), 289–310 (p. 290).
35. Stapp's article deals with the 'slippery' quality of 'fama' in that it is open to misinterpretation. '*El gallardo español*: La fama como arbitrio de la realidad'.
36. See Jonathan Brown, *The Golden Age of Painting in Spain* (Madrid: Nerea, 1990).
37. It should also be noted that audience conjecture is paradoxically established by a Moorish woman and by implication is, therefore, untrustworthy. This is, of course, not unlike the role which Cide Hamete Benengeli performs in the opening chapters of *Don Quijote*.

38. Jesús G. Maestro, 'Cervantes y Shakespeare: el nacimiento de la literatura metateatral', *Bulletin of Spanish Studies*, 81 (2004), 599–611 (p. 601).
39. See John A. Moore, 'Is Truth Relative for Cervantes?', *Hispania*, 44 (1961), 660–62 (p. 660).
40. Significantly, Don Fernando would appear to be more concerned with the Moor's opinion than that of his (Spanish) superiors. See Fastrup's comment on Don Fernando's desire to secure his enemy's recognition, 'Cross-cultural Movement in the Name of Honour', p. 358.
41. Canavaggio views Don Fernando's defection as a 'désobéissance momentanée' which is out of character for the gallant Spaniard. See *Cervantès Dramaturge*, p. 393. However, it is precisely because he is so lacking in character (an identity of his own) that Don Fernando defects.
42. Hughes, '*El gallardo español*: A Case of Misplaced Honour', p. 68.
43. Kartchner perceives that Guzmán helps Don Fernando to negotiate this gulf between desire and duty by manipulating his master's statement: 'Respondedle cortésmente / con el término prudente / que de vuestro ingenio fío'. See 'Dramatic Diegesis', p. 29.
44. For Francisco Márquez Villanueva, the soldier is trapped between an 'impasse entre el individualismo de la caballería y una disciplina militar a la moderna'. See *Moros, moriscos y turcos de Cervantes. Ensayos críticos* (Barcelona: Edicions Bellaterra, 2010), pp. 50–51.
45. Kartchner, 'Dramatic Diegesis', p. 31.
46. See Friedman, *The Unifying Concept*, p. 30.
47. Etienne Balibar, 'The Nation Form: History and Ideology', in *Race, Nation, Class: Ambiguous Identities*, ed. by Etienne Balibar and Immanuel Wallerstein (London: Verso, 1991), pp. 86–106 (p. 86).
48. Raymond Williams, *Marxism and Literature* (Oxford: Oxford University Press, 1977), pp. 121–22.
49. Elizabeth Davies states that the poem 'sets out to construct the fiction of a homogenous, Castilian self, in the process of attempting to suppress difference'. 'Rape and Redemption: Virués's *El Monserrate* and Reading Golden Age Foundational Myths', in *Myth and Identity in the Epic of Imperial Spain* (Missouri: University of Missouri Press, 2000), pp. 98–127 (p. 101).
50. Robledo's fate is not dissimilar to that of the rebel soldier in Calderón's *La vida es sueño*. The close of the *La vida* compels the spectator to reflect on the cyclical nature of the drama and the implications that this might have for the future stability of Segismundo's rule.
51. Claire Sponsler, *Drama and Resistance: Bodies, Goods, and Theatricality in Late Medieval England* (Minnesota: University of Minnesota Press, 1997), p. 2.
52. Fuchs, *Passing for Spain*, p. 4.
53. Kartchner, 'Dramatic Diegesis', p. 32.
54. Stapp, '*El gallardo español*: La fama como arbitrio de la realidad', p. 268.
55. Don Juan, therefore, represents a stark contrast to the audience in *El retablo de las maravillas* who would rather be deceived than admit that they cannot see the spectacle on stage.
56. Mary Malcolm Gaylord, 'Pulling Strings with Master Peter's Puppets: Fiction and History in *Don Quixote*', *Cervantes*, 18 (1998), 117–47 (pp. 127–28).
57. This observation, as made by Spadaccini with respect to *Pedro de Urdemalas*, can be just as readily applied to *El gallardo*. 'Cervantes and the Spanish comedia', p. 66.
58. See for instance Cotarelo y Valledor, *El teatro de Cervantes*.
59. See article in *El País* by Rosana Torres 2nd July 2010. <http://www.elpais.com/articulo/cultura/gran/sultana/visita/Estambul/elpepicul/20100702elpepicul_3/Tes>.

60. Ottmar Heygi, *Cervantes and the Turks: Historical Reality versus Literary Fiction in La gran sultana and El amante liberal* (Delaware: Juan de la Cuesta, 1992), p. 1.
61. Paul Lewis-Smith, 'La gran sultana Doña Catalina de Oviedo: A Cervantine Practical Joke', *Modern Language Studies*, 17 (1981), 68–81 (p. 69).
62. See Ottmar Heygi; Albert Mas, *Les turcs dans la literature espagnole de siècle d'or* (Paris: Centre des Recherches, 1967) and Canavaggio, *Cervantès dramaturge*, for studies which argue that *La gran sultana* does not 'mis-manage' its historical sources. Scholarship has associated some of *La gran sultana*'s protagonists with historical figures and it would appear that these might have functioned as the dramatist's prototypes. See Paul Lewis-Smith, 'La gran sultana Doña Catalina de Oviedo', p. 69.
63. The very title of the play alludes to the paradoxes with which a spectator must contend.
64. Lewis-Smith, 'La gran sultana', p. 69.
65. See 'Cervantes como poeta del heroismo: de la *Numancia* a *La gran sultana*', in *Memoria de la palabra: Actas del VI Congreso de la Asociación Internacional Siglo de Oro*, ed. by Maria Luisa Lobato and Francisco Domínguez Matito (Madrid; Frankfurt: Iberoamericana-Vervuert, 2004), pp. 1155–63 (p. 1162). Lewis-Smith views the drama as representative of 'idealismo nacionalista' and a 'bello sueño' which is degraded by Madrigal's speech which mocks the ignorance of the public.
66. Friedman, 'Female Presence, Male Prescience: The Creation of the Subject in *La gran sultana*', in *Estudios en homenaje a Enrique Ruiz-Fornells*, ed. by Juan Fernández Jiménez and others (Pennsylvania: Asociación de Licenciados & Doctores Españoles en Estados Unidos, 1990), pp. 218–25 (p. 224).
67. Catherine Connor (Swietlicki), 'La sexualidad, el 'orientalismo' cervantino y el caso de *La gran sultana*', in *Actas del Tercer Congreso de Hispanistas de Asia*, ed. by Hiroto Ueda (Tokyo: Asociación Asiática de Hispanistas, 1993), pp. 512–18 (p. 512). Also see Christopher B. Weimar, 'Going to extremes: Barthes, Lacan, and Cervantes' *La gran sultana*', in *Gender, Identity and Representation in Spain's Golden Age*, ed. by Anita K. Stoll and Dawn L. Smith (Lewisburg, Pennsylvania: Bucknell University Press, 2000), pp. 47–60.
68. McKendrick remarks: 'It is entirely possible that [*La gran sultana*] was not performed partly because it overstepped the bounds of decency or at least decorum [. . .] the theatre's opponents were always on the look-out for dramatic material which supported their contention that the playhouses represented a danger to public morals'. 'Writings for the stage', p. 142.
69. Barbara Fuchs, *Passing for Spain*, p. 86. See especially chapter 4, 'Passing Pleasures: Costume and Custom in "El amante liberal" and *La gran sultana*', pp. 63–86. Moisés Castillo contends that *La gran sultana* dismantles cultural centrality as Cervantes promotes 'síntesis racial' and encourages his spectator to view this as 'un acontecimiento más que no sólo se puede dar en Constantinopla, sino que se da, lo queramos o no, todos los días en la península'. 'Ortodoxia cervantina? Un análisis de *La gran sultana*, *El trato de Argel* y *Los baños de Argel*', *Bulletin of the Comediantes*, 56 (2004), 219–40 (p. 226).
70. George Mariscal, '*La gran sultana* and the issue of Cervantes's Modernity', *Revista de Estudios Hispánicos*, 28 (1994), 185–211. Susana Hernández Araico argues that in *La gran sultana* taboos of the 'other' vanish by means of love and humour. 'Estreno de *La gran sultana*: Teatro de lo otro, amor y humor', *Cervantes*, 14 (1994), 155–65.
71. Zimic, *El teatro de Cervantes*, pp. 183–84. See also Agapita Jurado Santos's study, *Tolerancia y ambigüedad en La gran sultana de Cervantes* (Kassel: Reichenberger, 1997).
72. J. Ignacio Díez Fernández, '"Sin discrepar de la verdad un punto". *La gran sultana*: ¿Un canto a la tolerancia?', *Lectura y Signo*, 1 (2006), 301–22 (pp. 303–04).
73. Hernández Araico, 'Estreno de *La gran sultana*', p. 163. María Francisca Vilches de Frutos states: 'en 1992, olvidados ya los intentos golpistas involucionistas, la sociedad

española recuperaba el orgullo de su identidad histórica como crisol de culturas, razas y religiones [...] sus miembros más activos comenzaban a preocuparse por un fenómeno que con los años acarrearía numerosas ventajas, pero también graves problemas. Me refiero a la emigración'. 'El teatro de Cervantes en la escena española contemporánea: Identidad y Vanguardia', *Anales de la Literatura Española Contemporánea*, 31 (2006), 5–39 (p. 11). See Luciano García Lorenzo for various reviews of how this 1992 production was received. '*La gran sultana* de Miguel de Cervantes: adaptación del texto y puesta en escena', *Anales Cervantinos*, 32 (1994), 117–36.

74. Adolfo Marsillach, 'Nuestro Cervantes', *Cuadernos de Teatro Clásico*, 7 (1992), 201–02. Interestingly, Pou, the play's 2010 director, claims that *La gran sultana*'s depiction of tolerance paints it as 'terriblemente moderno'.
75. See Felipe B. Pedraza Jiménez, 'El teatro mayor de Cervantes: Comentarios a contrapelo', in *Actas del VII Coloquio Internacional de la Asociación de Cervantistas*, ed. by José Ramón Fernández de Cano y Martín (El Toboso: Ayuntamiento de El Toboso, 1999), pp. 19–38 (p. 26).
76. Pedraza Jiménez, 'El teatro mayor de Cervantes', p. 28.
77. Pedraza Jiménez, 'El teatro mayor de Cervantes', p. 25 and p. 29.
78. For example see Hernández Araico, 'Estreno de *La gran sultana*', p. 156; Antonio Rey Hazas, 'Las comedias de cautivos de Cervantes'; Lewis-Smith, 'El humorismo de La gran sultana', *Donaire*, 3 (1994), 55–58 (p. 57).
79. *La española inglesa* shares many similarities with *La gran sultana*. Both works deal with the geographical displacement of a woman within the context of an amorous plot and each of the female protagonists are objectified as a 'spoil'. See Fuchs (*Passing for Spain*, pp. 64–65) who suggests that Sicily is a smokescreen for a critique of Imperial Spain in *El amante liberal*.
80. Lewis-Smith, 'La gran sultana', p. 72.
81. Francisco López Estrada, 'Vista a Oriente, la española en Constantinopla', *Cuadernos de Teatro Clásico*, 7 (1992), 31–46 (p. 36).
82. Friedman, 'Female Presence, Male Prescience', p. 222.
83. See Zimic, *El teatro de Cervantes*, p. 275.
84. El Saffar, 'Voces marginales y la visión del ser cervantino', p. 59.
85. Edwin Williamson, '*La gran sultana*: una fantasía política de Cervantes', *Donaire*, 3 (1994), 52–54 (p. 54).
86. A very blatant example of the play's intolerance is seen when Madrigal, a Spanish captive, breaks into a Jewish household and throws bacon into the stew pot. He commits this disrespectful act for no other reason than he can. I have not considered this episode given that it is repeatedly cited and analysed by critics and is obvious evidence of a world in which intolerance is the *raison d'être*.
87. Díez Fernández, 'Sin discrepar de la verdad un punto', p. 321.
88. See also *La española inglesa* in which Isabela is captured, taken to England and paraded as a 'riquísimo despojo'.
89. Mariscal, '*La gran sultana* and the issue of Cervantes's Modernity', p. 199 and p. 201.
90. Fuchs, *Passing for Spain*, p. 82.
91. Fuchs, *Passing for Spain*, p. 85.
92. Zimic contends that Catalina's jealousy is unfeigned: '[La sultana] está muy celosa: un repentino interés amoroso en una persona antes desdeñada, que surge por el mero hecho de que está manifiesta nuevas inclinaciones sentimentales, es un rasgo fundamental de la psicología amorosa'. *El teatro de Cervantes*, p. 194
93. Mariscal, '*La gran sultana* and the issue of Cervantes's Modernity', p. 201.
94. For detailed discussion of the statutes of *limpieza de sangre* see Albert A. Sicroff, *Los estatutos de limpieza de sangre: Controversias entre los siglos XV y XVII* (Madrid: Taurus,

1985). Sicroff argues that the statues are challenged in *Don Quijote* which expresses a preference for inherent rather than genealogical nobility.
95. Mariscal observes that the idea of 'limpieza de sangre' carries no cultural value for the Sultan but does not interrogate what this might mean for the contemporary audience. '*La gran sultana* and the issue of Cervantes's Modernity', p. 198.
96. Elliott comments: 'The expulsion of the Moriscos, carefully prepared, and carefully executed between 1609 and 1614, was to some extent the act of a weak Government anxious for easy popularity at a time of widespread national discontent'. See *Imperial Spain*, p. 300.
97. Friedman, 'Female Presence, Male Prescience', p. 222.
98. See Díez Fernández, 'Sin discrepar de la verdad un punto', pp. 315–16.
99. Castillo, 'Ortodoxia cervantina?', p. 220.
100. See María Antonia Garcés, *Cervantes in Algiers: A Captive's Tale* (Tennessee: Vanderbilt University Press, 2002), p. 127. It is thought that Cervantes composed *El trato* sometime between 1580–83. See Enrique Fernández, '*Los tratos de Argel*: obra testimonial, denuncia política y literatura terapéutica', *Cervantes*, 20 (2000), 7–26.
101. Willard King, 'Cervantes, El cautiverio y los renegados', *Nueva Revista de Filológia Hispánica*, 40 (1992), 279–91 (p. 284).
102. Nicholas Kanellos considers this topic in the context of two of Cervantes's *comedias*. See 'The Anti-Semitism of Cervantes' *Los baños de Argel* and *La gran sultana*: A Reappraisal', *Bulletin of the Comediantes*, 27 (1975), 48–52.
103. Américo Castro, *El pensamiento de Cervantes* (Madrid: Impr. de la librería y casa editorial Hernando, 1925), p. 306.
104. Zimic, *El teatro de Cervantes*, p. 143.
105. Canavaggio, 'La estilización del judío en *Los baños de Argel*', *Primer Acto: Cuadernos de Investigación Teatral*, 270 (1997), 129–37. Also see Or Hasson, '*Los baños de Argel*: Un análisis del tratamiento Cervantino de lo Hebreo y lo Judío desde un punto de vista Kleiniano', in *Cervantes y las religiones*, ed. by Ruth Fine and Santiago López Navia (Madrid; Frankfurt: Iberoamericana-Vervuet, 2008), pp. 473–502.
106. Anti-Semitism is, of course, a highly polemical issue. When Francisco Nieva (as part of the *Centro Dramático Nacional*) staged *Los baños* in Madrid in 1979, he elected to leave out the scenes in which Tristán ridicules the Jewish man. Nieva won the *Premio Nacional de Teatro* for his production.
107. Castillo, 'Ortodoxia cervantina?', p. 220.
108. Javier Irigoyen-García, '"La música ha sido hereje": Pastoral Performance, Moorishness, and Cultural Hybridity in *Los baños de Argel*', *Bulletin of the Comediantes*, 62 (2010), 45–62. The dismantling of 'centralidad culural' is also the focus of another recent article by the critic: 'El problema morisco en *Los baños de Argel*, de Miguel de Cervantes: De renegados a mártires cristianos', *Revista Canadiense de Estudios Hispánicos*, 32 (2008), 421–28.
109. The reasoning for Allen's and López-Vázquez's theory operates on opposing premises. See Allen, 'The division into acts of Cervantes's *Los baños de Argel*', *Symposium*, 17 (1963), 42–49 and Alfredo Rodríguez López-Vázquez, '*Los baños de Argel* y su estructura en cuatro actos', *Hispania*, 77 (1994), 207–14.
110. Kenneth Stackhouse, 'Beyond Performance: Cervantes's Algerian Plays, *El trato de Argel* and *Los baños de Argel*', *Bulletin of the Comediantes*, 52 (2000), 7–30.
111. Maryrica Ortiz Lottman, 'The Call of the Natural World in *Los baños de Argel*', *Bulletin of the Comediantes*, 56 (2004), 345–66.
112. Jorge Kühni, 'Aspectos de la realidad y la ilusión, juegos semánticos del metateatro en *Los baños de Argel* (1585-1595) de Miguel de Cervantes', in *El teatro dentro del teatro: Cervantes, Lope, Tirso y Calderón*, pp. 49–58 (p. 58). Although Kühni's is the only

concentrated study on this aspect of the play, other critics do make reference to the metatheatrical elements of the play. See for instance: Canavaggio, 'Cervantine Variations on the Theme of Theater within the Theater', in *Critical Essays on Cervantes*, ed. by Ruth El Saffar (Boston: G. K. Hall, 1986), pp. 147–62 and Maestro, 'Cervantes y Shakespeare'. Interestingly, Arboleda's *Teoría y Formas del Metateatro* makes no mention of *Los baños*. In a recent article, Irigoyen-García examines the drama's interlude in light of the instability of religious and national identities in the play. In the context of Spain's projection of an image of homogenous national identity, the critic argues that the play within the play 'deconstructs pastoral as one of the idealizing ideologies that promote the politics of ethnic and cultural cleansing in Spain'. See '"La música ha sido hereje"', p. 46.

112. Garcés, *Cervantes in Algiers*, p. 1. Garcés's work specifically explores the relation between fiction and memory as she considers 'the afterlife of trauma in Cervantes, especially its effects on his literary production', p. 3.

114. For instance, see Michael McGaha, 'Hacia la verdadera historia del cautivo Miguel de Cervantes', *Revista Canadiense de Estudios Hispánicos*, 20 (1996), 540–46.

115. Fernández, '*Los tratos de Argel*', p. 7. Mary Gaylord Randel notes: 'So striking is the presence of autobiographical references [in Cervantes's writings] that readers have often succumbed to the temptation to peer through the veil of fiction for glimpses of the historical Cervantes'. 'Cervantes' Portrait of the Artist', *Cervantes*, 3 (1983), 83–102 (p. 83).

116. Stackhouse comments that the play is 'very forceful, yet considering the actual conditions he knew in Algiers, Cervantes's restraint in presenting the fate of Christian slaves in Africa is remarkable'. 'Beyond Performance', p. 18. Again, we must carefully consider the relationship between literary depiction and reality. For Louise Fothergill-Payne, the forcefulness of the play emerges from Cervantes's desire to compete with Lope's *Los cautivos de Argel*. See '*Los tratos de Argel, Los cautivos de Argel y Los baños de Argel*: Tres "trasuntos" de un "asunto"', in *El mundo del teatro español en su Siglo de Oro*, ed. by José M. Ruano de la Haza (Ottawa: Dovehouse, 1989), pp. 177–84 (p. 181).

117. The brutality of *Los baños de Argel* makes the play very different from the vision of captivity as depicted in *La gran sultana* and *El gallardo español* where the Spaniard, for the most part, is physically free. Cervantes had no direct experience of Constantinople where *La gran sultana* is set and he visited Oran, the setting of *El gallardo* as an emissary for the Spanish Crown in 1581. It is, however, his first hand-experience as a prisoner in Africa which influences *Los baños de Argel*.

118. Rey Hazas, 'Las comedias de cautivos de Cervantes', p. 37. We must also consider the fact that although many captives were ransomed and allowed to return to Spain, they were often treated with suspicion and made to face inquisitors who suspected *cautivos* of having denounced their faith.

119. Stackhouse, 'Beyond Performance', p. 17.

120. Garcés, *Cervantes in Algiers*, p. 17. María Francisca Vilches de Frutos draws attention to the 'contemporaneidad' of *Los baños*'s message. She comments that the drama is 'una acérrima defensa de la libertad y de la tolerancia'. See 'El teatro de Cervantes en la escena española contemporánea', p. 8.

121. Juan Goytisolo, *Crónicas sarracinas* (Barcelona: Ibérica, 1982), p. 59.

122. 'The spectacular victory of the Christian forces at Lepanto in 1571 was to epitomize for contemporaries all that was most glorious in the crusade against Islam. It was an eternal source of pride to those who, like Miguel de Cervantes, had fought in the battle and could show the scars of their wounds, and of grateful wonder to the millions who saw in it a divine deliverance of Christendom from the power of the oppressor [. . .] But, in fact, the battle of Lepanto proved a curiously deceptive triumph, and the attempt to follow it up was peculiarly unsuccessful'. Elliott, *Imperial Spain*, p. 234.

123. See my introduction to *La gran sultana* for further analysis on this type of strategy as employed by Cervantes in the play and also in his exemplary novel, *La española inglesa*.
124. Goytisolo, *Crónicas sarracinas*, p. 61.
125. Goytisolo argues: 'ningún gran escritor sino Cervantes vivió el problema [el tema islámico] desde dentro ni supo dotarlo de una dimensión creadora tan genial como ambigua', *Crónicas sarracinas*, p. 59.
126. Kühni, 'Aspectos de la realidad y la ilusión', p. 56.
127. Alfredo Hermenegildo, 'Mirar en Cadena: Artificios de la Metateatralidad Cervantina', in *Cervantes y la puesta en escena de la sociedad de su tiempo* (Actas del Coloquio de Montreal, 1997), ed. by Catherine Poupeney Hart, Alfredo Hermenegildo and César Oliva (Murcia: Universidad de Murcia, 1999), pp. 77–91 (p. 79).
128. Cervantes, *Obra Completa*, ed. by Florencio Sevilla Arroyo and Antonio Rey Hazas (Madrid: Alianza, 1996–99), p. xi.
129. Celis Sánchez, 'Planos de comunicación en las comedias cervantinas', p. 91.
130. Celis Sánchez, 'Planos de comunicación en las comedias cervantinas', p. 93.
131. For Kühni, Tristán 'consigue emplear el juego de las máscaras y de los espejos con tanta perfección que llega a confundir y a embaucar, mediante su virtuosidad verbal, a Caurali'. 'Aspectos de la realidad y la ilusión', p. 57.
132. Kühni, 'Aspectos de la realidad y la ilusión', p. 57.
133. According to Covarrubias, the expression 'aquí fue Troya' connotes disastrous failure and defeat. *Tesoro de la lengua*, p. 979.
134. Iser, *The Act of Reading: A Theory of Aesthetic Response* (London: Routledge and Kegan Paul, 1978), p. 28.
135. Iser, *The Act of Reading*, p. 29.
136. Thacker remarks that Cervantes, amongst others, nostalgically misrepresented Rueda's theatre. See *A Companion to Golden Age Theatre*, p. 124.
137. Carroll Johnson comments that in the prologue: 'Cervantes se identifica con Rueda en un grupo un tanto arcaizante de dramaturgos a la vieja manera que prefieren guardar el arte, frente a Lope de Vega y sus secuaces de la comedia nueva, que prefieren abandonarlo'. See 'El arte viejo de hacer teatro', p. 250.
138. Jewish scripture speaks of the dog in negative and derogatory terms. The sexton, therefore, uses this slur to link the unnamed Jew with something he would find objectionable.
139. The boys speak in *lingua franca* in this scene. See chapter 41 of *Don Quijote I* (*historia del cautivo*) for a description of this dialect which represents a mix of languages spoken in North Africa.
140. Rey Hazas, 'Las comedias de cautivos de Cervantes', p. 36.
141. It is possible that the colloquy is one called *Gila*, published by Timoneda in 1567. See Rey Hazas and Sevilla Arroyo, *Teatro completo*, p. 257.
142. Canavaggio, 'Cervantine Variations on the Theme of the Theater', p. 148.
143. Irigoyen-García, '"La música ha sido hereje"', p. 54.
144. Irigoyen-García, '"La música ha sido hereje"', p. 55.
145. See the introduction to section 1.3 for an analysis of those readings which deal with the rustic scenes in *La casa de los celos*.
146. Barbara Mujica, *Iberian Pastoral Characters* (Washington: Scripta Humanistica, 1986), p. 173.
147. Space does not permit a fuller investigation of how pastoral here, and in other Cervantine works, emerges as a locus of investigation of selfhood and, therefore, a site of liberation. I have briefly touched on this in *La casa de los celos* and it is certainly a legitimate and fruitful area of exploration as demonstrated by Rosalie Hernández-Pecoraro's recent study *Bucolic Metaphors*.

148. See Encarnación de la Torre García, 'Los Austrias y el poder: la imagen en el siglo XVII', *Historia y Comunicación Social*, 5 (2000), 13–29 (p. 16). The solar trope was often associated with the king in Golden-Age Spain. Lope de Vega's *La Circe* (1624) addresses Olivares in the opening section and depicts him as moon to Felipe IV's sun. Olivares actively promoted the image of Felipe IV as 'rey planeta'; a king who would usher in a new Golden-Age. See Jonathan Brown and J. H. Elliott, *A Palace for a King: the Buen Retiro and the Court of Philip IV* (New Haven; London: Yale University Press, 1980), p. 33.
149. Alfredo Hermenegildo, *La 'Numancia' de Cervantes* (Madrid: Sociedad General Española de Librería, 1976), p. 43.
150. William Egginton, 'The Baroque as a Problem of Thought', *Publications of the Modern Language Association of America*, 124 (2009), 143–49 (pp. 144–45). The theorist sees Cervantes as belonging to the 'minor strategy' and employs *El retablo de las maravillas* as a case study.
151. Egginton, 'The Baroque as a Problem of Thought', p. 147.

CHAPTER 3

◦∼◦

Shaping the Self in *El rufián dichoso* and *Pedro de Urdemalas*

> 'Yo también, que soy un leño, príncipe y papa me sueño, emperador y monarca, y aún mi fantasía abarca de todo el mundo a ser dueño'
>
> *Pedro de Urdemalas*

Cervantes's *El rufián dichoso* and *Pedro de Urdemalas* are *comedias* which 'sit outside' easy categorisation. *El rufián* has traditionally been perceived as a *comedia de santos* and *Pedro de Urdemalas* as a pseudo-picaresque play. Nonetheless, as this chapter will elucidate, they have more in common than has been realised. What connects these plays, in particular, is their protean *pícaro* protagonists. Despite the fact that scholarship has conventionally viewed Cervantes and the picaresque as incongruous, something with which I will engage more fully in the analysis which follows, it is in the characterisation of the plays' protagonists that *El rufián dichoso* and *Pedro de Urdemalas* play on and with the picaresque genre. Both Cristóbal de Lugo and Pedro de Urdemalas exemplify the *theatrum mundi* motif, as artists who persistently create, forge and bring new 'realities' into being.

What is particularly significant about the protagonists of these plays is a perverse sense of self-fashioning. They experience and express stable selfhood in the face of life's fluctuations and instabilities. As we will see, what sets them apart from the conventional *pícaro* and typical Golden-Age anti-heroes is that Lugo and Pedro negotiate their situation and circumstances in performance without appearing to lose any sense of individuality. What is conveyed by the plays is that life itself is a set of performances which requires astute aptitude for acting, sharp perception and the ability to distinguish between reality and illusion.

The following analysis of these plays will, therefore, deal with a key paradox at the heart of the Baroque. That is, the 'problem of truth as a function of appearances'.[1] In other words, models and representations of truth may, in fact, be illusions which project a veneer of certainty. In these *comedias*, Cervantes's protagonists play on this instability in order to conjure up spectacles which their audiences readily accept as reality. However, Lugo and Pedro utilise their respective stages in very distinct ways. For *El rufián*, Lugo, *parecer* is the hallmark of his exploitative agenda. For Pedro, however, the stage serves its purpose for a moment of time, but is not permitted to deceive indefinitely. As such, the men are two very different creators through whom Cervantes presents a unique vision of how a differently conceived theatre might have the potential to interpret and question reality.

El rufián dichoso and *Pedro de Urdemalas* are, therefore, highly self-conscious dramas which illuminate Cervantes's preoccupation with art, with much to say about the artistic process on stage; how it functions, its potential influence and, particularly, the effect it might wield on the receiver. This approach will engage with questions concerning the validity of the stage's representations and interrogate how the seventeenth-century Spanish spectator might reflect upon and construct their experience of a world in which appearance disguises itself as something more credible.

3.1 'O sé rufián, o sé santo': Transformative Craft(iness) in *El rufián dichoso*

El rufián dichoso is Cervantes's only *comedia de santos*. As such, it has attracted considerable attention. To date, scholars have tended to focus on the play's hagiographic sources and content.[2] Considering both the condemnation which is made of religious theatre in the *Quijote* and Cervantine theatre's confrontation with the *comedia nueva*, it is surprising that the dramatist's dialogue with religious drama, a genre in which Lope was the prominent force, has remained unexplored until recently.[3] Spadaccini and Talens observe that *El rufián dichoso* deviates from the standard model of a hagiographic drama as practiced by Lope and his followers.[4] Childers has since offered a more sustained approach which views Cervantes's theatre as operating against the grain of established ideology (the Inquisition, theological discourse) and against Lope's drama which promotes the Counter-Reformation and the *comedia nueva* as 'separate but ultimately mutually reinforcing projects'.[5] Childers prioritises the inherently theatrical nature of sainthood and argues that the play depicts sainthood 'as a series of performances'.[6] *El rufián*'s protagonist, Cristóbal de Lugo, is deconstructed as a saint and replaced by a figure that merely represents the life of a converted sinner. In short, Childers sees Lugo as a role-player who dons interchangeable masks according to the situation in which he finds himself.

This self-conscious practice implies a process of self-fashioning or, in other words, the invention and performance of an identity; traits which are often associated with the picaresque. Although Childers acknowledges that Lugo 'uses picaresque techniques' in his life as a converted rogue, his focus is not on Lugo as a picaresque subject.[7] This is generally reflective of *El rufián*'s critical appraisal to date which has tended to identify the picaresque as a negative denominator restricted to the first act and has not explored the relationship between the protagonist and the genre beyond that. Zimic, for example, has observed: 'aunque el protagonista frecuente con preferencia a los pícaros y actúe a menudo como ellos, empeñándose en superarlos en la conducta impudente y antisocial, no tiene, sin embargo nada esencial en su personalidad que lo identifique como verdadero pícaro o rufián'.[8] Canavaggio draws a comparison between Lugo and *Guzmán de Alfarache* within the theological framework of the notion of free will, while Kartchner connects Lugo with the picaresque but offers no interrogation of the elements which designate the protagonist as *pícaro*.[9] Connections between the play and the picaresque have been, therefore, only superficially studied and can be best understood in the light of influential Cervantine criticism which has documented Cervantes's association with the genre in ambiguous terms. The outcome is an argument which has persuaded critics to accept that no palpable relationship exists between the dramatist and the genre.

Américo Castro was the first to express the opinion that Cervantes cannot be considered a picaresque author.[10] This judgement was extended in a seminal article by Carlos Blanco Aguinaga which, according to Peter Dunn, was 'decisive in convincing a generation of readers that Cervantes and picaresque were absolutely incompatible'.[11] Blanco Aguinaga contends: 'Cervantes no escribió jamás una novela picaresca [. . .] porque su manera de ver el mundo y de novelar, es decir, su realismo, es esencialmente antagónico al de los autores de las picarescas más famosas'.[12] Nonetheless, more recent criticism deems Blanco Aguinaga's judgement rash; and offers qualifying arguments which point to picaresque elements in Cervantes's work, highlighting in particular the importance of parody in the creation of Cervantes's 'picaresque' texts.[13] Dunn's view is typical of this approach, arguing that although Cervantes rejected many of the aesthetic, ideological and philosophical elements which are synonymous with the foundational picaresque texts,[14] *novelas ejemplares* such as *Rinconete y Cortadillo* and *La ilustre fregona* are testament to 'a bricolage of picaresque formal and narrative techniques'.[15] Manuel Durán takes this further:

> Cervantes makes use of fragments, materials taken from the picaresque quarry, without building a picaresque house for his own characters. Since he does not reject picaresque materials, for he finds them useful and much in demand among his contemporary readers, and yet he considers them ultimately unacceptable, debasing, even abhorrent, he is forced to neutralise them the best way he can.[16]

Helen Reed's study contests this 'counter' picaresque stance and engages with the feature which she believes distinguishes Cervantes's picaresque from that of others:

> The fact that Cervantes frequently brings his *pícaros* to the stage indicates in the most obvious way *the theatricality of his vision of the picaresque* [. . .] As

fictional characters, Cervantes' *pícaros* often become actors or are otherwise engaged in the theatre; on a more philosophical level, they play out their lives on the world stage self-consciously (emphasis mine).[17]

According to Reed, Cervantes created a 'metapicaresque' through which the *pícaro* can be seen to embrace and abandon roles 'whose scripts are based on previous picaresque texts'.[18] Reed's study makes only passing reference to *El rufián dichoso*, commenting that elements of *Rinconete y Cortadillo* are repeated in its first act. The drama, however, merits a more sustained interrogation which would allow us to reconcile both Reed's and Childers's analysis. The former's theory of theatricality, viewed in the light of Childers's interpretation of *El rufián*'s protagonist as a consummate role-player, serves to illuminate Cervantes's concern with how the *pícaro* plays out his roles on the world's stage or, in other words, with the 'performability' of the picaresque. In *El rufián*, Cervantes extracts theatrical elements from narrative, transfers them to the stage, thereby exploiting the potential of the stage and its actor/audience dynamic to dramatise the implications of manipulative dramatic art. Thus the picaresque becomes the vehicle through which the very processes of art are displayed. The ramifications of these manipulable processes are particularly evident in Acts II and III in which Lugo fashions a false selfhood via a highly calculating and unscrupulous linguistic strategy. The *pícaro*'s use, and misuse, of speech facilitates his 'transformation' from *rufián* to *santo*; a central aspect of the drama which I explore in greater depth elsewhere.[19]

Cervantes's *pícaro* is, therefore, a role-player who carves out an identity which sees him exchange his sense of displacement for a role which demands deference and social recognition, seeking 'la social estimación visible' which Maravall sees as fundamental to the *pícaro*.[20] Lugo, as will be argued here, does not fit the conventional portrayal of the *pícaro* who flits from master to master seeking to *medrar*. He is, however, characterised by a trait which, according to Marcel Bataillon, is synonymous with all *pícaros*: 'su insolente usurpación de identidades honradas'.[21] Cervantes, in *El rufián*, subverts both this fundamental component and the idea of the *pícaro* as a peripheral character living in society's underworld. He creates a protagonist who not only performs a representation of the identity he has usurped in order to assume a vitally central social role but who, significantly, does not lose sight of 'quién es' — *rufián*, not *santo*.

Critics are almost unanimous about Lugo's conversion as evidence of genuine repentance.[22] Only Stapp disputes Lugo's religious experience as 'authentic' and asserts that the ruffian retains his prideful nature: 'sigue siendo el hombre orgulloso, lidiando en hábitos de religioso'.[23] For Stapp the spiritual transformation is merely an illusion created by the protagonist. Developing Stapp's view, I will argue that in the context of Lugo's performance as *pícaro*, religious discourse replaces material and financial gain as the medium which disguises his delinquent character. Throughout Act I intertextual triggers support the notion of a relationship between the drama and picaresque genre. Significantly, these triggers signpost and anticipate the non-redemption of the *pícaro* protagonist. This deliberately self-reflexive device dialogues with, and deconstructs, the play's dramatic (and artistic) processes. Analysis of Act I will, therefore, allow us to observe how Cervantes's *comedia* engages in a type of meta-communication. As we will see, Cervantes employs such a strategy not only to alert his audience to the nuanced messages at play, but to the act of representation itself.[24]

The 'Performing' pícaro

Early twentieth-century criticism tended to focus on Act I of *El rufián dichoso* as a showcase for Cervantes's writing abilities. For Schevill and Bonilla, it represented: 'lo mejor que la pluma de Cervantes ha escrito, por su variado lenguaje, por su brío, por la incomparable pintura de los caracteres, por la naturalidad del diálogo, por el realismo del ambiente'.[25] The 'idealistic' character of the latter half of the drama was condemned in comparison: 'el primer acto hubiera constituído por sí solo un excelente entremés'.[26] This reading of a schism between Act I and Acts II and III has since been denounced by scholars such as Casalduero[27] and, more recently, by Zimic who censures the opinion that the second and third acts are less convincing:

> el sentido fundamental de *El rufián dichoso* se realiza precisamente por el contraste áspero, totalmente intencionado, entre los episodios "realistas" de la primera jornada y los "idealistas" de los dos siguientes; entre el ambiente sevillano del pecado y el claustral del arrepentimiento, del recogimiento y de la apoteosis espiritual.[28]

Undoubtedly, recognition of this 'shift' in the play is fundamental to an understanding of Cervantes's intentions. However, I would argue that the gulf between the 'realistic' and 'idealistic' is not indicative of the protagonist's spiritual metamorphosis, as Zimic would have us understand, but reflects Lugo's successful usurpation of a saintly identity. Act I determines our response to Lugo's transformation and consequent conduct in light of the picaresque elements which are encoded throughout the opening scenes.

The word '*pícaro*' is used only once in the first act and is spoken by Lugo in defiant reply to a *corchete*'s order:

Corchete: ¡Téngase a la Justicia!
Lugo: ¡Tente, pícaro! (I. 27–28)

An *alguacil*, who is also in attendance, is made aware of Lugo's identity by the *corchete* who asks: '¿No conoce que es el señor Cristóbal el delinque?' (I. 32). Throughout the opening act, Lugo is, in fact, depicted as synonymous with criminal behaviour. As Parker observed, Cervantes's protagonist is 'an offender against the moral and civil laws, [...] someone who is dishonourable and anti-social'.²⁹ It transpires that Lugo has been confined to prison on numerous occasions as a result of his reprobate ways. His master, Tello de Sandoval, states: 'Siete veces te he librado de la cárcel' (I. 787). Lugo's misbehaviour is so extreme that he is labelled 'Satanás' (I. 844), 'el diablo' (I. 37) and 'un Barrabás' (I. 56). His criminal conduct, then, is so counter-productive and oppressive that it is symbolic of hell itself. Act I, in fact, represents a sort of hell on earth; a sordid environment which is peopled by law-breakers, prostitutes and *pícaros* who epitomise the under-classes of Sevillan society.³⁰ It is a world reminiscent of the base atmosphere of Fernando de Rojas's *La Celestina*. Lugo's song in Act I refers to the protagonist of Rojas's work: 'Escucha, la que veniste / de la jerezana tierra / a hacer a Sevilla guerra / en cueros, como valiente; [. . .] la que en vieja y en astuta / da quinao a Celestina;' (I. 567–70; 583–84). Moreover, Lugo manifests characteristics similar to those of Celestina. For instance, he displays the same reckless attitude exhibited by Rojas's protagonist who persistently exhorts others to pursue happiness and procure pleasure; advice which does not consider the moral implications of such behaviour: 'Por deleyte: semejable es, como seays en edad dispuestos para todo linaje de plazer, en que más los moços que los viejos se juntan, assí como para jugar, para vestir, para burlar, para comer y bever, para negociar amores junctos de compaña'.³¹ In the immoral world represented in Act I of *El rufián*, civil laws are broken by Lugo and Lagartija and rules of propriety are violated by Antonia, a prostitute and by the *dama*, a married woman who desires Lugo as her lover. Lugo's world, then, is lawless and his disparaging attitude toward authoritative bodies constitutes a picaresque mentality. Lugo must serve somebody in order to live, but he infuses this service with a roguery which is redolent of disrespect. Having managed to escape incarceration on account of the fact his master is an inquisitor, he revels in social disorder without fear of recrimination and treats his boss with contempt (I. 832–44). In Act I, authority is given a superficial representation in the form of an *alguacil* who occupies little space on-stage and rapidly loses patience with Lugo's anti-social behaviour. He makes almost no attempt to challenge Lugo and leaves the scene exasperated, willing to leave the protagonist to his own devices. In short, the first act depicts an anarchic environment where Lugo is free and 'freed' to rebel against authority and to take pleasure in his lack of responsibility.

Lugo's confrontational and aggressive conduct mirrors that of the archetypal *pícaro*. His behaviour, in fact, stems from a desire to escape his lowly and humble origins. Act I particularly depicts Lugo's reaction to his background, much in the same way the opening chapters of *El buscón* detail the shame felt by Pablos on learning that his father is a thief and his mother a prostitute and witch.³² *El rufián*'s protagonist exemplifies the picaresque rupture with origin and family and, as we have already identified, with social responsibilities. Although the notion of rupture is essential to realising social integration, Lugo paradoxically becomes 'other' than what he is in order to be perceived as who he wants to be, which results in the deception of others. Lugo moves through life motivated by an inherent need to escape the past by fabricating an alternate identity. Especially concerned with forging an identity which will ensure that he no longer lives under the shadow of his father and employer, he exhibits 'un fuerte complejo de inferioridad personal'.[33] This is supported by a telling moment in which the rogue laments: 'Que sólo me respeten por mi amo / y no por mí, no sé esta maravilla; [...] Cuelgue mi padre de su puerta el ramo, / despoje de su jugo a Manzanilla, / conténtese en su humilde y bajo oficio' (I. 73–74; 77–79). It is clear, then, that Lugo's behaviour masks insecurity and a feeling of displacement. He rejects a peripheral role and desires to form part of established society.

Aside from the traits which Lugo shares with stock *pícaros*, the possibility is presented that the protagonist may spend his future and thus, the remaining acts of the drama, in New Spain; a place to which *El buscón*'s Pablos also flees to escape the consequences of crime. Tello remarks upon the prospect on two occasions: 'Mas lo mejor es quitalle / de aquesta tierra y llevalle / a Méjico' (I. 531–33) and '¡Bien iré a la Nueva España / cargado de ti, malino' (I. 854–55). The idea that Lugo will move to the New World is also implied by the *padre*: 'Nuevo español bravonel / con tus bravatas bizarras / me has librado de las garras / de aquel tacaño Luzbel' (I. 985–88). The suggestion of Lugo's departure from Seville to Mexico parallels the conclusion of *El buscón* when the reader is informed of Pablos's decision to leave for the Indies. However, Pablos does not manage to attain the new beginning which he craves and the *pícaro*'s purgatorial position is summarised in the haunting Senecan line with which the novel closes: 'Y fueme peor, como v. m. verá en la segunda parte, pues nunca mejora su estado quien muda solamente de lugar, y no de vida y costumbres'.[34] Kartchner argues that in *El rufián dichoso*: 'the New World becomes a place where true transformations are possible, where *pícaros* can become saints, where sinners can be exalted, where men can rise from socially restrictive circumstances of their birth to become famous, powerful, and internally changed'.[35] The critic acknowledges, however, that Cervantes's narrative does not always represent the New World in such a positive light. Speaking of *El celoso extremeño*, Kartchner observes that Carrizales leaves the New World 'with no indication of having left it better than he found it' and that 'even in Spain he dies a lonely, dishonoured, miserable man [...] remembered for his weakness — his jealousy'.[36] An 'internal' change is also in no way representative of the 'new life' of *El buscón*'s protagonist. In the context of Lugo's picaresque behaviour and attitude it is, therefore, entirely possible that relocation to Mexico may not connote any possibility of reform. Kartchner's argument does not consider the picaresque dimensions of the protagonist's characterisation and how this might impinge on the viewer's understanding of his impending immigration. These picaresque elements emblematise the conventional *pícaro*'s failed attempt to fabricate a fresh start in life precisely because he is resistant to 'internal change'. Such conduct is also exemplified by

Lazarillo de Tormes whose journey from *pícaro* to town-crier is only apparently progressive. The acquisition of social and economic ascent results in moral descent as Lázaro is willing to turn a blind eye to the relationship between his wife and the archpriest. He attains a semblance of respectability and economic security at the expense of becoming a cuckold. Unlike Pablos or Lazarillo, however, Lugo engages only superficially with façade.

Cervantes's ruffian departs from the conventional portrayal of the *pícaro* in that his aspiration for social recognition is not bound up with material and financial gain. Quevedo's Pablos, for instance, feigns noble ancestry by tipping his hat to gentlemen in Madrid and is intent on getting his father's money in order that he might finance his future. The *pícaro*'s single focus on material concerns is also often depicted through a lack of food. Lugo is much less concerned with hunger or accruing wealth than with his powerlessness to control the way in which others perceive him. In *El rufián* an appetite for food is transformed into an appetite for control and domination. Unconcerned with the *accoutrements* of society, Lugo gambles his money, offers his last *real* to the needy and refuses money from the wealthy husband of the *dama* (I. 435–38). Moreover, unlike Lázaro or Pablos, Lugo is neither motivated by economic nor social mobility. His desires are summarised in his vow that: 'yo haré que salga de mí un bramo / que pase de los muros de Sevilla [. . .] yo seré famoso en mi ejercicio' (I. 75–76, 80). Wardropper aptly comments that: 'el móvil del rufián es el deseo de fama'.[37] For Lugo, 'fama' connotes recognition or, in other words, acknowledgement of what he sees as his worth and importance.[38] His vow to be 'famoso' demonstrates Lugo's refusal to be immobilised by his state of affairs; a determination to be controller of his circumstances rather than to be controlled by them. Pablos and Lázaro, however, are ironically enslaved to social codes and values; Pablos (in the wake of murder and in company of a prostitute) is unable to break free of the corrupt system he paradoxically longed to be a part of and Lázaro (the cuckolded husband of the Archpriest's mistress) gains 'honra' stripped of integrity and reduced to the level of finance.

David Boruchoff's analysis of Cervantes's treatment of free will in the *novelas ejemplares* proposes that material and social factors place constraints upon freedom.[39] Boruchoff's interpretation of *novelas* such as *Rinconete y Cortadillo*, *La gitanilla* and *La ilustre fregona* highlights how freedom is defined by the negation of social convention or, in other words, by absence. For example, *La ilustre fregona*'s Carriazo, who leaves home because he is 'llevado de una inclinación picaresca, sin forzarle a ello algún mal tratamiento que sus padres le hiciesen, sólo por su gusto y antojo, se desgarró' is described by Boruchoff as 'free, not only of the social constraints that typically bind "decent" society, but also of the determinism and misery [. . .] that picaresque precursors such as Lázaro de Tormes would have us see in their adventures'.[40] In light of this argument, Lugo can be interpreted as unshackled by social and corporeal concerns and, as a result, Cervantes's *pícaro* is able to resist subjugation by the picaresque lifestyle. Lugo is disconnected from the socio-economic context of the picaresque and is free to make a wilful decision to become what he wants. For Boruchoff, this is, 'the essence of free will or, more properly, free choice (*liberum arbitrium, libre albedrío*), an imperative that consists in the capacity of all human beings to distinguish and, therefore, choose between right and wrong, and also in the power to act upon this decision'.[41] Lugo's determination to forge his own identity demonstrates a high degree of inner freedom which, according to Durán, 'is always lacking in the true picaresque hero'.[42] Cervantes grants his protagonist license to create his own path in life, thus emphasising the individuality of the subject. Lugo is not interested in 'collective' fashioning but rather focuses on subjectivity. He cloaks this essential self in guises and controlled performances in order to attain power and control. Cervantes's *pícaro* is distinct, therefore, from the archetypal *pícaro* who gradually vanishes as an individual and disintegrates into role or social status. For instance, *pícaros* often engage with the stage to perform roles and identities as is fitting to their particular situation. Quevedo's *pícaro*, Pablos, becomes so increasingly entrenched in illusion, always casting himself as the leading role, that he is incapable of discerning what is real. In short, Cervantes's protagonist is a self-fashioned individual who is free to forge a destiny of his own choosing and making.

A central component of the performance which Lugo will stage in Acts II and III is insincere engagement with religious devotion. Significantly, the religious elements of Act I are completely subsumed and nullified by Lugo's picaresque character. The protagonist's self-interested nature is exposed through his treatment of a blind man to whom he gives money in anticipation of reward: 'Las ánimas me llevan cuanto tengo; / mas yo tengo esperanza que algún día / lo tienen de volver ciento por uno' (I. 646–48). Cristóbal nonchalantly comments that his religious activities carry little personal importance and that his concern for souls in purgatory constitutes a desire that they might one day come to his aid: 'Estas y otras cosas tales / hago por mi pasatiempo, / demás que rezo algún tiempo / los psalmos penitenciales; / y, aunque peco de ordinario, / pienso, y ello será ansí, / dar buena cuenta de mí / por las de aqueste rosario' (I. 814–21). For Varas, Lugo's defence of the *padre* and reluctance to be involved with the *dama* or Antonia, redeem his ruffian behaviour: 'sirven para desarrollar la ascendencia del rufián hacia la santidad de una manera verosímil y artística'.[43] Nevertheless, rather than view Lugo's religious activity as a means through which Cervantes creates a seamless conversion from sinner to saint, developing Stapp's view of 'caridad militar' serves to elicit the improbability of Lugo's redemption.[44] This interpretation is reinforced by the fact that Lugo's insubordinate attitude is reminiscent of that of another trickster from Seville, Don Juan; a figure whose anti-social ways meet with destruction as opposed to salvation.[45] Both Lugo and Don Juan hold in contempt the divine powers which may ultimately punish them for their rebellious ways. Lugo's approach toward his insubordinate behaviour is outlined by Tello's probing questions: 'Dime, simple: ¿y tú no ves / que desa tu plata y cobre, / es dar en limosna al pobre / del puerco hurtado los pies? / Haces a Dios mil ofensas, / como dices, de ordinario, / ¿y con rezar un rosario / sin más, ir al cielo piensas?' (I. 822–29). Don Juan also lives in wilful disobedience of civil and moral laws, despite admitting that he realises death will be his ultimate reward: 'si el galardón en la muerte / tan largo me lo guardáis' (III. 119–20). Like Lugo, the nobleman is warned that his recalcitrant ways will incur divine punishment.

The two men also share a common disdain for others which is brought more sharply into focus in their relationships with women. Don Juan seduces women with fraudulent promises of marriage in return for sexual favours and spares little thought for their honour. Although Lugo does not become involved with Antonia or the *dama*, his attitude toward them is also one of derision. Clearly Lugo defies the characterisation of philanderer. However, his seemingly abnormal behaviour should be analysed in relation to his driving ambition.[46] Lugo categorically rejects the *dama*, but this rejection is not on account of her marital status, for Lugo possesses no moral compass. He makes no attempt to conceal his lack of interest interest and his would-be lover wonders at his apathy: '¿Para qué arrugas la frente / y alzas las cejas? ¿Qué es esto?' (I. 295–96). Lugo's indifferent behaviour is a clear reflection of his arrogance. He attempts to dissuade the woman by emphasising his roughish ways and base background: 'Yo soy un pobre criado' (I. 311), 'ocúpome en bajas cosas' (I. 319), 'soy tan terrible' (I. 320). Zimic rightly comments that we should not consider that Lugo sincerely believes his lowliness to be an impediment to a relationship.[47] In Zimic's opinion, Lugo merely uses his origins as an excuse to avoid any sort of entanglement which may hinder his ultimate goal. However, the *dama*'s reply is very telling: '*No te pintes con más faltas, / porque en mi imaginación / te tiene amor retratado / del modo que tú has contado, / pero con más perfección*' (I. 326–330). Her retort highlights that Lugo is constructing an image through his protestations of humble origins. In fact, Lugo's repeated use of the first person 'soy' suggests a deliberate process of subjective self-fashioning. His encounter with the *dama* provides the first opportunity to forge an identity following his vow to be 'famoso en mi ejercicio'. It is, therefore, unsurprising that he rejects the *dama* and instead chooses to converse about himself. The *pícaro*'s behaviour, then, is utterly self-seeking. Moreover, Lugo seems to find perverse satisfaction in spurning her advances. His rejection not only indicates arrogance, but displays his yearning for dominance. In light of this, Lugo's protestations are, in fact, a type of *engaño con la verdad*. Lugo exploits the power of suggestion seemingly paying respect to the *dama* by foregrounding the incompatibility of their social positions, but elicits an obsequious response which fuels his pride. Lugo, then, would appear to be even more furtive than Don Juan. The latter operates on the premise of blatant lies which cannot be sustained indefinitely. Lugo's *modus operandi*, on the other hand, shrewdly functions in a way which not only invites admiration as opposed to recrimination, but crucially provides a strategy which withstands protracted manipulation.[48]

Lugo's life as a religious man enables him to transcend the limitations of the picaresque and sustain a judicious performance which resists any insinuation of spuriousness. In this sense, Lugo is much more intelligent and astute than both Quevedo's Pablos and Tirso's Don Juan. The protagonists of *El buscón* and *El burlador* are unable to perform indefinitely and meet with disaster and death respectively. Pablos will not procure a life of prosperity in the New World, whilst Don Juan is eventually punished for his care-free mind-set: 'quien tal hace, que tal pague' (III. 957). Ultimately Pablos and Don Juan are unable to circumvent their fate. Lugo, however, successfully secures his objective and is in fact, revered to the extent that upon his death the *ciudadanos* keep the bandages which covered his leprosy (III. 2800–03). His success stems from an astute understanding that a performance results in either negative or positive consequences: 'quien vive bien, muere bien, / quien mal vive, muere mal.' (II. 1403–04). His appraisal of the links between life and art reflects the Baroque obsession with the 'life as stage' metaphor. Friedman remarks that: 'those who play their roles well are emulating the Christian who recognizes that to act one's role is to win the eternal life; the effective actor in society is analogous to the good Christian on the road to paradise'.[49] Lugo's skilful ability to fashion himself as the 'good Christian' is anticipated by the scene in which he wins a game of cards by cheating; an episode which functions as a microcosm of his life. For the *pícaro*, life is a game of wits which demands that he constantly outmanoeuvre his circumstances. The card game, in fact, serves to highlight the extent of Lugo's autonomy. Fundamental to the concept of 'game' is chance but significantly, this does not apply in this case. The rogue's actions are governed by reason and will and not by fate or fortune. Evidence of his linguistic ability to mislead wilfully is demonstrated by his ironic and dishonest claim that: 'Sucesos son de fortuna' (I. 1096). At the close of Act I we are, therefore, aware that Lugo, far from being a product of social and moral discourses, is neither a victim nor a puppet of society.[50] Rather, he is a shrewd and immoral puppeteer controlling the strings of both his on-stage and off-stage audience.[51]

The picaresque elements dramatised within this opening act cast a prolonged and sinister shadow over the rest of the play. Not only do they expose the hypocrisy and religious duplicity which is disguised by an unethical manipulation of *parecer*, but allow us to consider how one might create a distorted and self-serving 'reality' in such a society. This cannot be explored apart from the fact that in *El rufián dichoso* Cervantes draws attention to the mechanisms of theatrical production. In fact, this *comedia* becomes a type of 'arte de *deshacer* teatro'. In Cervantes's play, what is signified is deconstructed, pulled apart and exposed as we become privy to the very processes with which Lugo engages to create a counterfeit persona. Just as Velázquez's *Las meninas* portrays what appears 'behind the scene', Cervantes dramatises how the stage simultaneously makes, unmakes, constructs and deconstructs. In the context of a fraudulent 'reality', this can only lead to a more radical questioning of macro power structures masquerading as 'invariable truth'. As such, *El rufián dichoso* functions as a mirror both reflecting inward and outward; ultimately provoking heightened scrutiny of the complexities of the time.

3.2 *Pedro de Urdemalas*: A Cervantine Counter-Perspective

Billed as 'la comedia más original que salió del taller de Cervantes', *Pedro de Urdemalas* is arguably the best known of the *Ocho comedias* and is generally recognised as Cervantes's most innovative play.[52] Most likely written toward the end of his second dramatic writing period, the drama showcases the playwright's ability to produce comic, creative and highly self-conscious theatre. As one of Cervantes's more performable *comedias*, *Pedro de Urdemalas* has found success on the contemporary stage. It premiered in Barcelona in 1968 and was staged again in 1998 as part of the *Festival de Almagro*.[53] In recent years, the Royal Shakespeare Company presented an English verse translation of the play (2004). Had it been staged in Cervantes's time, the *corral* audience would have been familiar with the drama's protagonist, Pedro de Urdemalas as a stock picaresque figure from Spanish folklore who also features in works by authors such as Salas Barbadillo.[54] Schevill and Bonilla trace Pedro de Urdemalas's roots in order to recover the influence and impact of the character on popular cultural imagination:

> Ya era muy antiguo, en tiempo de Cervantes, el nombre de un personaje legendario y popular, llamado Pedro de Urdemalas. Con tal nombre se relacionaba, a causa de su propio sentido, una serie de burlas, enredos y tretas que, en algunas tradiciones, tendrían cierta significación moral y fueron luego denominadas *consejas*.[55]

The name of Pedro de Urdemalas consequently became synonymous with a stock figure who would eventually be termed a *pícaro*. Cervantes incorporates this prototype into his play and, as noted by both Fernando García Salinero and Ángel Estévez Molinero, the dramatist subverts literary and folkloric portrayals of the time to render Pedro de Urdemalas more positively.[56] As Anderson observes: 'Cervantes has subtly but significantly changed the quasi-picaresque character [...] into a trickster who apparently harms no one'.[57]

Cervantes's Pedro is, in fact, a highly likeable, seductive character and a paradoxically gallant charlatan; a type of Golden-Age Robin Hood and jack-of-all-trades who outwits others with his ingenious tricks. Ronald Surtz observes that in the hands of Cervantes, Pedro 'is transformed into an artist-figure [...]

a magician and creator'.⁵⁸ Certainly the swindler overcomes and makes possible circumstances and situations which appear insurmountable to both the on-stage and off-stage audience. The drama details Pedro's pursuit of the perfect 'modus vivendi' and utilises a decidedly episodic and, therefore, as noted by Friedman, anti-*comedia* structure.⁵⁹ Anderson has also explored the play's relationship with Lope; a pertinent area of investigation in light of the fact that Lope also composed a *Pedro de Urdemalas* play sometime between 1597–1606.⁶⁰

Outside Lopean parameters, criticism has engaged with the drama's depiction of society. For Zimic, *Pedro de Urdemalas* is a biting satire which exposes corruption and vice. He argues that Pedro, as 'un artista en la vida', utilises theatre as a space through which he can both counter-act the failings of society and assist those in need.⁶¹ Shawn O. Smith's recent study of monarchical authority in the play exposes 'the fraudulent state of a realm that relies on the discourse of blood as its *raison d'être*'.⁶² Collectively these analyses demonstrate that the play's rural environment, which is peopled by scribes, peasants and shepherds, superficially masks sinister undertones of fraud, greed and hypocrisy. Undoubtedly, the drama's slapstick humour and comic farce not only poke fun at the political and legislative structures of the day, but call attention to the deficiencies of the system.

Pedro's ability to 'role play' his way from one situation to the next has also been noted. In fact, mobility (which is more apparent than real) underpins Pedro de Urdemalas's portrayal. He has long been identified by critics as a skilful, benevolent Proteus who dons guises and fabricates personas in rapid response to ever-changing circumstances.⁶³ The protagonist himself draws attention to his role as a 'master of disguise': 'Bien logrado iré del mundo / cuando Dios me lleve dél, / pues podré decir que en él / un Proteo fui segundo' (III. 2672–75). As such, the world is quite literally Pedro's stage and he is often concomitantly author and actor. In this complex metatheatrical environment, Cervantes's role-player assumes the central role of dramatist and becomes the linchpin around which the three acts develop.

There has been a general failure, however, to recognise that what Pedro embodies is, in fact, constancy in motion. Like Lugo in *El rufián dichoso*, Pedro exemplifies stable selfhood, fully cognizant that his roles are just that — 'roles'. As a self-defined and autonomous individual, Pedro is an anomaly in an epoch which, according to Maravall, 'possessed acute consciousness of the multiplicity and variability of the human'.⁶⁴ Rey Hazas perceives that Pedro: 'es hijo de sus obras [. . .] un personaje independiente y libre'.⁶⁵ In fact, as a self-made man who is wholly unaffected by any authority that would determine who or what he is, Pedro is the very antithesis of the difficult and often problematic relationship between the conflicted Baroque subject and his/her world. To date, Fernández-Morera, Canavaggio and Maestro are the only critics who address this issue, but have little to say on the matter.⁶⁶ For instance, Maestro observes:

Pedro de Urdemalas es, en medio de tanto conservadurismo, un símbolo de alteración y heterodoxia, a través de las burlas del teatro y de las ficciones de la literatura [...] es paradigma del cambio y la mutación actanciales y accidentales, es decir, funcional y circunstancial, *pero nunca esencial*, que puede experimentar el sujeto en una de las épocas más inflexibles y moralmente más resistentes a cualquier transformación que ha conocido el mundo referencial y axiológico del arte y la literatura europeos (emphasis mine).[67]

Clearly Maestro's stance, in its negation of any possibility of essential selfhood, does not take into account how Pedro's self-conscious transformations function emblematically within and beyond his performance of them.

McKendrick's appraisal of Pedro as the 'ultimate self-fashioner, admitting no indelible definitions, responsive to chance and change, free and in control of himself and his life' opposes the definition of self-fashioning as theorised by Greenblatt.[68] Greenblatt's term denotes self-fashioning as the creation of oneself according to and against a set of socially acceptable standards. Dialectical tension is, therefore, implicit in this, given that selfhood is dependent on the recognition of authorities that exist outside of the self. It involves the 'experience of being moulded by forces outside one's control'.[69] Although Cervantes's trickster Pedro assumes many shapes and forms throughout the play, he never self-consciously adopts a role in order to fashion an identity that is either distinct from self or, indeed, determined by his relationship with authority. In other words, 'Yo sé quién soy' could as easily be proclaimed by Pedro as by Don Quijote. Pedro remains rooted in his own perception of what is real and his changeability is contained within the context of what is, undoubtedly, a subjectively-driven performance. In fact, he functions as a mirror reflecting back upon both the on-stage and off-stage audience the Baroque mentality of modification. Pedro's ability to produce transformations without suffering any sense of self-loss is subject to more sustained symbolism in this final *comedia*. As such, Pedro is presented as the culmination of a dramatic art which functions without the imposition of stage-managed mediums upon its receiver.

A cluster of orthodox tensions exist around the drama's secondary characters. However, conflict is unconventionally absent between self and society, desire and duty in Cervantes's depiction of his protagonist. Pedro's nonconformist attitude toward social structures and codes catapults the individual to the forefront of the drama; and so where more conventional conflict is lacking, the play derives its dramatic impact from Pedro's personal convictions regarding freedom.[70] This analysis will interrogate two issues in particular which inform Pedro's complex characterisation and which are clearly connected to the theme of freedom: self-fashioning and role-play. Contrary to Carroll Johnson's hypothesis that: 'el proyecto de Pedro es factible porque él abandona la idea de un ser auténtico o una persona por debajo de los varios personajes que encarna', my study of *Pedro del Urdemalas* will explore role-play as a strategy which ironically draws out self-confirmation.[71] In fact, from the play's opening scenes Pedro is clearly depicted as a 'ser auténtico' and as such, is free in and of himself. This analysis will consider how Pedro, as mirror, is deliberately subverted and distorted; his apparent inconstancy operates as an antagonistic response both to the prevailing world view where the individual is repressed and constrained, and the dominant public stage, the Lopean space where *ser* is often determined by *parecer*. As such, my argument highlights *Pedro de Urdemalas* as a counter-perspective; a play which demands a discerning response toward the dualities of the age.

Pedro: 'a contrapelo del siglo de oro'[72]

Pedro de Urdemalas's self-determination and ability to fashion himself is clearly seen within the sphere of his picaresque lifestyle, as this is the existence that he has embraced. However, as a nonthreatening and obliging ruffian, Pedro does not fit the traditional portrayal of the *pícaro*. Unlike *El rufián dichoso*'s Lugo, Pedro's behaviour is redeemed by the fact that his tricks have no sting, even in the light of the episode in which he swindles a widow out of her fortune. His actions are excused by the widow's thriftiness and ingenuousness, her worship of money and Pedro's own plans to use his loot to provide fine clothes for Belica, the gypsy girl (II. 2322–26). Unlike Lugo, whose religious life as a servant of God and others is a hoax designed to bring self-glorification, Pedro de Urdemalas is driven by a desire to serve others. The opening lines of the play laud the rogue for his compassionate intervention on behalf of Clemente: 'De tu ingenio, Pedro amigo, / y nuestra amistad se puede / fiar más de lo que digo, / porque él al mayor excede, / y della el mundo es testigo' (I. 1–5). The depiction of Pedro's conscientious care for others contrasts greatly to *pícaros* such as *Lazarillo de Tormes*'s Lázaro and *El buscón*'s Pablos, who are entirely self-serving. Lázaro, of course, comes to blame society for its negative impact on his life, whilst Pablos lashes out at the world and determines revenge on a society which alienated him. Pedro, too, suffered injustice at the hands of unscrupulous people who abused their positions as 'care-givers'. In picaresque fashion, he relays his life story:

> Yo soy hijo de la piedra,
> que padre no conocí:
> desdicha de las mayores
> que a un hombre pueden venir.
> No sé dónde me criaron;
> pero sé decir que fui
> destos niños de dotrina
> sarnosos que hay por ahí (I. 600–07)

In full, this speech demonstrates that Pedro is not conditioned by his origins and is the author of his own life (I. 600–60; 664–767). As a child of nobody but a product of 'sus obras', Pedro has wilfully and self-consciously fashioned himself into a person of his own choice. What is particularly interesting is that Cervantes's protagonist has fashioned a noble self that we might term 'other'-seeking:

> las muchas vicisitudes de la vida de Pedro, en que padeció con frecuencia un trato cruel por parte de los hombres, no logran afectar su generosa naturaleza y no le impiden que se dedique a realizar los deseos y las aspiraciones de los que solicitan su ayuda.[73]

Whereas Quevedo's Pablos is sordidly realistic in his base and depraved behaviour, Pedro is wholly idealistic, selfless in his ways and the product of self-cultivation.

Unscathed by oppressive dictates, Pedro de Urdemalas embodies freedom as a way of life and advocates that the individual should choose their path in life at will. Hayek, a theorist who advocated the preservation of individual freedom, believed that the individual will best serve himself if he is free and that if he is free 'he will best serve his fellow man'.[74] In fact, the drama is composed of various episodes which see Pedro coming to the rescue of those who are denied the right to make discriminating decisions regarding their future. A prime example of such is his intervention in the lives of Clemente and Clemencia; a trick which involves duping his employer, the *alcalde*, Martín Crespo. As father and authorial body, Crespo exercises judgement on both domestic and social affairs. Clemencia is denied her choice of husband as a result of her father's (Crespo) belief that marriage to Clemente would be economically incompatible. Clemente laments: 'A hurto de su padre / que es de su libertad duro tirano, / que ella no tiene madre, / de esposa me entregó la fe y la mano; / y agora, temerosa, / del padre, no confiesa ser mi esposa' (I. 394–99). The embodiment of power and coercion, Crespo embraces his role as administrator of his daughter's affairs and complies with a system that dictates her freedom of choice as subservient to his own. The mayor's displeasure with his daughter's choice of husband is paralleled by Maldonado's, the gypsy chief's, assertion that the gypsy girl Belica should cease to entertain fantasies of an elevated social status: 'Así que, gitana loca, / pon freno al grande deseo / que te ensalza y que te apoca, / y no busques por rodeo / lo que en nada no te toca' (II. 1575–79). He dismisses her lofty claims of grandeur and asserts that Belica should heed her rank: 'Cásate, y toma tu igual' (II. 1580). Pedro functions as Belica's spokesperson as he vehemently defends her freedom to make her own choice in spite of the fact that he had hoped to win her over: 'Déjala, que muy bien hace, / y no la estimes en menos / por eso: que a mí me aplace / que con soberbios barrenos / sus máquinas suba y trace' (II. 1595–99). Sympathetic to her determination and indomitable spirit, Pedro goes so far as to orchestrate a hoax in order that he can elicit money to help Belica pursue her goals. Maldonado, on the other hand, becomes increasingly frustrated with Belica's ambitions and demands that she sustain her group identity as gypsy. When he attempts to pair her with Pedro against her will, Belica retorts: 'Fácilmente te acomadas / a tu gusto y a mi afrenta' (II. 1553-54). Moreover, when Belica is given the opportunity to meet the king, Maldonado endeavours to discredit her behaviour as 'necedad' (II. 1659-65). Through involvement in the lives of Clemencia and Belica, Pedro emerges as both liberator and liberated. Significantly, Pedro's schemes enable these marginalised women to express themselves in the way that they choose. He is not dissimilar in this respect to Don Quijote who declares his unconditional support for Marcela, the shepherdess, and demands that her decision to shun marriage be respected:

> Ella ha mostrado con claras y suficientes razones la poca o ninguna culpa que ha tenido en la muerte de Grisóstomo y cuán ajena vive de condescender con los deseos de ninguno de sus amantes; a cuya causa es justo que, en lugar de ser seguida y perseguida, sea honrada y estimada de todos los buenos del mundo (p. 128).

Jorge Urrutia comments: 'Don Quijote comprende que esa voz de mujer es también la suya porque, feminina o masculina, es una voz que reclama el derecho a elegir'.[75] Like Don Quijote, Pedro's philanthropic nature extends to all, but particularly to those who have negligible control over their own destinies.

Significantly, it is not the advocation of liberty which undercuts authority in the play, rather that the bodies which exemplify the hierarchical structures of the day are seen to undermine themselves. In fact, Martín Crespo is an inept civic leader who craves recognition but relies heavily on Pedro's ingenuity. The magistrate refers to Crespo: 'porque, en efeto, es mancilla / que se rija aquesta villa / por la persona más necia / que hay desde Flandes a Grecia / y desde Egipto a Castilla' (I. 250-54). The King and Queen are equally as flawed. The Queen is a resentful, jealous person and has Belica, whom she perceives as a threat, imprisoned on a whim. The King is characterised as a lecherous man fuelled by a desire for the gypsy girl which is not diminished by the revelation that she is his niece: 'El parentesco no afloja / mi deseo; antes, por él / con ahínco más cruel / toda el alma se congoja' (III. 2964-67). Regardless of a person's station in life, Cervantes's drama unapologetically depicts the foibles of human nature on every rung of the social ladder. In fact, the monarchs and Crespo provoke our laughter rather than our respect.[76] Notably, the power they wield to curb the desires of their subjects is in each case overcome by Pedro. The rogue concocts a scheme which allows Clemente and Clemenica to fool the mayor and Belica, encouraged and championed by Pedro, is so persuaded of her noble status that incarceration proves no obstacle.[77] The authority exhibited by Crespo and the Queen is self-serving and does not stand up to the confidence and passions of those they would repress. In contrast, free will knows no bounds and is seen to be an agent of progress exemplified by Pedro and Belica who both achieve the goals that they set out to attain. To inhibit individual freedom, then, as Crespo, Maldonado and the monarchs would have done, is to inhibit progress and render the community stagnant. Such a state belongs to picaresque characters whose journey through life amounts to circular entrapment; in the case of *Lazarillo de Tormes* the shift is from inherited dishonour to acquired dishonour, while *El buscón*'s Pablos' sense of social alienation intensifies into alienation from self. Pedro de Urdemalas, on the other hand, does not require any set of standards against which to measure or define himself. He is, in fact, an incongruity in a society which invested in a system that demanded conformity to illusory values.

Although role-play is particularly useful for 'escaping social obligations and developing one's sense of self', Pedro does not adopt various identities during the course of the play in order to rebel against or evade social obligations.[78] In fact, the protagonist fashions alternate selves not only because he can do so successfully, but ultimately because he desires to sustain permanently a transitional state. It is precisely because Pedro, and those around him, are conscious that his metamorphoses constitute art that he remains grounded in reality. Fernández-Morera comments: 'Las transformaciones de Pedro dependen de la realidad. Pedro nunca se transforma en un ser fantástico. En medio de sus vuelos imaginativos, permanence atado a la tierra'.[79] Moreover, Pedro recognises that his performances carry both power and limit. There are numerous references throughout the drama that inform us of Pedro's appreciation of his roles as illusion. In the play's opening scenes, Crespo petitions Pedro for his help, to which the trickster replies: 'Es aqueso tan verdad, / cual lo dirá la experiencia, / porque con facilidad / luego os mostraré una ciencia' (I. 220–23). Pedro's clinical definition of his skill reveals the self-conscious nature of his role as architect of these schemes. More evidence of his detachment from fantasy can be observed in the scene in which Pedro determines to deceive the thrifty widow, Marina. He refers to his plan as an 'embuste' (I. 1207) and declares to Maldonado: 'voime a vestir de ermitaño, / con cuyo vestido honesto / daré fuerzas a mi engaño' (II. 1695–97). In each instance, Pedro is quick to affirm role-play as illusion. Moreover, in defence of Belica's lofty ambitions Pedro rebukes Maldonado for his derision of the gypsy girl's hopes. The protagonist states: 'Yo también, que soy un leño, / príncipe y papa me sueño, / emperador y monarca, / y aún mi fantasía abarca / de todo el mundo a ser dueño' (II. 1600–04). Pedro's subject-centred speech embraces plurality of expression but is not indicative of a fluid or inconsistent personality. It is, rather, a dynamic expression of stable selfhood, grounded in something more substantial than appearance. He locates 'fantasía' and 'sueño' within a world of illusion where any role, apart from his true self, is contained.

Pedro is author as well as actor but crucially realises where one role ends and one begins. The deceiver is, therefore, never deceived. The dramatist in Pedro invents various personae, all the while fully understanding the fabricated quality of these illusions. As Pedro is not a 'contradictory subject' as defined by Mariscal, I would see this ability to perform and not lose sight of self, reflected in his evaluation of his metamorphoses as art.⁸⁰ Pedro fully appreciates that his protean talents are best suited to the stage and that his ability in this dramatic context gives him the power of influence over others; he is able to deduce, for instance, that the widow Marina is his audience and he, for the duration of that hoax, is an actor. The very mechanisms of Pedro's trick are displayed on stage as he directs his play and orders Maldonado to prepare what is necessary for him to outwit Marina (I. 1196–1207). Moreover, when he decides that he has had enough of 'playing' gypsy, he informs Maldonado that it is time for him to adopt a new disguise: 'que a compás retiro el paso / del gitanesco progreso. / Un bonete reverendo/ y el eclesiástico brazo / sacarán deste embarazo / mi persona, a lo que entiendo' (II. 2093–98). Pedro's appreciation of his chameleon-like behaviour is fully realised in the final act when Cervantes's protagonist becomes a professional performer: 'hecho estoy una quimera' (III. 3142). The closing scenes see the trickster, now turned actor, recite the qualities of a 'farsante':

> Sé todo aquello que cabe
> en un general farsante;
> sé todos los requisitos
> que un farsante ha de tener
> para serlo, que han de ser
> tan raros como infinitos.
> De gran memoria, primero;
> Segundo, de suelta lengua; [. . .]
> Ha de recitar de modo,
> con tanta industria y cordura [. . .]
> Ha de sacar con espanto
> las lágrimas de la risa (III. 2894–901; 2912–13; 2920–21)

The fact that Pedro can maintain distance from his illusion and define it as such, not only conveys confident individuality, but equally significant, emphasises his conception of the stage as both transitory and temporal. Pedro's trickery is designed for a moment in time. As such, he is an ethical creator whose stage magic does not masquerade as anything else. Just as Alonso Quijano kills off Don Quijote at the end of book two, in *Pedro de Urdemalas*, illusion is allotted its time and its place and ultimately is not allowed to replace the real world.

Pedro de Urdemalas is the antithesis of characters who deliberately fabricate alternate selves and indulge in role-playing in order to achieve a sense of identity and/or to realise their own desires. In fact, the drama is peopled by such characters. Crespo, for instance, 'plays' at being mayor.⁸¹ Foolish and inept, Crespo is unable to judge discerningly and relies on Pedro to place written judgements in a hood from which he can choose and pronounce his verdict. When approached by Clemencia and Clemente, disguised as shepherds, Crespo pulls a sentence from the hood: '"Yo, Martín Crespo, alcalde, determino / que sea la pollina del pollino"' (I. 436–37). Unwittingly, Crespo approves their marriage.

The mayor perceives Clemente to be of inferior rank (I. 61–63), yet in his role as mayor he can raise no objection. Interestingly, like Rosamira in *El laberinto*, Clemencia lets Clemente ventriloquise her request while she stays silent: 'Su proceder honesto / la tendrá muda, por mi mal, agora; / pero señales puede / hacer con que su intento claro quede' (I. 420–23). In the guise of a *pastora* Clemencia remains undetected and her father executes judgement based on the 'reality' which faces him. When the truth is discovered Clemencia protests against her father's reaction: 'Pues, con ese seguro, padre mío, / el velo quito y a tus pies me postro. / Mal haces en usar deste desvío, / pues soy tu hija, y no espantable mostro' (I. 454–57). Similar to the reaction of Rosamira's father, Crespo perceives female agency as something 'monstrous'. Nonetheless, like the heroines of *El laberinto*, the shepherdess's strategic use of silence ensures that she is powerfully free as she counter-acts her father's wishes for her future. Her shrewd manipulation of the situation and ability to expose the injustice at the heart of her father's attitude is evident in the remark: 'Tú has dado la sentencia a tu albedrío' (I. 458). Clemencia's pointed comment exposes the pitfalls of a value system based on elusive and external signifiers. Such a system is fortified by the individual's (for instance, Crespo's) refusal to interrogate it intelligently but, crucially, is challenged by the subject's own free will. Moreover, Crespo's roles as father and mayor are clearly blurred in this scene and his acceptance of Clemente is muddled, stranded somewhere between obligations to the murky worlds of self and duty. Unlike Pedro, he is unable to discern where one role ends and another begins.

Crespo, caught in a trap of entirely his own doing, exemplifies the conflict between self-determination and social position. For Zimic: 'La vanidad del alcalde es enorme: sumido en su apariencia, embriagándose con ella, llega a perder todo sentido de su verdadera personalidad'.[82] Crespo becomes so embroiled in playing a role — that of mayor — that he loses sight of himself. Coerced by society to embrace an attitude disdaining disparity of rank, he is the victim of his own stupidity when his roles mingle. One only has to look at Calderón's *El alcalde de Zalamea* to witness a parallel situation, although explored with much greater depth. Fully persuaded that 'el honor es patrimonio del alma', the Crespo of Calderón's drama, who will also become mayor, executes the army captain who rapes his daughter. While there is some masking of this in the legal proceedings, I would argue that Calderón defends the individual and the personal over and above the social, as Pedro Crespo's situation accentuates the tension between natural inclination and the other legislative spheres supported by society. Ángel Valbuena Briones asserts that Crespo's infamous lines 'defienden la libertad del individuo para tomar venganza en las querellas personales del honor, las cuales no conciernen al estado'.[83] Yet despite what has been generally considered by commentators as a radical action, in the resolution of Calderón's play, the mayor of Zalamea ultimately bows to social conditioning and his dishonoured daughter leaves for a convent. In both cases, society's ability to infiltrate and impinge on all aspects of the individual's life is revealed. In the case of *Pedro de Urdemalas* the mayor's willingness to indulge in a role which is so alien from who he is as an individual, exposes the societal tendency to compel an individual to assume a different role and then to punish him for doing so. Such a paradox not only serves to highlight the precarious nature of early modern Spain's value system, but emphasises precisely why the individual Baroque subject is both alienated from this and conflicted as a result.

Pedro, however, does not suffer any sense of displacement and the stability of his characterisation is heightened by identity crises in characters such as Crespo and Pascual. For instance, when Benita mistakenly pledges herself to a man called Roque, Pedro advises Pascual to change his name and, thus, secure Benita's hand: 'Puede Pascual confirmarse, / y puede el nombre mudarse / de Pascual en Roque, y luego, / con su gusto y tu sosiego, / puede contigo casarse' (I. 933–37). In order to marry Benita, Pascual must surrender his name. Like Crespo, Pascual's identity is no longer certain. It is now founded on that of another man and his goal is won at the expense of himself. Pedro, on the other hand, understands that roles are layers worn by actors which can be discarded after a performance. This is often conveyed in a visual sense by stage directions that show Pedro to have changed into his own clothes after a hoax or into another costume. This is particularly pertinent in the play's final scenes where directions denote: '*Sale Pedro de Urdemalas, con manteo y bonete, como estudiante*' (III. 2659). *El buscón*'s swindler, Pablos, who also becomes a professional actor, is once again a useful point of comparison. For Quevedo's protagonist, however, acting reflects the fantastical environment into which he flees upon his release from prison; and into which he has fled throughout the novel at the first sign of confrontation with reality. Like Pedro he dons disguises, such as passing himself off as a wealthy man pretending to be poor, yet Pablos never really steps back out of this world. In fact, the world of Quevedo's *pícaro* is a perpetual façade and Pablos' fabricated selves are an obstacle to true self-knowledge. In Cervantes's drama, however, Pedro embraces transient appearances as a statement of self-affirmation. Depicting 'stability' in such ironic terms, renders a deviant portrayal of what is ordinarily a mutable world.

In this idealistic universe, Cervantes shows the individual's free will to triumph; Clemencia and Clemente win the approval of the mayor, Belica proves herself to be the long lost niece of the Queen and Pedro enters a profession which permits perpetual metamorphoses. Yet art ensures that reality is seen to rule. Clemencia and her husband face the possibility that their marriage will be rejected (I. 454–55) and Belica's royal blood is no illusion (III. 2620–22).[84] The same cannot be said for Lope's protagonist Teodoro in the closing scene of *El perro del hortelano* whose aristocratic self is designed by an elaborate deceit. The contrast between illegitimate and legitimate anagnorisis is reflective of the gulf between Cervantes's and Lope's theatre. As exemplified in *El perro*, Lope's *comedia nueva* depicts selfhood as fluid, as characters become what is necessary in order to extract maximum advantage from a given situation. Awareness of distance between art and the real world is a prime destabiliser deliberately manipulated by Lope. In *El perro del hortelano*, it serves to undermine the 'closure' of the conclusion as an illusion in which the audience is compliant. In the case of *Pedro de Urdemalas*, Cervantes subsumes reality into his art in order to produce stable entities who fully embrace self-realisation. There is no flux between art and life as represented in the non-conflictive self-role relationship. Individual freedom is seen to possess the ability to supersede set limits, therefore rendering the individual potentially limitless, while also underscoring the boundless potential of art. Cervantes's drama makes the real ideal and thus exposes Pedro as symbolic of the transformative power of art. Art is now seen to subvert Lope's 'stage as mirror' in order to present an idealised portrayal of a world where the individual is neither alienated nor displaced.

Via his portrayal of Pedro's stability as an antidote to the transience of the age and the illusory nature of the public stage, Cervantes comments, once again, on art's didactic potential. The author of the exemplary novels chooses to put on stage an exemplary figure in the form of his unconventionally stable protagonist. Pedro embodies a state of freedom to the extent that he is a self-fashioned subject in a world where the individual readily buckles to external pressure and attempts to affiliate him/herself with a status and societal position via role-play. In a perverse fashion, then, Cervantes responds to the Baroque's vision of the mutability of man. This serves to emphasise the dramatist's prominent focus on the individual's impact on society, rather than a concern with society's influence on the individual. Ultimately, however, Pedro's distortion of the mirror image cannot advocate a model of life. Pedro de Urdemalas is, after all, a dramatic representation and, as Spadaccini and Talens would have it, therefore, 'an interpretation of reality'.[85] In fact, as in *La entretenida* and *El gallardo español*, the artificiality of the spectacle is driven home by Pedro's final lines which confront the audience with the drama's generic status in its condemnation of conventional endings and the *comedia*'s disrespect for unities of time and place:

> Mañana, en el teatro, se hará una,
> donde por poco precio verán todos
> desde principio al fin toda la traza,
> y verán que no acaba en casamiento,
> cosa común y vista cien mil veces,
> ni que parló la dama esta jornada,
> y en otra tiene el niño ya sus barbas,
> y es valiente y feroz, y mata y hiende,
> y venga de sus padres cierta injuria,
> y al fin viene a ser rey de un cierto reino
> que no hay cosmografía que le muestre.

> Destas impertinencies y otras tales
> ofreció la comedia libre y suelta,
> pues llena de artificio, industria y galas,
> se cela del gran Pedro de Urdemalas. (III. 3166–80)[86]

Pedro is shown to be a creation *for* the stage, emphasised in this case *by* the stage. It would appear, then, that the dramatist's final play has much to say about the nature of the relationship between art and life. In this final foregrounding of artistic process *Pedro de Urdemalas* emerges as perhaps Cervantes's greatest challenge to contemporary theatre. The drama's exceptional protagonist successfully works against the grain of established parameters and forges a stage which is, in fact, a picture of the Cervantine stage itself: free, ethical and antipropagandistic. As such, it both confronts and counter-acts conventional artistic imaginings of the day.

Ultimately *El rufián dichoso* and *Pedro de Urdemalas* are useful contrasting models in understanding Cervantes's view of seventeenth-century 'reality' as an artificial construct; one that depends on consumer participation and operates on the basis of what is seen and/or said and is, therefore, inherently insecure. These two plays taken together depict a world which pressures the individual to conform and integrate. This requirement to conform results in a deliberate, and often desperate, attempt to mould oneself according to societal values and standards. Cervantes distorts this impulse to self-fashion in response to, or against, existing authorities by placing centre stage two powerfully autonomous and articulate individuals who express authentic selfhood in distinct ways. Pedro de Urdemalas places little stock on demands to comply with the fictions created by others, while Lugo wilfully creates an alternate self based on the power structures which underpin society. On one hand, Pedro's impulse to self-fashion is inherently selfless. On the other, Lugo's conduct is entirely self-serving. However, despite their differences, both these Cervantine protagonists resist the control which the dominant socio-cultural and political infrastructures would impose upon them. This resistance is a product of the 'inner' freedom which both Lugo and Pedro clearly possess. It allows the characters to make cognizant decisions regarding their role in, and contribution to, society. Pedro and Lugo, then, not only stand in contradiction to Greenblatt's theory, but suggest that it is not tenable in the context of the subject's ability to mobilise free will. Moreover, it fails to take account of the human being's capacity to perceive and engage with the ways in which the state or community might enforce compliance. Lugo and Pedro withstand pressure to conform precisely because they recognise and actively combat coercion. It is this potent combination of scrutiny and self-conscious detachment which is presented in these two plays as a solution to the oppression experienced by the Baroque subject.

SHAPING THE SELF 151

The strategies employed by Cervantes in *El rufián dichoso* and *Pedro de Urdemalas* identify the Cervantine stage as a theatre which theorises about art and, in particular, about theatre. As Arboleda observes:

> con Cervantes la idea del teatro tomará un rumbo distinto a la de sus antecesores en el sentido en que ya no hará referencia única y exclusivamente a la representación de un mundo fingido o imaginado en palabras. Este tipo de teatro que se referirá mayormente a sí mismo, al proceso de representación misma. Será un metateatro.[87]

Not only does metatheatre function in these *comedias* as a device which reveals and comments on the manipulative potential of the stage (as it also does in *La casa de los celos*), but it exposes Cervantes's protagonists as always firmly in control; they are much more than consummate role-players. As creators and architects of their own schemes who retain authorial power, they are distinct to characters conventionally portrayed on the Golden-Age stage. The illusions which Lugo and Pedro project are, in fact, the reality of others who cannot distinguish truth from fiction. For instance, Pedro's 'inconstancy' is a reflection of the process of making and unmaking in which *pícaros* and other individuals around him engage in order to fashion a definable self. Such illusion-making tactics are not dissimilar to the spectacle created in *El retablo de las maravillas* which operates as a mirror reflecting back the attempts of an audience to construct selfhood on the basis of (elusive) signifiers which connote honour and reputation. Chanfalla and Chirinos's trick capitalises on the spectator's desire to protect the appearance of legitimacy. In the dramatic universe of *El rufián dichoso* and *Pedro de Urdemalas*, art and life cannot be disconnected. Cervantes's stage engages with the tensions between illusion and reality, challenging the spectator's understanding of their own world. The metamorphoses of Cervantes's protagonists portray, above all, the instabilities of the modifiable and suspect world of appearances at the heart of the Baroque.

Notes to Chapter 3

1. Egginton, 'Reason's Baroque House (Cervantes, Master Architect)', in *Reason and Its Others*, pp. 186–203 (p. 186).
2. *El rufián dichoso* constitutes a Cervantine dramatisation of the conversion of Fray Agustín Dávila Padilla, *Historia de la Fundación y Discurso de la Provincia de Santiago de México de la Orden de Predicadores, por las Vidas de sus Varones Insignes* (Madrid, 1596). According to Canavaggio, Cervantes would also have been familiar with, and influenced by, stories on the life of Cristóbal de Lugo published in a treatise by Fray Antonio de San Román, *Consuelo de Penitentes o Mesa franca de spirituales manjares* (Salamanca, 1583). See *Cervantès dramaturge*, p. 47.
3. Although studies of *El rufián dichoso* have neglected to interrogate its relationship to contemporary religious theatre, Thacker's recent study suggests that Cervantes wanted to comment upon and parody the form of Lopean drama: '"Véote, y no te conozco": The Unrecognizable Form of Cervantes's *El rufián dichoso*', *Hispanic Research Journal*, 3

(2009), 206–26. See Elaine Canning for an analysis of Lope de Vega's religious plays: *Lope de Vega's comedias de tema religioso* (Woodbridge: Tamesis, 2004).
4. Spadaccini and Talens, *Through the Shattering Glass*, p. 91.
5. William Childers, '"Ese Tan Borrado Sobrescrito": The Deconstruction of Lope's Religious Theater in *El retablo de las maravillas* and *El rufián dichoso*', *Bulletin of the Comediantes*, 56 (2004), 241–69 (p. 262). In a climate in which religious fervour reached fever pitch, saints plays in seventeenth-century Spain were given every opportunity for dramatic success and such enthusiasm for this theatre 'can be seen as a result of efforts by both Church and State to make sure that the people were uniform and orthodox in matters of their faith'. See Robert R. Morrison, *Lope de Vega and the Comedia de Santos* (New York: Peter Lang, 2000), p. 26.
6. Childers, 'Ese Tan Borrado Sobrescrito', p. 251.
7. Childers, 'Ese Tan Borrado Sobrescrito', p. 260.
8. Zimic, '"La caridad jamás imaginada" de Cristóbal de Lugo. Estudio de *El rufián dichoso* de Cervantes', *Boletín de la Biblioteca Menéndez y Pelayo*, 56 (1980), 85–171 (p. 87).
9. Jean Canavaggio, 'La conversión del *rufián dichoso*: Fuentes y Recreación', in *On Cervantes: Essays for L. A. Murillo*, ed. by James A. Parr (Newark: Juan de la Cuesta, 1991), pp. 11–19 and Eric J. Kartchner, 'Pícaros, Saints, and the New World in Cervantes's *El rufián dichoso*', in *Crosscurrents: Transatlantic Perspectives on Early Modern Hispanic Drama*, ed. by Mindy E. Badía and Bonnie L. Gasior (Lewisburg, Pennsylvania: Bucknell University Press, 2006), pp. 85–103.
10. Castro, *El pensamiento de Cervantes*.
11. Peter N. Dunn, 'Cervantes De/Re-Constructs the Picaresque', *Cervantes*, 2 (1982), 109–31 (p. 112).
12. Carlos Blanco Aguinaga, 'Cervantes y la picaresca: Notas sobre dos tipos de realismo', *Nueva Revista de Filología Hispánica*, 11 (1957), 313–42 (pp. 313–14). This study was to have a decisive impact on both general and specific analyses of Cervantes's work and analysis of the picaresque. See, for example, Claudio Guillén, *Literature as System: Essays Toward the Theory of Literary History* (Princeton: Princeton University Press, 1971) and Ann Wiltrout, 'Ginés de Pasamonte: The Pícaro and his Art', *Anales Cervantinos*, 17 (1978), 11–17.
13. See Dunn, 'Cervantes De/Re-Constructs the Picaresque'.
14. Anon., *La vida de Lazarillo de Tormes*, ed. by Francisco Rico (Madrid: Cátedra, 1987); Mateo Alemán, *Guzmán de Alfarache*, ed. by Benito Brancaforte (Madrid: Cátedra, 1979); Francisco de Quevedo, *Historia de la vida del Buscón llamado Don Pablos*, ed. by Américo Castro (Madrid: Espasa Calpe, 1973).
15. Dunn, 'Cervantes De/Re-Constructs the Picaresque', p. 111.
16. Manuel Durán, 'Picaresque elements in Cervantes's works', in *The Picaresque: Tradition and Displacement*, ed. by Giancarlo Maiorino (Minneapolis: University of Minnesota Press, 1996), pp. 226–47 (p. 237).
17. Helen H. Reed, 'Theatricality in the Picaresque of Cervantes', *Cervantes*, 7 (1987), 71–84 (p. 72). Reed examines *Rinconete y Cortadillo*, *La ilustre fregona*, *El casamiento engañoso*, *El coloquio de los perros*, *Don Quijote*, *Persiles* and *Pedro de Urdemalas*.
18. Reed, 'Theatricality in the Picaresque of Cervantes', p. 76.
19. My analysis of Cervantes's protagonist develops Childers's application of J. L. Austin's speech act theory in order to explore how Lugo utilises language in a performative discourse that allows him to usurp the identity of a religious man. By examining Lugo's violation of the rules which govern effective communication I determine how the trickster effects a transformation from sinner to saint. This line of enquiry not only underscores the active nature of speech, but also expounds upon how language functions in drama to produce and complicate conflict and, more significantly, to lead and control audience

response. Ultimately Cervantes flaunts *El rufián dichoso* as an artificial construct by persistently displaying the ways in which language and, therefore, dramatic art operates. See Melanie Henry, 'Cervantine Theater as Counter-Perspective Aesthetic: Reconsidering *El rufián dichoso*', *Cervantes*, 31 (2011), 105–24.
20. José Antonio Maravall, *La literatura picaresca desde la historia social* (Madrid: Taurus, 1986), p. 536.
21. Marcel Bataillon, *Pícaros y Picaresca* (Madrid: Taurus, 1969), p. 210.
22. See, for instance, Zimic, 'La caridad jamás imaginada'; Patricia Varas, '*El rufián dichoso*: Una 'comedia' de santos diferente', *Anales Cervantinos*, 29 (1991), 9–19; Spadaccini and Talens, *Through the Shattering Glass*; Kartchner, 'Pícaros, Saints, and the New World'; and Miñana, '"Veréis el monstruo": La nueva "comedia" de Cervantes'.
23. William Stapp, 'Dichoso por confiado', *Anales Cervantinos*, 25 (1987), 413–52 (p. 431).
24. This approach fits with what I have identified as Cervantes's attempt to create an 'ideal spectator' for his theatre. See section 2.3 of this book.
25. Cervantes, *Comedias y Entremeses Vol. 6*, p. 124.
26. Cervantes, *Comedias y Entremeses Vol. 6*, pp. 126–27.
27. Casalduero, *Sentido y forma*, p. 108.
28. Zimic, *El teatro de Cervantes*, p. 171.
29. A. A. Parker, *Literature and the Delinquent: The Picaresque Novel in Spain and Europe 1599–1753* (Edinburgh: Edinburgh University Press, 1967), p. 4.
30. For further discussion of seventeenth-century Seville's underworld, see Mary Elizabeth Perry, *Crime and Society in Early Modern Seville* (Hanover, New Hampshire: University Press of New England, 1980). See especially 'The Underworld', pp. 19–32.
31. Fernando de Rojas, *La Celestina*, ed. by Dorothy S. Severin (Madrid: Cátedra, 1989), p. 124.
32. Quevedo, *Historia de la vida del buscón llamado Don Pablos*, pp. 17–19.
33. Zimic, 'Una caridad jámas imaginada', p. 91.
34. Quevedo, *Historia de la vida del buscón llamado Don Pablos*, p. 270. The book's closing sentence has been described as 'a pithy *sententia* with a proverbial ring, significantly and strikingly placed in a position which is sure to catch the eye'. See Dale B. J. Randall, 'The Classical Ending of Quevedo's *Buscón*', *Hispanic Review*, 32 (1964), 101–08 (p. 101). In Randall's opinion, the closest parallel to *El buscón*'s ending is found in Seneca's twenty-eighth epistle. See *L. Annaei Senecae Ad Lucilium epistulae morales*, ed. by L. D. Reynolds (Oxonii: E Typographeo Clarendoniano, 1965). The critic also notes that Quevedo's conclusion may have been influenced by Horace.
35. Kartchner, 'Pícaros, Saints and the New World', p. 101.
36. Kartchner, 'Pícaros, Saints and the New World', p. 99.
37. Bruce Wardropper, 'Comedias', in *Suma cervantina*, ed. by J. B. Avalle-Arce & E. C. Riley (London: Tamesis, 1973), pp. 147–69 (p. 166).
38. Zimic observes: 'Lugo tiene vergüenza de que su humilde familia no haya hecho nada para honrarlo a él, y se propone así lograr grandes éxitos personales para hacerla olvidar. No se trata, pues, de un sano, positivo, deseo de mejorarse, de superarse personal y cívicamente, sino tan sólo de imponerse y, sobre todo, de convencer a todo el mundo de su gran valía e importancia'. 'Sobre el arte dramático de Cervantes en *El rufián dichoso*', in *Cervantes 1547–1997: Jornadas de Investigación Cervantina*, ed. by Aurelio González (Mexico: Colegio de México, Fondo Eulalio Ferrer, 1999), pp. 87–101 (p. 88).
39. Boruchoff, 'Free Will'. See also *Novelas ejemplares II*, p. 139.
40. Boruchoff, 'Free Will', p. 382.
41. Boruchoff, 'Free Will', p. 377.
42. Durán, 'Picaresque elements in Cervantes's work', p. 240.
43. Varas, '*El rufián dichoso*: Una 'comedia' de santos diferente', p. 16.

44. Stapp comments that the protagonist's conduct 'le permite cumplir la obligación de la caridad sin establecer íntimas relaciones humanas, las cuales parecen serle desagradables. En fin, la suya es una 'caridad' militar basada en el canje y no en el amor y la compresión'. 'Dichoso por confiado', p. 423.
45. Zimic draws a parallel between the two figures noting that Lugo exemplifies 'dotes donjuanescas'. See 'La caridad jamás imaginada', p. 106.
46. Varas sees Lugo's reluctance to be involved with the women as positive indication that he is not a womaniser. 'Una comedia de santos diferente', p. 15.
47. Zimic, 'La caridad jámas imaginada', p. 104.
48. This scene with the *dama* functions as a 'precursor' to the linguistic strategies which Lugo employs in Acts II and III in order to secure success in his role as saint.
49. Friedman, *The Unifying Concept*, p. 114.
50. This reading opposes that of Parker who argues that the *pícaro* 'becomes a rogue mainly through society's fault'. See 'The Psychology of the *pícaro* in *El buscón*', *The Modern Language Review*, 42 (1947), 58-69 (p. 61). My analysis of Lugo identifies Cervantes's rogue an 'hijo de sus obras'; an independent, autonomous individual who makes his own path in life and is more in line with Boruchoff's argument outlined above. In another article, Boruchoff contends that Cervantes was unable to 'aceptar la premisa de determinismo circunstancial y hereditario a la que apela Lázaro [. . .] para justificar sus acciones'. See 'La malograda invención de la picaresca', in *Homenaje a Francisco Márquez Villanueva*, ed. by Pedro M. Piñero Ramírez (Seville: Universidad de Sevilla, 2005), pp. 497-511 (p. 498).
51. A parallel with the *Quijote*'s Maese Pedro and the notion of authorial manipulation is apparent here. For further discussion of the similarities between Lugo and Pedro see 'Cervantine Theater as Counter-Perspective Aesthetic', pp. 116-17.
52. Miguel de Cervantes, *La entretenida. Pedro de Urdemalas*, ed. by Florencio Sevilla Arroyo and Antonio Rey Hazas (Madrid: Alianza, 1998), p. xxxiii. McKendrick judges that *Pedro de Urdemalas* is Cervantes's 'most original play and significantly it is the most completely conceived and achieved. While his other plays represent to varying degrees a distracted compromise between personal inclination and precept or formula, here one feels that Cervantes was working fully in his element'. 'Writings for the Stage', p. 148.
53. See Jerónimo López Mozo, 'De pícaro a cómico', *Reseña*, 301 (1999), 18-19 for a review of the Almagro production.
54. See Salas Barbadillo, *El subtil cordobés Pedro de Urdemalas* (1620) and Cristóbal de Villalón, *Viaje de Turquía (la odisea de Pedro de Urdemalas)* (1557).
55. *Comedias y Entremeses*, p. 137.
56. Fernando García Salinero's study focuses on the history of the literary figure: 'Dos perfiles paralelos de Pedro de Urdemalas', in *Cervantes: Su obra y su mundo. Actas del I Congreso Internacional sobre Cervantes*, ed. by Manuel Criado de Val (Madrid: EDI-6, 1981), pp. 229-34. Ángel Estévez Molinero also subscribes to the view that Cervantes's protagonist is a deviation from literary portrayals of Pedro de Urdemalas of the time. The critic sees Pedro as someone who can change his own destiny. 'La (re)escritura Cervantina de *Pedro de Urdemalas*', *Cervantes*, 15 (1995), 82-93.
57. Anderson, 'Articulate Characters: Gender, Genre, and Genius in Cervantes's *El coloquio de los perros and Pedro de Urdemalas*', *Romance Languages Annual*, 5 (1993), 349-55 (p. 352). Anderson contends that Pedro adopts a decidedly marginal feminine position given that it is usually Cervantes's heroines who utilise role-play and disguise, as evidenced by *El laberinto de amor* and *El gallardo español*.
58. Ronald E. Surtz, 'Cervantes's *Pedro de Urdemalas*: The Trickster as Dramatist', *Romanische Forschungen*, 92 (1979), 118-25 (p. 118). For Forcione, Pedro is also a type of artist. Taking into account the contemporary worldview, Forcione sees Pedro's

imagination as overcoming the normality of everyday life. Pedro, then, should be viewed as a 'grand spectacle in God's comedy'. *Cervantes, Aristotle and the Persiles* (Princeton: Princeton University Press, 1970), p. 331.

59. See *The Unifying Concept*; in particular chapter IV, 'Dramatic structure in Cervantes and Lope: The *Pedro de Urdemalas* Plays', pp. 81–102.
60. Lope's play was, therefore, most likely written before Cervantes's *Pedro de Urdemalas*. See Friedman, *The Unifying Concept*, p. 158. Anderson examines how gender and rank intersect in very different places in the plays. 'The Gentility and Genius of *Pedro de Urdemalas*, engendered by Lope de Vega and Cervantes', in *Brave New Words: Studies in Spanish Golden Age Literature*, ed. by Edward H. Friedman and Catherine Larson (New Orleans: University Press of the South, 1996), pp. 175–89.
61. Zimic, *El teatro de Cervantes*, p. 265.
62. Shawn O. Smith, '*Pedro de Urdemalas*: Contesting the Spanish Hapsburg Discourse of Blood', *Vanderbilt e-Journal of Luso-Hispanic Studies*, 2 (2005).
63. On this topic see, amongst others, Zimic, 'El gran teatro del mundo y el gran mundo del teatro en *Pedro de Urdemalas* de Cervantes', *Acta Neophilologica*, 10 (1977), 55–105; McKendrick, 'Writings for the stage', p. 149; and Maestro, 'Cervantes y Shakespeare', pp. 606–07.
64. Maravall, *Culture of the Baroque*, p. 170.
65. Rey Hazas, *Poética de la libertad*, p. 305.
66. Darío Fernández-Morera, 'Algunos aspectos del universo Cervantino en la comedia *Pedro de Urdemalas*', in *Cervantes: su obra y su mundo. Actas del I Congreso Internacional sobre Cervantes*, ed. by Manuel Criado de Val (Madrid: Edi-6, 1981), pp. 239–42; Cervantes, *Los baños de Argel. Pedro de Urdemalas*, ed. by Jean Canavaggio (Madrid: Taurus, 1992), p. 56; and Maestro, 'Cervantes y Shakespeare'.
67. Maestro, 'Cervantes y Shakespeare', pp. 606–07.
68. McKendrick, 'Writings for the Stage', p. 149.
69. Greenblatt, *Renaissance Self-fashioning*, p. 3.
70. '*Pedro de Urdemalas* es una muestra de una forma diferente de hacer las cosas y, sobre todo, una forma diferente de pensar. Lo primero que llama la atención, en contraste con el teatro de Lope y sus seguidores, es la libertad, tanto técnica como temática, que preside esta obra'. Raquel Arias Careaga, '*Pedro de Urdemalas*: Otro ejemplo de libertad Cervantina', *Annali di Ca' Foscari: Rivista della Facoltà di Lingue e Letterature Straniere dell'Università di Venezia*, 31 (1992), 43–59 (p. 43).
71. Carroll B. Johnson, 'La construcción del personaje en Cervantes', *Cervantes*, 15 (1995), 8–32 (p. 16).
72. See Rey Hazas, *Poética de la libertad*, p. 305.
73. Zimic, 'El gran teatro del mundo', p. 58.
74. Calvin M. Hoy, *A Philosophy of Individual Freedom: The Political Thought of F. A. Hayek* (Connecticut: Greenwood, 1984), p. 23.
75. Jorge Urrutia, 'La libertad del yo feminino o la libertad de don Quijote', in *El Quijote en clave de mujer/es*, ed. by Fanny Rubio (Madrid: Editorial Complutense, 2005), pp. 475–79 (p. 478).
76. Zimic argues that it is impossible not to see parallels with Felipe III and Margarita de Austria. According to the critic, Cervantes dramatises 'el lamentable desprestigio social, político y moral de una clase reinante'. 'El gran teatro del mundo', p. 89.
77. Clemencia's and Belica's rejection of an identity against the individual will is mirrored in Act II by the failure of the dance of the young men, dressed as women, in front of the King and Queen (II. 1860–94). See Friedman, *The Unifying Concept*, p. 86.
78. Thacker, *Role-Play and the World as Stage*, p. 48.
79. Darío Fernández-Morera, 'Algunos aspectos del universo Cervantino', p. 242. Surtz

comments: 'Make-believe is, in a sense, truer than reality because Pedro knows that he is acting'. 'The Trickster as Dramatist', p. 121.
80. See *Contradictory Subjects* and 'The Interlude: Play on Play' (*La entretenida*) of this study.
81. Friedman, *The Unifying Concept*, p. 84.
82. Zimic, 'El gran teatro del mundo', p. 68.
83. Pedro Calderón de la Barca, *El alcalde de Zalamea*, ed. by Ángel Valbuena Briones (Salamanca: Anaya, 1971), p. 98.
84. As Sevilla Arroyo and Rey Hazas succinctly comment: 'La relación con *La gitanilla* es indudable'. *Teatro completo*, p. xxxv.
85. Spadaccini and Talens, *Through the Shattering Glass*, p. 80.
86. The play which Pedro will perform could possibly be the very one the audience has just watched or *La entretenida*.
87. Arboleda, *Teoría y Formas del Metateatro*, p. 86.

CONCLUSION

'Lo que te sé decir es que no hay fortuna en el mundo, [. . .] que cada uno es artífice de su ventura'

Don Quijote, II, LXVI

In this study I have aimed, via an analysis of freedom, to draw conclusions regarding Cervantes's *Ocho comedias* as a counter-perspective to contemporary Golden-Age drama. Despite the fact that the dramatist's writings for the stage clearly flout conventional Lopean parameters, it is not indicative of a theatre which is deficient or inferior. Rather, Cervantes constructs an aesthetic which permits free expression of seditious voices and an alternative stage for those discourses normally quashed by prevailing dramatic monopoly. It is precisely because of the restrictive nature of seventeenth-century Spanish theatre that Cervantes advocates a strategy of authorial liberty. For instance, in *La entretenida* and *El laberinto de amor* the tight rein on the freedom of the individual is the driving force behind the women's creative performance. Malgesí's conditioned audience in *La casa de los celos* motivates the magician to fashion a spectacle which demands a discerning response and in *Los baños de Argel* the captives' play is forged from within a highly oppressive environment. If, as I have argued in this study, Cervantes fashions his aesthetic self on-stage via these creators, then their ability to create in the light of confinement must have a bearing on how we perceive Cervantes's drama. This is a theatre, then, which emerges from a refusal to operate within the limiting boundaries of inhibiting conditions of contemporary dramatic practise; not from a negative competitive impulse born of Cervantes's inability to contend with Lope's 'monarquía cómica'. It is this desire to transcend prevailing trends which has left an 'anti-Lope' imprint on Cervantes's theatre. However, to view it solely within 'anti-Lope/*comedia*' 'confines' is not only misleading, but greatly ironic and denies us any sense of what Cervantes's drama endorses.

Cervantes not only undermines the dominant *corral* stage but attempts to create a spectator specifically suited to the messages transmitted by his own drama. In fact, investigation of the *Ocho comedias* has revealed that the spectator is at the heart of Cervantes's dramatic project. Although by its very nature all theatre depends upon the producer/consumer relationship between stage and audience, Cervantes's plays explicitly involve and prioritise the nature of reception. By thematising illusion and deconstructing illusion-making apparatus, Cervantes's *comedias* are designed to provoke a heightened level of audience discrimination. If seventeenth-century Spanish theatre can be said to be a testing ground for society,[1] Cervantes's stage is one which equips the spectator to recognise and interrogate the 'deceiving senses' which permeated the Baroque.[2]

This book demonstrates that the Cervantine aesthetic promotes plurality of expression and multivalency of characters on a symbolic level. In fact, Cervantes's characters would appear to signify several things concomitantly. For instance, Marcela Osorio is not only emblematic of the prejudice experienced by the seventeenth-century woman but is an expression of Cervantes's own marginality, in dramatic terms. Likewise, the heroines' rebellious schemes in *El laberinto* are resonant of the playwright's dissident voice. In *El gallardo español*, Don Fernando is representative of Spain whilst Cervantes's *pícaro* protagonist in *Pedro de Urdemalas* illustrates the Cervantine stage itself. Malgesí is not only a magician but becomes symbolic of Cervantes as he deconstructs his own illusions. Such a multilayered approach fits appropriately with what criticism has long determined as multiperspectivism in Cervantes's work. In his drama, Cervantes offers a host of (counter) perspectives from which to perceive and better understand a complex world constituted by conflicting and competing discourses. It is a theatre, then, which precludes a single resting place for the viewer's gaze. It is, perhaps, in this more enhanced and plural mode of characterisation that Cervantes is especially distinct from Lope de Vega.

Cervantes's dialogue with the discourses and structures which inform seventeenth-century Spanish 'reality' renders his stage one which persistently questions, interrogates and probes the limits of Baroque consciousness. Cervantes's vigorous resistance to the myths (both socio-cultural and political) that disingenuously underpin Golden-Age Spain affirms the 'anti-propagandistic' dimension of his drama. However, as my analyses have confirmed, such a strategy is not designed as an end in itself, but is a device which critiques the illusions constructed by an equally illusive ideological infrastructure. The playwright's theatre, therefore, demands and provokes an astute reaction to the mechanisms of representation. Cervantes's extensive involvement in such a project is anchored by a persistent focus on freedom as theme and symbol; explored on occasions with contradictory ramifications. My examination of Cervantes's *Ocho comedias* has sought to conceptualise freedom within the dramatist's own historical time and place. As such, we can conclude that Cervantes offers a depiction of freedom that challenges and destabilises the subject's conflictive engagement with austere social structures, but which cannot be termed radical by our own standards. For instance, Georges Bataille comments:

> The impossible is that phenomenon which breaks free from the established norms of society [. . .] such a moment of defiance leads to the abyss, but it is only by embracing such a moment of defiance, by ignoring the established limits of society, that we achieve freedom.[3]

Cervantine freedom, however, does not advocate upheaval or blatant disregard for the 'established limits of society'. Rather, it offers a sense of how these limits sometimes operate antagonistically. In *El laberinto* and *La entretenida*, for instance, we encounter women who are denied the right to express freely how they might better fulfil their societal role. In the *comedias de cautivos*, the individual is admonished to conform to a world which promotes illusory values; an act which plunges the subject into labyrinthine confusion. This is played out especially in *El rufián dichoso*, in which a 'devalued' subject is so driven to attain a sense of significance that he wilfully orchestrates a dangerous hoax that exploits and deceives others. Cervantes, then, endorses the autonomy of the individual insofar as he promotes perceptive engagement with the norms and assumptions of the day, so that the individual might escape burdening deception. Rather than displace the spectator into the 'abyss', Cervantes enables his audience to navigate the oppressive demands of their world and to express a subjectivity not unlike Don Quijote's, 'Yo sé quién soy'; an assertion which encapsulates the independence of the Cervantine aesthetic itself.

It has been my aim to offer a broad evaluation of Cervantes's theatre, but one which is more systematic than any study to date and which may allow for further scrutiny of the field. Over three decades ago, Canavaggio labelled Cervantes's drama 'un théâtre à naître'; an observation which underscored the validity of critical analysis. This book hopes to have allowed the *Ocho comedias* to take their first positive steps forward, and to have gone some way to establishing the Cervantine stage as an aesthetic which demands and merits our attention.

Notes to the Conclusion

1. See Jodi Campbell, *Monarchy, Political Culture, and Drama in Seventeenth-Century Madrid: Theatre of Negotiation* (Aldershot: Ashgate, 2006), p. 5.
2. Foucault calls the time in which Cervantes was writing the 'age of the deceiving senses'. *The Archaeology of Knowledge*, translated by A. M. Sheridan Smith (New York: Pantheon Books, 1972), p. 23.
3. Georges Bataille, *The Impossible* (San Francisco: City Lights Books, 1991), p. 10.

BIBLIOGRAPHY

Primary References

ALEMÁN, MATEO, *Guzmán de Alfarache*, ed. by Benito Brancaforte (Madrid: Cátedra, 1979)
ANON., *La vida de Lazarillo de Tormes*, ed. by Francisco Rico (Madrid: Cátedra, 1987)
CALDERÓN DE LA BARCA, PEDRO, *El alcalde de Zalamea*, ed. by Ángel Valbuena Briones (Salamanca: Anaya, 1971)
—— *La vida es sueño*, ed. by Ciriaco Morón Arroyo (Madrid: Cátedra, 1989)
CERVANTES SAAVEDRA, MIGUEL DE, *Comedias y Entremeses*, ed. by Rodolfo Schevill and Adolfo Bonilla (Madrid: Impr. de B. Rodríguez, 1915–22)
—— *La Galatea*, ed. by Juan Bautista Avalle-Arce (Madrid: Espasa-Calpe, 1961)
—— *Obras dramáticas de Miguel de Cervantes*, ed. by Francisco Ynduráin (Madrid: Biblioteca de Autores Españoles, 1962)
—— *Los trabajos de Persiles y Sigismunda*, ed. by Juan Bautista Avalle-Arce (Madrid: Castalia, 1969)
—— *Poesías Completas, I. Viaje del Parnaso y Adjunta al Parnaso*, ed. by Vicente Gaos (Madrid: Castalia, 1973)
—— *Novelas ejemplares*, ed. by Harry Sieber (Madrid: Cátedra, 1980)
—— *Teatro completo*, ed. by Florencio Sevilla Arroyo and Antonio Rey Hazas (Barcelona: Planeta, 1987)
—— *La Numancia*, ed. by Robert Marrast (Madrid: Cátedra, 1989)
—— *Los baños de Argel. Pedro de Urdemalas*, ed. by Jean Canavaggio (Madrid: Taurus, 1992)
—— *Obra Completa*, ed. by Florencio Sevilla Arroyo and Antonio Rey Hazas (Madrid: Alianza, 1996–99)
—— *La entretenida. Pedro de Urdemalas*, ed. by Florencio Sevilla Arroyo and Antonio Rey Hazas (Madrid: Alianza, 1998)
—— *Don Quijote de la Mancha*, ed. by Francisco Rico (Madrid: Ediciones Alfaguara, 2004)
MOLINA, TIRSO DE, *El burlador de Sevilla*, ed. by Antonio Prieto (Madrid: Editorial Biblioteca Nueva, 1997)
OVIDIUS NASO, PUBLIUS, *Heroides and Amores*, with an English translation by Grant Showerman (Cambridge; London: Harvard University Press, 1921)
—— *Metamorphoses VIII*, with an English translation and notes by D. E. Hill (Warminster: Aris & Phillips, 1992)
PÉREZ DE MOYA, JUAN, *Philosofía secreta de la gentilidad*, ed. by Carlos Clavería (Madrid: Cátedra, 1995)
QUEVEDO, FRANCISCO DE, *Historia de la vida del Buscón llamado Don Pablos*, ed. by Américo Castro (Madrid: Espasa Calpe, 1973)

Rojas, Fernando de, *La Celestina*, ed. by Dorothy S. Severin (Madrid: Cátedra, 1989)
Salas Barbadillo, Alonso Jerónimo de, *El subtil cordobés Pedro de Urdemalas*, ed. by Marcel Charles Andrade (Chapel Hill: University of North Carolina, 1974)
Seneca, Lucius Annaeus, L. *Annaei Senecae Ad Lucilium epistulae morales*, ed. by L. D. Reynolds (Oxonii: E Typographeo Clarendoniano, 1965)
Vega, Lope de, *El arte de hacer comedias en este tiempo*, ed. by Juana de José Prades (Madrid: Consejo Superior de Investigaciones Científicas, 1971)
—— *El perro del hortelano*, ed. by Victor Dixon (London: Tamesis, 1981)
Villalón, Cristóbal de, *Viaje de Turquía (la odisea de Pedro de Urdemalas)*, ed. by Fernando G. Salinero (Madrid: Cátedra, 1980)

Secondary References

Alcalá Galán, Mercedes, '"Dios te dé salud y a mí paciencia". Teoría del teatro en Cervantes', in *La media semana del jardincito: Cervantes y la reescritura de los códigos*, ed. by José María Manuel Morán (Padova: Unipress, 2002), pp. 255–75
Allen, John J., 'The division into acts of Cervantes's *Los baños de Argel*', *Symposium*, 17 (1963), 42–49
—— 'Some aspects of the staging of Cervantes's play', *Crítica Hispánica*, 9 (1989), 7–16
—— '*La casa de los celos* and the 1605 *Quijote*', in *Cervantes for the 21st Century: Studies in Honor of Edward Dudley*, ed. by Francisco Rubia Prado (Delaware: Juan de la Cuesta, 2000), pp. 1–9
Amat, Illuminada, '"And These Be the Fruits of Play": Sexuality in *La casa de los celos y selvas de Ardenia*', *Bulletin of the Comediantes*, 52 (2000), 31–51
Anderson, Ellen M., 'Articulate Characters: Gender, Genre, and Genius in Cervantes's *El coloquio de los perros* and *Pedro de Urdemalas*', *Romance Languages Annual*, 5 (1993), 349–55
—— 'Refashioning the Maze: The Interplay of Gender and Rank in Cervantes's *El laberinto de amor*', *Bulletin of the Comediantes*, 46 (1994), 165–85
—— 'The Gentility and Genius of *Pedro de Urdemalas*, engendered by Lope de Vega and Cervantes', in *Brave New Words: Studies in Spanish Golden Age Literature*, ed. by Edward H. Friedman and Catherine Larson (New Orleans: University Press of the South, 1996), pp. 175–89
—— 'Mothers of Invention: Toward a Reevaluation of Cervantine Dramatic Heroines', *Bulletin of the Comediantes*, 62 (2010), 1–44
Arboleda, Carlos Arturo, *Teoría y Formas del metateatro en Cervantes* (Salamanca: Universidad de Salamanca, 1991)
Arias Careaga, Raquel, '*Pedro de Urdemalas*: Otro ejemplo de libertad Cervantina', *Annali di Ca' Foscari: Rivista della Facoltà di Lingue e Letterature Straniere dell'Università di Venezia*, 31 (1992), 43–59
Astrana Marín, Luis, *Vida ejemplar y heroica de Miguel de Cervantes Saavedra, con mil documentos hasta ahora inéditos y numerosas ilustraciones y grabados de época* (Madrid: Instituto Editorial Reus, 1948)
Avalle-Arce, Juan Bautista, 'On *La entretenida* of Cervantes', *Modern Language Notes*, 74 (1959), 418–21

BALIBAR, ETIENNE, 'The Nation Form: History and Ideology', in *Race, Nation, Class: Ambiguous Identities*, ed. by Etienne Balibar and Immanuel Wallerstein (London: Verso, 1991), pp. 86–106
BATAILLE, GEORGES, *The Impossible* (San Francisco: City Lights Books, 1991)
BATAILLON, MARCEL, *Pícaros y Picaresca* (Madrid: Taurus, 1969)
BATESON, GREGORY, *Steps to an Ecology of Mind* (New York: Ballentine, 1972)
BERGMANN, EMILIE L., 'Acts of Reading, Acts of Writing', in *Heavenly Bodies: The Realms of La estrella de Sevilla*, ed. by Frederick A. De Armas (Lewisburg, Pennsylvania: Bucknell University Press, 1996), pp. 221–34
BERNAT VISTARINI, ANTONIO, ed., *Actas del Tercer Congreso Internacional de la Asociación de Cervantistas* (Palma: Universitat de Illes Balears, 1998)
BLANCO AGUINAGA, CARLOS, 'Cervantes y la picaresca: Notas sobre dos tipos de realismo', *Nueva Revista de Filología Hispánica*, 11 (1957), 313–42
BLOOM, HAROLD, *A Map of Misreading* (New York: Oxford University Press, 1975)
BORUCHOFF, DAVID A., 'La malograda invención de la picaresca', in *Homenaje a Francisco Márquez Villanueva*, ed. by Pedro M. Piñero Ramírez (Seville: Universidad de Sevilla, 2005), pp. 497–511
—— 'Free Will, the Picaresque, and the Exemplarity of Cervantes's *Novelas ejemplares*', *Modern Language Notes*, 124 (2009), 372–403
BROWN, JONATHAN and J.H. ELLIOTT, *A Palace for a King: the Buen Retiro and the Court of Philip IV* (New Haven; London: Yale University Press, 1980)
BROWN, JONATHAN, *The Golden Age of Painting in Spain* (Madrid: Nerea, 1990)
BUCHANAN, M. A., 'The works of Cervantes and their dates of composition', *Transactions of the Royal Society of Canada*, 32 (1938), 23–39
BUTLER, JUDITH, *Gender Trouble and the Subversion of Identity* (London: Routledge, 1999)
BYRON, WILLIAM, *Cervantes: A Biography* (London: Cassell, 1979)
CAMAMIS, GEORGE, *Estudios sobre el cautiverio en el Siglo de Oro* (Madrid: Gredos, 1977)
CAMPBELL, JODI, *Monarchy, Political Culture, and Drama in Seventeenth-Century Madrid: Theatre of Negotiation* (Aldershot: Ashgate, 2006)
CANAVAGGIO, JEAN, *Cervantès dramaturge: un thèâtre à naître* (Paris: Presses Universitaires de France, 1977)
—— 'Las figuras del donaire en las comedias de Cervantes', in *Risa y sociedad en el teatro español del Siglo de Oro. Actes du III Colloque du Groupe d'études sur le Théâtre Espagnol, Toulouse* (Paris: Éditions du Centre National de la Recherche Scientifique, 1981), pp. 51–67
—— *Cervantes* (Madrid: Espasa Calpe, 1987)
—— 'La conversión del *rufián dichoso*: Fuentes y Recreación', in *On Cervantes: Essays for L. A. Murillo*, ed. by James A. Parr (Newark: Juan de la Cuesta, 1991), pp. 11–19
—— 'La estilización del judío en *Los baños de Argel*', *Primer Acto: Cuadernos de Investigación Teatral*, 270 (1997), 129–37
—— 'De un Lope a otro Lope: Cervantes ante el teatro de su tiempo', *Anuario Lope de Vega*, 6 (2000), 51–59
CANNING, ELAINE, *Lope de Vega's comedias de tema religioso* (Woodbridge: Tamesis, 2004)

CARRASCO URGOTI, MARÍA SOLEDAD, 'Cervantes en su comedia *El laberinto de amor*', *Hispanic Review*, 48 (1980), 77-90

CASALDUERO, JOAQUÍN, *Sentido y forma del teatro de Cervantes* (Madrid: Aguilar, 1951)

CASEY, JAMES, *Early Modern Spain: A Social History* (London; New York: Routledge, 1999)

CASTILLO, DAVID R., *(A)Wry Views: Anamorphosis, Cervantes, and the Early Picaresque* (Indiana: Purdue University Press, 2001)

—— and NICHOLAS SPADACCINI, 'Cervantes y la 'comedia nueva': lectura y espectáculo', *Theatralia: Revista de Teoría del Teatro*, 5 (2003), 153-63

—— and MASSIMO LOLLINI, eds, *Reason and Its Others: Italy, Spain, and the New World* (Tennessee: Vanderbilt University Press, 2006)

CASTILLO, MOISÉS, 'Ortodoxia cervantina? Un análisis de *La gran sultana, El trato de Argel* y *Los baños de Argel*', *Bulletin of the Comediantes*, 56 (2004), 219-40

CASTRO, AMÉRICO, *El pensamiento de Cervantes* (Madrid: Impr. de la librería y casa editorial Hernando, 1925)

CAUDWELL, CHRISTOPHER, *Studies in a Dying Culture* (London: John Lane, 1938)

CELIS SÁNCHEZ, MARÍA ÁNGELA, 'Planos de comunicación en las comedias cervantinas: el juego metateatral', in *El teatro en tiempos de Felipe II: Actas de las XXI Jornadas de Teatro Clásico* (Almagro, Julio de 1998), ed. by Felipe B. Pedraza Jiménez and Rafael González Cañal (Almagro: Universidad de Castilla-La Mancha, 1999), pp. 83-98

CHILDERS, WILLIAM, '*Correr la pluma*: Multigeneric composition in *Don Quijote* and *Persiles*', *Mester*, 25 (1996), 119-46

—— '"Ese Tan Borrado Sobrescrito": The Deconstruction of Lope's Religious Theater in *El retablo de las maravillas* and *El rufián dichoso*', *Bulletin of the Comediantes*, 56 (2004), 241-69

CHITWOOD, SHELLEY, 'Calderón's Labyrinth: *La vida es sueño*', in *Looking at the Comedia in the Year of the Quincentennial: Proceedings of the 1992 Symposium on Golden Age Drama at the University of Texas, El Paso, March 18-21*, ed. by Barbara Mujica and Sharon D. Voros (Lanham, Maryland: University Press of America, 1993), pp. 179-86

CLOSE, ANTHONY, 'La idea cervantina de la comedia', *Theatralia: Revista de Teoría del Teatro*, 5 (2003), 331-49

CONNOR (SWIETLICKI), CATHERINE, 'Lope's Dialogic Imagination: Writing Other Voices of "Monolithic Spain"', *Bulletin of the Comediantes*, 40 (1988), 205-26

—— 'La sexualidad, el 'orientalismo' cervantino y el caso de *La gran sultana*', in *Actas del Tercer Congreso de Hispanistas de Asia*, ed. by Hiroto Ueda (Tokyo: Asociación Asiática de Hispanistas, 1993), pp. 512-18

—— 'Marriage and Subversion in Comedia Endings: Problems in Art and Society', in *Gender, Identity, and Representation in Spain's Golden Age*, ed. by Anita K. Stoll and Dawn L. Smith (Lewisburg, Pennsylvania: Bucknell University Press, 2000), pp. 23-46

CORREA, GUSTAVO, 'El doble aspecto de la honra en el teatro del siglo XVII', *Hispanic Review*, 26 (1958), 99-107

COTARELO Y VALLEDOR, ARMANDO, *El teatro de Cervantes* (Madrid: Revista de Archivos, Bibliotecas y Museos, 1915)

Covarrubias, Sebastián de, *Tesoro de la lengua castellana o española*, ed. by Martín de Riquer (Barcelona: Alta Fulla, 1996)

Cruz, Anne J., 'Deceit, Desire, and the Limits of Subversion in Cervantes's Interludes', *Cervantes*, 14 (1994), 119-36

Cubero, Carmen, 'En torno a La entretenida de Cervantes. El teatro dentro del teatro y el teatro sobre el teatro', in *El teatro dentro del teatro: Cervantes, Lope, Tirso y Calderón. Actas del 'Grand Séminaire' de la Universidad de Neuchâtel, 18–19 de Mayo de 1995*, ed. by Irene Andrés-Suárez, José Manuel López de Abiada and Pedro Ramírez Molas (Madrid: Editorial Verbum, 1997), pp. 59-72

Davis, Elizabeth, *Myth and Identity in the Epic of Imperial Spain* (Missouri: University of Missouri Press, 2000)

De Armas, Frederick A., 'Los excesos de Venus y Marte en *El gallardo español*', in *Cervantes: Su obra y su mundo. Actas del I Congreso Internacional sobre Cervantes*, ed. by Manuel Criado de Val (Madrid: Edi-6, 1981), pp. 249-60

—— *Cervantes, Raphael and the Classics* (Cambridge: Cambridge University Press, 1998)

—— *Ovid in the Age of Cervantes* (Toronto: University of Toronto Press, 2010)

Díez Borque, José María, *Sociedad y Teatro en la España de Lope de Vega* (Barcelona: Antoni Bosch, 1978)

—— 'La historia del teatro según Cervantes', in *Cervantes y la puesta en escena de la sociedad de su tiempo* (Actas del Coloquio de Montreal, 1997), ed. by Catherine Poupeney Hart, Alfredo Hermenegildo and César Oliva (Murcia: Universidad de Murcia, 1999), pp. 17-53

Díez Fernández, J. Ignacio, '"Sin discrepar de la verdad un punto". *La gran sultana*: ¿Un canto a la tolerancia?', *Lectura y Signo*, 1 (2006), 301-22

DiPuccio, Denise, *Communicating Myths of the Golden Age Comedia* (Lewisburg, Pennsylvania: Bucknell University Press, 1998)

Doob, Penelope Reed, *The Idea of the Labyrinth from Classical Antiquity through the Middle Ages* (Ithaca: Cornell University Press, 1990)

Dunn, Peter N., 'Cervantes De/Re-Constructs the Picaresque', *Cervantes*, 2 (1982), 109-31

Egginton, William, 'The Baroque as a Problem of Thought', *Publications of the Modern Language Association of America*, 124 (2009), 143-49

Elliott, J. H., *Imperial Spain 1469-1716* (London: Edward Arnold Publishers, 1963)

El Saffar, Ruth, 'Tracking the trickster in the works of Cervantes', *Symposium*, 37 (1983), 106-24

——, ed. *Critical Essays on Cervantes* (Boston: G.K. Hall, 1986)

—— 'Voces marginales y la visión del ser cervantino', *Anthropos*, 98-99 (1989), 59-62

—— and Diana de Armas Wilson, eds, *Quixotic Desire: Psychoanalytic Perspectives on Cervantes* (Ithaca: Cornell University Press, 1993)

Estévez Molinero, Ángel, 'La (re)escritura Cervantina de *Pedro de Urdemalas*', *Cervantes*, 15 (1995), 82-93

Fastrup, Anne, 'Cross-cultural Movement in the Name of Honour: Renegades, Honour and State in Miguel de Cervantes' Barbary Plays', *Bulletin of Spanish Studies*, 89 (2012), 347-67

FERNÁNDEZ, ENRIQUE, '*Los tratos de Argel*: obra testimonial, denuncia política y literatura terapéutica', *Cervantes*, 20 (2000), 7-26

FERNÁNDEZ-LOZA, PILAR ALCALDE, 'La verdad y la mentira en el teatro de Cervantes: El caso del *Laberinto de amor*', in *Memoria de la palabra: Actas del VI congreso de la asociación internacional Siglo de Oro*, ed. by María Luisa Lobato and Francisco Domínguez Matito (Madrid; Frankfurt: Iberoamericana-Vervuert, 2004), pp. 193-99

FERNÁNDEZ-MORERA, DARÍO, 'Algunos aspectos del universo Cervantino en la comedia *Pedro de Urdemalas*', in *Cervantes: su obra y su mundo. Actas del I congreso Internacional sobre Cervantes*, ed. by Manuel Criado de Val (Madrid: Edi-6, 1981), pp. 239-42

FORCIONE, ALBAN, 'Cervantes and the Freedom of the Artist', *The Romantic Review*, 61 (1970), 243-55

—— *Cervantes and the Humanist Vision: A Study of Four Exemplary Novels* (Princeton: Princeton University Press, 1982)

FOTHERGILL-PAYNE, LOUISE, '*Los tratos de Argel, Los cautivos de Argel* y *Los baños de Argel*: Tres "trasuntos" de un "asunto"', in *El mundo del teatro español en su Siglo de Oro*, ed. by José M. Ruano de la Haza (Ottawa: Dovehouse, 1989), pp. 177-84

FOUCAULT, MICHAEL, *The Archaeology of Knowledge*, translated by A. M. Sheridan Smith (New York: Pantheon Books, 1972)

FRIEDMAN, EDWARD H., 'An Archetype and its modifications: Cervantes's dramatic theory and practice', *The American Hispanist*, 15 (1978), 9-11

—— 'Double Vision: Self and Society in *El Laberinto de amor* and *La entretenida*', in *Cervantes and the Renaissance*, ed. by Michael D. McGaha (Pennsylvania: Juan de la Cuesta, 1980), pp. 157-66

—— '*La casa de los celos*: Cervantes' Dramatic Anomaly', in *Cervantes: Su obra y su mundo. Actas del I Congreso Internacional sobre Cervantes*, ed. by Manuel Criado de Val (Madrid: EDI-6, 1981), pp. 281-89

—— *The Unifying Concept: Approaches to the Structure of Cervantes' Comedias* (South Carolina: Spanish Literature Publications Company, 1981)

—— 'Perspectivism on Stage: Don Quijote and the Mediated Vision of Cervantes' *Comedia*', in *Ideologies and Literature. Plays and Playhouses in Imperial Decadence*, ed. by Anthony Zahareas (Minneapolis: Institute of Ideologies and Literature, 1985), pp. 69-86

—— 'Female Presence, Male Prescience: The Creation of the Subject in *La gran sultana*', in *Estudios en homenaje a Enrique Ruiz-Fornells*, ed. by Juan Fernández Jiménez and others (Erie, Pennsylvania: Asociación de Licenciados & Doctores Españoles en Estados Unidos, 1990), pp. 218-25

—— 'Sign Language: The Semiotics of Love in Lope's *El perro del hortelano*', *Hispanic Review*, 68 (2000), 1-20

—— 'The Comic Vision of Cervantes's *La entretenida*', *Theatralia: Revista de Teoría del Teatro*, 5 (2003), 351-59

FRYE, NORTHROP, *A Natural Perspective: The Development of Shakespearean Comedy and Romance* (New York: Harcourt, Brace and World, 1965)

—— 'The Argument of Comedy', in *Comedy: Developments in Criticism*, ed. by D. J. Palmer (London: Macmillan, 1984)

FUCHS, BARBARA, *Passing for Spain: Cervantes and the Fictions of Identity* (Urbana; Chicago: University of Illinois Press, 2003)

FULKERSON, LAUREL, *The Ovidian Heroine as Author: Reading, Writing, and Community in the Heroides* (Cambridge: Cambridge University Press, 2005)

GARCÉS, MARÍA ANTONIA, *Cervantes in Algiers: A Captive's Tale* (Tennessee: Vanderbilt University Press, 2002)

GARCÍA LORENZO, LUCIANO, 'La gran sultana de Miguel de Cervantes: adaptación del texto y puesta en escena', *Anales Cervantinos*, 32 (1994), 117–36

GARCÍA SALINERO, FERNANDO, 'Dos perfiles paralelos de Pedro de Urdemalas', in *Cervantes: Su obra y su mundo. Actas del I Congreso Internacional sobre Cervantes*, ed. by Manuel Criado de Val (Madrid: EDI-6, 1981), pp. 229–34

GAYLORD, MARY MALCOLM, 'Pulling Strings with Master Peter's Puppets: Fiction and History in Don Quixote', *Cervantes*, 18 (1998), 117–47

GERLI, E. MICHAEL, 'Aristotle in Africa: History, Fiction, and Truth in *El gallardo español*', *Cervantes*, 15 (1995), 43–57

—— *Refiguring Authority: Reading, Writing, and Rewriting in Cervantes* (Lexington: University of Kentucky Press, 1995)

GOFFMAN, ERVING, *The Presentation of Self in Everyday Life* (Harmondsworth: Penguin, 1969)

GOYTISOLO, JUAN, *Crónicas sarracinas* (Barcelona: Ibérica, 1982)

GREENBLATT, STEPHEN, *Renaissance Self-Fashioning: From More to Shakespeare* (Chicago; London: University of Chicago Press, 1980)

GUILLÉN, CLAUDIO, *Literature as System: Essays Toward the Theory of Literary History* (Princeton: Princeton University Press, 1971)

GUTIÉRREZ, CARLOS M., 'Cervantes o la relocalización del sujeto teatral', *Bulletin of the Comediantes*, 56 (2004), 289–310

HABERMAS, JÜRGEN, *The Structural Transformation of the Public Sphere* (Cambridge: Polity, 1989)

HASSON, OR, '*Los baños de Argel*: Un análisis del tratamiento Cervantino de lo Hebreo y lo Judío desde un punto de vista Kleiniano', in *Cervantes y las religiones*, ed. by Ruth Fine and Santiago López Navia (Madrid; Frankfurt: Iberoamericana-Vervuet, 2008), pp. 473–502

HENRY, MELANIE, 'Cervantine Theater as Counter-Perspective Aesthetic: Reconsidering *El rufián dichoso*', *Cervantes*, 31 (2011), 105–24

HERMENEGILDO, ALFREDO, *La 'Numancia' de Cervantes* (Madrid: Sociedad General Española de Librería, 1976)

—— 'Mirar en Cadena: Artificios de la Metateatralidad Cervantina', in *Cervantes y la puesta en escena de la sociedad de su tiempo* (Actas del Coloquio de Montreal, 1997), ed. by Catherine Poupeney Hart, Alfredo Hermenegildo and César Oliva (Murcia: Universidad de Murcia, 1999), pp. 77–91

HERNADI, PAUL, 'Re-presenting the Past: A note on narrative historiography and historical drama', *History and Theory*, 15 (1976), 45–51

HERNÁNDEZ ARAICO, SUSANA, 'Estreno de *La gran sultana*: Teatro de lo otro, amor y humor', *Cervantes*, 14 (1994), 155–65

HERNÁNDEZ-PECORARO, ROSALIE, '*La casa de los celos y selvas de Ardenia*: The Pastoral Metaphor Disrupted', in *Bucolic Metaphors: History, Subjectivity, and*

Gender in the Early Modern Spanish Pastoral (Chapel Hill: University of North Carolina Press, 2006), pp. 202–10

HEYGI, OTTMAR, *Cervantes and the Turks: Historical Reality versus Literary Fiction in La gran sultana and El amante liberal* (Newark, Delaware: Juan de la Cuesta, 1992)

HORNBY, RICHARD, *Drama, Metadrama and Perception* (Lewisburg, Pennsylvania: Bucknell University Press, 1986)

HOY, CALVIN M., *A Philosophy of Individual Freedom: The Political Thought of F. A. Hayek* (Connecticut: Greenwood, 1984)

HUGHES, GETHIN, '*El gallardo español*: A Case of Misplaced Honour', *Cervantes*, 13 (1993), 65–75

HUTCHEON, LINDA, *A Theory of Parody: The Teachings of Twentieth Century Art Forms* (New York; London: Methuen, 1985)

IRIGOYEN-GARCÍA, JAVIER, 'El problema morisco en *Los baños de Argel*, de Miguel de Cervantes: De renegados a mártires cristianos', *Revista Canadiense de Estudios Hispánicos*, 32 (2008), 421–28

—— '"La música ha sido hereje": Pastoral Performance, Moorishness, and Cultural Hybridity in *Los baños de Argel*', *Bulletin of the Comediantes*, 62 (2010), 45–62

ISER, WOLFGANG, 'The Reading Process: A Phenomenological Approach', *New Literary History*, 3 (1972), 279–99

—— *The Act of Reading: A Theory of Aesthetic Response* (London: Routledge and Kegan Paul, 1978)

JACOBSON, HOWARD, *Ovid's Heroides* (Princeton: Princeton University Press, 1974)

JAUSS, HANS ROBERT, *Toward an Aesthetic of Reception* (Brighton: Harvester, 1982)

JOHNSON, CARROLL B., 'El arte viejo de hacer teatro: Lope de Rueda, Lope de Vega y Cervantes', *Cuadernos de Filología*, 3 (1981), 247–59

—— 'La construcción del personaje en Cervantes', *Cervantes*, 15 (1995), 8–32

JURADO SANTOS, AGAPITA, *Tolerancia y ambigüedad en La gran sultana de Cervantes* (Kassel: Reichenberger, 1997)

—— 'Silencio/Palabra: Estrategias de algunas mujeres cervantinas para realizar el deseo', *Cervantes*, 19 (1999), 140–53

KAHN, AARON, *The Ambivalence of Imperial Discourse. Cervantes's La Numancia within the 'Lost Generation' of Spanish Drama (1570–90)* (Bern: Peter Lang, 2008)

KAMEN, HENRY, *Spain 1469–1714: A Society of Conflict* (Harlow: Longman, 1991)

KANELLOS, NICHOLAS, 'The Anti-Semitism of Cervantes' *Los baños de Argel* and *La gran sultana*: A Reappraisal', *Bulletin of the Comediantes*, 27 (1975), 48–52

KARTCHNER, ERIC J., 'Dramatic Diegesis: Truth and Fiction in Cervantes's *El gallardo español*', *Yearbook of Comparative and General Literature*, 47 (1999), 25–35

—— 'Empty Words: Promises and Deception in *La entretenida*', *Bulletin of the Comediantes*, 56 (2004), 327–43

—— 'Pícaros, Saints, and the New World in Cervantes's *El rufián dichoso*', in *Crosscurrents: Transatlantic Perspectives on Early Modern Hispanic Drama*, ed. by Mindy E. Badía and Bonnie L. Gasior (Lewisburg, Pennsylvania: Bucknell University Press, 2006), pp. 85–103

KIDD, MICHAEL, 'The Rise of the *Comedia Nueva*', in *Stages of Desire: The Mythological Tradition in Classical and Contemporary Spanish Theater* (Pennsylvania: The Pennsylvania State University Press, 1999), pp. 63-123

KING, WILLARD, 'Cervantes, El cautiverio y los renegados', *Nueva Revista de Filológia Hispánica*, 40 (1992), 279-91

KISACKY, JULIA M., *Magic in Boiardo and Ariosto* (New York: Peter Lang, 2000)

KOSELLECK, REINHART, *Futures Past: On the Semantics of Historical Time* (Massachusetts: Massachusetts Institute of Technology, 1985)

KÜHNI, JORGE, 'Aspectos de la realidad y la ilusión, juegos sémanticos del metateatro en *Los baños de Argel* (1585-1595) de Miguel de Cervantes', in *El teatro dentro del teatro: Cervantes, Lope, Tirso y Calderón. Actas del 'Grand Séminaire' de la Universidad de Neuchâtel, 18-19 de Mayo de 1995*, ed. by Irene Andrés-Suárez, José Manuel López de Abiada and Pedro Ramírez Molas (Madrid: Editorial Verbum, 1997), pp. 49-58

LARSON, DONALD R., '*La Dama Boba* and the comic sense of life', *Romanische Forschungen*, 85 (1973), 41-62

LÉVI-STRAUSS, CLAUDE, *Tristes Tropiques*, translated by John and Doreen Weightman (New York: Atheneum 1979)

LEWIS-SMITH, PAUL, 'La gran sultana Doña Catalina de Oviedo: A Cervantine Practical Joke', *Modern Language Studies*, 17 (1981), 68-81

—— 'Cervantes and Inversimilar Fiction: Reconsidering *La casa de los celos y selvas de Ardenia*', in *Golden-Age Spanish Literature: Studies in Honour of John Varey by his Colleagues and Pupils*, ed. by Charles Davis and Alan Deyermond (London: Westfield College, 1991), pp. 127-36

—— 'Cervantes on Human Absurdity: The Unifying Theme of *La casa de los celos y selvas de Ardenia*', *Cervantes*, 12 (1992), 93-103

—— 'El humorismo de La gran sultana', *Donaire*, 3 (1994), 55-58

—— '*La casa de los celos* y la Commedia dell'Arte', *Theatralia: Revista de Teoría del Teatro*, 5 (2003), 375-84

—— 'Cervantes como poeta del heroismo: de la *Numancia* a *La gran sultana*', in *Memoria de la palabra: Actas del VI Congreso de la Asociación Internacional Siglo de Oro*, ed. by Maria Luisa Lobato and Francisco Domínguez Matito (Madrid; Frankfurt: Iberoamericana-Vervuert, 2004), pp. 1155-63

LINDHEIM, SARA H., *Mail and Female: Epistolary Narrative and Desire in Ovid's Heroides* (Madison: University of Wisconsin Press, 2003)

LOFTIS, JOHN, *Renaissance Drama in England and Spain* (Princeton: Princeton University Press, 1987)

LÓPEZ ALFONSO, FRANCISCO JOSÉ, '*La entretenida*, parodia y teatralidad', *Anales Cervantinos*, 24 (1986), 193-205

LÓPEZ ESTRADA, FRANCISCO, 'Vista a Oriente, la española en Constantinopla', *Cuadernos de Teatro Clásico*, 7 (1992), 31-46

LÓPEZ MOZO, JERÓNIMO, 'De pícaro a cómico', *Reseña*, 301 (1999), 18-19

LÓPEZ-VÁZQUEZ, ALFREDO RODRÍGUEZ, '*Los baños de Argel* y su estructura en cuatro actos', *Hispania*, 77 (1994), 207-14

LOTTMAN, MARYRICA ORTIZ, 'The Call of the Natural World in *Los baños de Argel*', *Bulletin of the Comediantes*, 56 (2004), 345-66

MADRIGAL, JOSÉ A., ed., *New Historicism and the Comedia: Poetics, Politics and*

Praxis (Boulder, Colorado: Society of Spanish and Spanish-America Studies, 1997)
MAESTRO, JESÚS G., *La escena imaginaria: poética del teatro de Miguel de Cervantes* (Madrid; Frankfurt: Iberoamericana-Vervuert, 2000)
—— 'El triunfo de la heterodoxia. El teatro de Cervantes y la literatura europea', *Theatralia: Revista de Teoría del Teatro*, 5 (2003), 19–48
—— 'Cervantes y Shakespeare: el nacimiento de la literatura metateatral', *Bulletin of Spanish Studies*, 81 (2004), 599–611
MAIORINO, GIANCARLO, ed., *The Picaresque: Tradition and Displacement* (Minneapolis: University of Minnesota Press, 1996)
MARAVALL, JOSÉ ANTONIO, *Culture of the Baroque: Analysis of a Historical Structure* (Manchester: Manchester University Press, 1986)
—— *La literatura picaresca desde la historia social* (Madrid: Taurus, 1986)
MARISCAL, GEORGE, *Contradictory Subjects: Quevedo, Cervantes and Seventeenth-Century Spanish Culture* (Ithaca; London: Cornell University Press, 1991)
—— '*La gran sultana* and the issue of Cervantes's Modernity', *Revista de Estudios Hispánicos*, 28 (1994), 185–211
—— 'Woman and Other Metaphors in Cervantes's comedia famosa de *La entretenida*', *Theatre Journal*, 46 (1994), 213–30
MARKS, MORLEY HAWKS, 'Deformación de la tradición pastoril en *La casa de los celos* de Miguel de Cervantes', in *Cervantes and the Pastoral*, ed. by José J. Labrador Herraiz and Juan Fernández Jiménez (Cleveland: Cleveland State University, 1986), pp. 129–38
MÁRQUEZ VILLANUEVA, FRANCISCO, *Moros, moriscos y turcos de Cervantes. Ensayos críticos* (Barcelona: Edicions Bellaterra, 2010)
MARRAST, ROBERT, *Miguel de Cervantès: Dramaturge* (Paris: L'Arche, 1957)
MARSILLACH, ADOLFO, 'Nuestro Cervantes', *Cuadernos de Teatro Clásico*, 7 (1992), 201–02
MAS, ALBERT, *Les turcs dans la literature espagnole de siècle d'or* (Paris: Centre des Recherches, 1967)
MCCRORY, DONALD, *No Ordinary Man: The Life and Times of Miguel de Cervantes* (London: Peter Owen, 1999)
MCGHAHA, MICHAEL D., 'Hacia la verdadera historia del cautivo Miguel de Cervantes', *Revista Canadiense de Estudios Hispánicos*, 20 (1996), 540–46
MCKENDRICK, MELVEENA, *Women and Society in the Spanish Drama of the Golden Age: A Study of the Mujer Varonil* (London: Cambridge University Press, 1974)
—— *Cervantes* (Boston: Little, Brown, 1980)
—— 'Women against Wedlock. The Reluctant Brides of Golden Age Drama', in *Women in Hispanic Literature: Icons and Fallen Idols*, ed. by Beth Miller (Berkeley: University of California Press, 1983), pp. 115–46
—— *Playing the King: Lope de Vega and the Limits of Conformity* (London: Tamesis, 2000)
—— 'Writings for the stage', in *The Cambridge Companion to Cervantes*, ed. by Anthony J. Cascardi (Cambridge: Cambridge University Press, 2002), pp. 131–59
MEIXELL, AMANDA S., 'The Espíritu de Merlín, Renaissance Magic, and the Limitations of Being Human in *La casa de los celos*', *Cervantes*, 24 (2004), 93–118

MIÑANA, ROGELIO, '"Veréis el monstruo": La nueva 'comedia' de Cervantes', *Bulletin of the Comediantes*, 56 (2004), 387-411

MOIR, DUNCAN, 'The Classical Tradition in Spanish Dramatic Theory and Practice in the Seventeenth Century', in *Classical Drama and Its Influence*, ed. by M. J. Anderson (London: Methuen, 1965), pp. 193-228

MOORE, JOHN A., 'Is Truth Relative for Cervantes?', *Hispania*, 44 (1961), 660-62

MORIARTY, MICHAEL, 'Theory and the Early Modern: Some Notes on a Difficult Relationship', *Paragraph*, 29 (2006), 1-11

MORRISON, ROBERT R., *Lope de Vega and the Comedia de Santos* (New York: Peter Lang, 2000)

O'CONNOR, THOMAS AUSTIN, 'Is the Spanish Comedia a Metatheater?', *Hispanic Review*, 43 (1975), 275-89

PARKER, A. A., 'The Psychology of the *pícaro* in *El buscón*', *The Modern Language Review*, 42 (1947), 58-69

—— *The Approach to the Spanish Drama of the Golden Age* (London: Hispanic & Luso-Brazilian Councils, 1957)

—— *Literature and the Delinquent: The Picaresque Novel in Spain and Europe 1599-1753* (Edinburgh: Edinburgh University Press, 1967)

PAZ GAGO, JOSÉ MARÍA, 'Texto y representación en el teatro español del último cuarto del siglo XVI (Cervantes y Lope: una perspectiva comparada)', *Bulletin of the Comediantes*, 45 (1993), 255-75

PEDRAZA JIMÉNEZ, FELIPE B., 'El teatro mayor de Cervantes: Comentarios a contrapelo', in *Actas del VII coloquio internacional de la Asociación de Cervantistas*, ed. by José Ramón Fernández de Cano y Martín (El Toboso: Ayuntamiento de El Toboso, 1999), pp. 19-38

PÉREZ FERNÁNDEZ, DESIRÉE, '*El laberinto de amor* de Cervantes: análisis del texto y su puesta en escena', *Estudios humanísticos. Filología*, 28 (2006), 143-60

PERRY, MARY ELIZABETH, *Crime and Society in Early Modern Seville* (Hanover: University Press of New England, 1980)

PHIDDIAN, ROBERT, *Swift's Parody* (Cambridge: Cambridge University Press, 1995)

RANDALL, DALE B. J., 'The Classical Ending of Quevedo's *Buscón*', *Hispanic Review*, 32 (1964), 101-08

REED, CORY A., 'Cervantes and the Novelization of Drama: Tradition and Innovation in the *Entremeses*', *Cervantes*, 11 (1991), 61-86

REED, HELEN H., 'Theatricality in the Picaresque of Cervantes', *Cervantes*, 7 (1987), 71-84

REY HAZAS, ANTONIO, 'Las comedias de cautivos de Cervantes', in *Los imperios orientales en el teatro del Siglo de Oro, Actas de XVI Jornadas de Teatro Clásico, Almagro Julio de 1993*, ed. by Felipe B. Pedraza Jiménez and Rafael González Cañal (Almagro: Universidad Castilla-La Mancha y Festival de Almagro, 1994), pp. 29-56

—— *Poética de la libertad y otras claves cervantinas* (Madrid: Ediciones Eneida, 2005)

RICOEUR, PAUL, 'Narrative Time', *Critical Enquiry*, 7 (1980), 169-90

RITCHIE, B., 'The Formal Structure of the Aesthetic Object', in *The Problems of Aesthetics*, ed. by Eliseo Vivas and Murray Kreiger (New York: Rineheart, 1965), pp. 225-33

ROBBINS, JEREMY, *The Challenges of Uncertainty: An Introduction to Seventeenth-Century Spanish Literature* (London: Duckworth, 1998)
—— *Arts of Perception: The Epistemological Mentality of the Spanish Baroque, 1580-1720* (New York: Routledge, 2007)
ROKEM, FREDDIE, *Performing History: Theatrical Representations of the Past in Contemporary Theatre* (Iowa: University of Iowa Press, 2000)
ROSALES, LUIS, *Cervantes y la Libertad*, 2 vols. (Madrid: Instituto de Cooperación Iberoamericana, 1985)
ROSE, MARGARET A., *Parody: Ancient, Modern, and Post-modern* (Cambridge: Cambridge University Press, 1993)
ROSE, MARY BETH, 'Gender, Genre, and History: Seventeenth-Century English Women and the Art of Autobiography', in *Women in the Middle Ages and the Renaissance: Literary and Historical Perspectives*, ed. by Mary Beth Rose (New York: Syracuse University Press, 1986), pp. 245-74
RUIZ PÉREZ, PEDRO, 'Dramaturgia, teatralidad y sentido en *La casa de los celos*', in *Actas del II Coloquio de la Asociación de Cervantistas* (Alcalá de Henares, 6-9 de noviembre de 1989), (Barcelona: Anthropos, 1991), pp. 657-72
—— *La distinción cervantina. Poética e historia* (Alcalá de Henares: Centro de Estudios Cervantinos, 2006)
SAWHNEY, MINNI, 'Cervantes' Cosmopolitan *El gallardo español* during an Earlier Clash of Civilizations', *Theatralia: Revista de Teoría del Teatro*, 5 (2003), 167-75
SICROFF, ALBERT A., *Los estatutos de limpieza de sangre: Controversias entre los siglos XV y XVII* (Madrid: Taurus, 1985)
SIMERKA, BARBARA, 'Early Modern Skepticism and Unbelief and the Demystification of Providential Ideology in *El burlador de Sevilla*', *Gestos*, 23 (1997), 39-66
SMITH, SHAWN O., '*Pedro de Urdemalas*: Contesting the Spanish Hapsburg Discourse of Blood', *Vanderbilt e-Journal of Luso-Hispanic Studies*, 2 (2005)
SPADACCINI, NICHOLAS, 'Cervantes and the Spanish comedia', in *Ideologies and Literature. Plays and Playhouses in Imperial Decadence*, ed. by Anthony Zahareas (Minneapolis: Institute of Ideologies and Literature, 1985), pp. 53-67
—— and JENARO TALENS, 'Introduction: The Construction of the Self. Notes on Autobiography in Early Modern Spain', in *Autobiography in Early Modern Spain*, ed. by Nicholas Spadaccini and Jenaro Talens (Minneapolis: University of Minnesota Press, 1985)
—— and JENARO TALENS, *Through the Shattering Glass: Cervantes and the Self-Made World* (London; Minneapolis: University of Minnesota Press, 1993)
SPONSLER, CLAIRE, *Drama and Resistance: Bodies, Goods, and Theatricality in Late Medieval England* (Minnesota: University of Minnesota Press, 1997)
STACKHOUSE, KENNETH, 'Beyond Performance: Cervantes's Algerian Plays, *El trato de Argel* and *Los baños de Argel*', *Bulletin of the Comediantes*, 52 (2000), 7-30
STAPP, WILLIAM A., 'Dichoso por confiado', *Anales Cervantinos*, 25 (1987), 413-52
—— 'El gallardo español: La fama como arbitrio de la realidad', in *Cervantes: Su obra y su mundo. Actas del I Congreso Internacional sobre Cervantes*, ed. by Manuel Criado de Val (Madrid: Edi-6, 1981), pp. 261-72
STERN, CHARLOTTE, 'Lope de Vega, Propagandist?', *Bulletin of the Comediantes*, 34 (1982), 1-36

SULLIVAN, HENRY W., *Tirso de Molina & the Drama of the Counter-Reformation* (Amsterdam: Editions Rodopi, 1981)

SURTZ, RONALD E., 'Cervantes's *Pedro de Urdemalas*: The Trickster as Dramatist', *Romanische Forschungen*, 92 (1979), 118–25

SWANSEY, BRUCE, 'From Allegory to Mockery: Baroque Representations of the Labyrinth', in *Rewriting Classical Mythology in the Hispanic Baroque*, ed. by Isabel Torres (Woodbridge: Tamesis, 2007), pp. 128–38

TADDEO, SARA, 'De vox extremada: Cervantes's women characters speak for themselves', in *Women in the Discourse of Early Modern Spain*, ed. by Joan F. Cammarata (Gainesville, Florida: University Press of Florida, 2003), pp. 183–98

TALENS, JENARO, 'Narrating Theatricality', in *Ideologies and Literature. Plays and Playhouses in Imperial Decadence*, ed. by Anthony Zahareas (Minneapolis: Institute of Ideologies and Literature, 1980), pp. 87–101

THACKER, JONATHAN, *Role-Play and the World as Stage in the Comedia* (Liverpool: Liverpool University Press, 2002)

—— *A Companion to Golden Age Theatre* (Woodbridge: Tamesis, 2007)

—— 'La figura de la Comedia en *El rufián dichoso* de Cervantes', in *La comedia de santos*, ed. by Felipe B. Pedraza Jiménez and Almudena García González (Almagro: Universidad de Castilla-La Mancha, 2008), pp. 121–34

—— '"Véote, y no te conozco": The Unrecognizable Form of Cervantes's *El rufián dichoso*', *Hispanic Research Journal*, 3 (2009), 206–26

THOMPSON, EARL, 'Shepherds as Spanish Society: Cervantes' View in One *comedia*', in *Varia hispánica: Homenaje a Alberto Porqueras Mayo*, ed. by Joseph L. Laurenti and Vern G. Williamsen (Kassel: Reichenberger, 1989), pp. 7–15

TORRE GARCÍA, ENCARNACIÓN DE LA, 'Los Austrias y el poder: la imagen en el siglo XVII', *Historia y Comunicación Social*, 5 (2000), 13–29

TORRES, ISABEL, '"Pues no entiendo tus palabras / y tus bofetones siento". Linguistic subversion in Lope de Vega's *El perro del hortelano*', *Journal of Hispanic Research*, 5 (2004), 197–212

——, ed., *Rewriting Classical Mythology in the Hispanic Baroque* (Woodbridge: Tamesis, 2007)

TRABADO CABADO, JOSÉ MANUEL, 'Lírica, mundo pastoril y discurso dramático en *La casa de los celos*', *Theatralia: Revista de Teoría del Teatro*, 5 (2003), 385–96

TRAMBAIOLI, MARCELLA, 'Una protocomedia burlesca de Cervantes: *La casa de los celos*, parodia de algunas piezas del primer Lope de Vega', in *Cervantes y su mundo I*, ed. by Eva Reichenberger and Kurt Reichenberger (Kassel: Reichenberger, 2004), pp. 407–38

TRAUGOTT, ELIZABETH CLOSS and MARY LOUISE PRATT, *Linguistics for Students of Literature* (San Diego; London: Harcourt Brace Jovanovich, 1980)

URRUTIA, JORGE, 'La libertad del yo feminino o la libertad de don Quijote', in *El Quijote en clave de mujer/es*, ed. by Fanny Rubio (Madrid: Editorial Complutense, 2005), pp. 475–79

VALBUENA PRAT, ÁNGEL, 'Las *ocho comedias* de Cervantes', in *Homenaje a Cervantes*, ed. by Francisco Sánchez-Castañer (Valencia: Mediterráneo, 1950), pp. 257–66

VARAS, PATRICIA, '*El rufián dichoso*: Una 'comedia' de santos diferente', *Anales Cervantinos*, 29 (1991), 9–19

VERNAY, PHILIPPE, *Maugis d'Aigremont: chanson de geste* (Berne: Francke, 1980)

VILCHES DE FRUTOS, MARÍA FRANCISCA, 'El teatro de Cervantes en la escena española contemporánea: Identidad y Vanguardia', *Anales de la Literatura Española Contemporánea*, 31 (2006), 5–39

VOSSLER, KARL, *Lope de Vega y su tiempo* (Madrid: Revista de Occidente, 1933)

WARDROPPER, BRUCE, 'Cervantes' Theory of the Drama', *Modern Philology*, 52 (1955), 217–21

—— 'Comedias', in *Suma cervantina*, ed. by J. B. Avalle Arce and E. C. Riley (London: Tamesis, 1973), pp. 147–69

WILLIAMS, RAYMOND, *Marxism and Literature* (Oxford: Oxford University Press, 1977)

WILLIAMSON, EDWIN, '*La gran sultana*: una fantasía política de Cervantes', *Donaire*, 3 (1994), 52–54

WILTROUT, ANN, 'Ginés de Pasamonte: The Pícaro and his Art', *Anales Cervantinos*, 17 (1978), 11–17

ZIMIC, STANISLAV, 'Algunas observaciones sobre *La casa de los celos*', *Hispania*, 49 (1973), 51–58

—— 'Sobre la técnica dramática de Cervantes en *El gallardo español*', *Boletín de la Real Academia Española*, 54 (1974), 505–18

—— 'Cervantes frente a Lope y a la comedia nueva: Observaciones sobre *La entretenida*', *Anales Cervantinos*, 15 (1976), 19–119

—— 'El gran teatro del mundo y el gran mundo del teatro en *Pedro de Urdemalas* de Cervantes', *Acta Neophilologica*, 10 (1977), 55–105

—— 'El laberinto y el lucero redentor: Estudio de *El laberinto de amor* de Cervantes', *Acta Neophilologica*, 13 (1980), 31–48

—— '"La caridad jamás imaginada" de Cristóbal de Lugo. Estudio de *El rufián dichoso* de Cervantes', *Boletín de la Biblioteca Menéndez y Pelayo*, 56 (1980), 85–171

—— 'Sobre la clasificación de las comedias de Cervantes', *Acta Neophilologica*, 14 (1981), 63–83

—— *El teatro de Cervantes* (Madrid: Castalia, 1992)

—— 'Sobre el arte dramático de Cervantes en *El rufián dichoso*', in *Cervantes 1547–1997: Jornadas de Investigación Cervantina*, ed. by Aurelio González (Mexico: Colegio de México, Fondo Eulalio Ferrer, 1999), pp. 87–101